AFROCENTRIC THEATRE

AFROCENTRIC THEATRE

CARLTON W. MOLETTE
AND
BARBARA J. MOLETTE

Copyright © 2013 by Carlton W. Molette and Barbara J. Molette.

Library of Congress Control Number: 2013908358
ISBN: Hardcover   978-1-4836-3740-2
              Softcover   978-1-4836-3739-6
              Ebook   978-1-4836-3741-9

All rights reserved. No part of this book may be reproduced or transmitted in any form or by any means, electronic or mechanical, including photocopying, recording, or by any information storage and retrieval system, without permission in writing from the copyright owner.

This book was printed in the United States of America.

Rev. date: 05/17/2013

To order additional copies of this book, contact:
Xlibris Corporation
1-888-795-4274
www.Xlibris.com
Orders@Xlibris.com
133596

ON THE COVER: Sankofa means go back to retrieve it. African people often use the image of a long necked bird looking to its rear to reinforce the idea that it is wise to look back and consider the past before moving forward in the present and into the future.

Sankofa symbols occur in different styles from relatively realistic depictions to abstract symbols. This image is reproduced from African Design From Traditional Sources by Geoffrey Williams, Dover Publications, Inc.

CONTENTS

PREFACE ix

PREMISE 1
1. Culture and Values 15
    Culture 18
    Values and How They are Acquired 23
2. Race is a Social Construction 32
    Acknowledging White Racism 33
    Location and Agency 42
3. Foundations of Interpretation 51
    The First Theatre 52
    The First African American Theatre 61
    The Oldest Extant African American Script 68
    The Minstrel Tradition 75
4. Foundations of Evaluation 79
    Creators and Imitators of Art 83
    Cherished Beliefs 92
    Objectivity and Universality 97
5. Evaluation of Art 106
    Aesthetics 106
    Fine vs. Applied Art 107
    Artists and Responders to Art 114
    Other Factors that Influence Evaluation 116

PRESENTATION 127
6. Rituals 133
    Religious Rituals 139
    Word Power 142
    Vocality 145

  Rhythm and Movement 149
  Spirituality 153
7. Space and Time 156
  Afrocentric Space 157
  Acting in Afrocentric Space 163
  Afrocentric Time 165
  Visual and Rhythmic Asymmetry 169
8. Heroes 174
  Heroic Values 175
  Traditional Afrocentric Heroes 178
  Scripted Heroes 185
9. Characterization 204
  Hip-Hop Characterization 204
  Values and Character Motivation 207
  How Character Shapes Theme 220
10. Images in Theatre and Media 226
  Visual Cues 227
  Eunuchs are Safe 230
  Functions of the Fool 235
  The Supernegro 243
11. Asking Critical Questions 248
  Fundamental Issues 249
  Foundation Questions 252
  Style Questions 253
  Texture Questions 256
  Structure Questions 258
  Constructing Themes 262

END NOTES 267

BIBLIOGRAPHY 279
  Works Cited 279
  Additional Works Recommended 285

INDEX 291

ABOUT THE AUTHORS 299

PREFACE

While a great deal has changed since the second edition of *Black Theatre: Premise and Presentation* was published in 1992, much remains the same. We have an African American president but we also have the Tea Party, a concerted effort to keep people of color from voting, and the Trayvon Martin murder. The term "Afrocentric" is a more comfortable part of the American lexicon than it was twenty years ago. While the terms "Black" and "Afrocentric" seem to be used almost interchangeably, evolving social discourse recognizes subtle differences between the two terms. The term "Black" is more suggestive of the physical characteristics associated with race, whereas the term "Afrocentric" is fundamentally based in culture and point of view. *Afrocentric Theatre* continues our quest to enhance thinking about and understanding the nature of Afrocentric theatre as expressions of culture and media for communicating values. Our effort to describe Afrocentric theatre and culture is not intended to prescribe rules for what is or is not Afrocentric or Black. Our goal remains to honor Afrocentric theatre and Afrocentric culture without dishonoring any other theatre or culture, to describe without devaluing. Variances exist within and across cultural groups. These variances do not indicate that any one person or group is better or worse or inferior or superior to any other.

This book is divided into two sections. Part 1, "Premise," describes terms and concepts that aid in examining Afrocentric theatre from an Afrocentric point of view. Essential to that discourse is understanding how culture and values shape points of view, which in turn shape interpretations and evaluations of theatre arts. Afrocentric theatre deserves to be defined, interpreted, and evaluated in a context of Afrocentric culture and values.

AFROCENTRIC THEATRE

Interpreters and evaluators shape the standards they use to interpret and evaluate creative works. But their results are immaterial, no matter how sincere, if their culture and values differ significantly from those of the artist and the audience for whom the work of art is intended.

Individuals purported to be experts often praise or discredit work by asserting the presence or absence of universality or objectivity or both. Using objectivity and universality as standards for determining a work's worth says very little about the work itself and exposes a great deal about the evaluator's cultural biases, especially when the work's creator and intended audience are culturally different from the evaluator. Since we say objectivity and universality are "myths," and since the term "myth" is sometimes used to infer fiction or falsehood, we need to explain the context in which we use the term. Myths are traditional stories that invigorate and authenticate the worldview of a specific cultural group. While a group's myths often seem benign on the surface, these traditional stories are much more powerful than they seem. If cultural group A persuades cultural group B that group A's mythology, artifacts, and behaviors are objective and universal, group B may come to accept group A's worldview as superior to its own, thereby granting cultural dominance to group A.

Part 2, "Presentation," delineates values that have, over time, influenced Afrocentric theatrical presentations and characteristics of style, form, physical parameters of the performance environment, concepts of space and time, and expectations about how people perceive and respond to such presentations. These characteristics form a describable systematic arrangement that is uniquely Afrocentric. Afrocentric and Eurocentric values, concepts, and performance characteristics are described in order to distinguish between the two theatrical presentation conventions.

Traditional Afrocentric rituals, religious and secular, are recounted from a point of view of dramatic theory. An examination of these rituals provides a basis for understanding Afrocentric heroic values, characterization, and

PREFACE

how space, time, and visual imagery impacts performance. Afrocentric rituals and the values they communicate are related to plays that exhibit similar values and presentation styles.

While racism fosters negative stereotypical images of Black people, good intentions do not guarantee accuracy of perception. The reasons that perceptions of cultural others are often erroneous are too complex to attribute to a single cause. Readily accessible images in film and television drama illustrate how images of Black people in Eurocentric theatre and media differ from those Afrocentric audiences consider valid, real, true, or appropriate.

The nature of Afrocentric theatre can be illustrated by citing the work of various playwrights from the USA and elsewhere in the African diaspora. While there are many excellent Afrocentric plays that could be used to illustrate each point we make, we mention only a few such plays. Since this is not a compendium of all the plays we think deserve wider recognition, many of the plays we hold in high regard are not mentioned.

Most people's evaluative competencies do not go astray as a result of deficiencies in answering questions but from reticence to ask them. The chapter entitled "Asking Critical Questions" is a result of several decades of seeking to enable students to increase their capacity to appreciate and evaluate Afrocentric theatre by increasing their capability to form pertinent questions.

While we will undoubtedly fail to mention some of the many who have contributed to the endeavors that led to this publication, we cannot fail to mention those who come to mind. Many theatre professionals have encouraged us when their encouragement was very much needed. We are especially grateful to William Branch, Alice Childress, Abram Hill, Douglas Turner Ward, Loften Mitchell, Woodie King, Jr., and Garland Thompson for welcoming and encouraging us as playwrights.

AFROCENTRIC THEATRE

To our former professors and mentors, especially Baldwin Burroughs, J. P. Cochran, S. Randolph Edmonds, Arnold Gillete, Richard Fallon, William Harlan Shaw, and Arthur Dorlag, this opportunity to say thank you is far too little too late. Insightful questions and comments from Richard Long, Kariamu Welch Asante, Molefi Asante, Hoyt Fuller, Oscar Brockett, Errol Hill, James Hatch, John Scott, Thomas Pawley, Orlando Taylor, and Samuel Andrews provided immeasurable assistance in transforming amorphous thoughts into more intelligible statements. We owe a large debt of gratitude to our professors in all the academic disciplines we encountered, as well as our former colleagues at the historically Black colleges we attended as undergraduates and where we spent much of our careers as professors.

Most of all, we are grateful to our daughters, Carla and Andrea, and our grandchildren, Courtney and Conrad.

Barbara and Carlton Molette, March 2013

PART ONE
PREMISE

n. 1 Logic. a statement assumed to be true and used to draw a conclusion; 2 any assumption or presupposition; postulate
v.t. 1 to set forth as an introduction or explanation; mention beforehand

A friend of ours had a T-shirt that read "Theatre is life. Film is art. Television is furniture." If theatre is life, then life lessons, issues, and dilemmas raised by works of theatre are appropriate subject matter for a book about theatre. When focusing on Afrocentric theatre, racial identity is life whether we wish it to be or not. Yet objections often arise when racism becomes an unmentioned surrogate antagonist in a Black play because its pervasive presence affects the lives of the play's characters. For example, if one fails to appreciate the pervasive presence of racial discrimination evidenced in both job opportunity and home ownership in *A Raisin in the Sun*, one may conclude the play is about people who whine about easily solvable problems that result from their own laziness or incompetence. Failure to appreciate the magnitude of racism as a play's unheralded antagonist can result in shallower perceptions than one would otherwise have.

Afrocentric theatre is a thread in the fabric of African American culture. All theatre reflects a culture, the time, place, and social strata of those who present theatre and those for whom it is presented. Understanding a culture's theatre is more effectively accomplished by a broadly based inquiry into the characteristics of the society from which that theatre emerges. Therefore, a serious study of Afrocentric theatre must include the societal forces that shape it and cannot be limited to the study of activities within the theatre itself.

Insights into artistic creations of a culture are more likely to be valid when they occur after exposure to that culture's values and dominant creative motifs. A culture's values establish qualitative standards by which its art is judged. Understanding of a play or group of plays is best developed by first acquiring an appreciation of the culture that produced the dramatic art and the values that form the foundation of that culture. Most importantly, the aesthetic values of the culture must be understood before its art or any specific work of art that grows out of that culture may be understood.

Differences in culture generate differences in theatre and the aesthetic standards by which a culture's theatre is evaluated. Mavor Moore, former chairman of the Canada Council, suggests, when one responds to art from a different cultural context, the interpretations that follow are so inextricably connected to one's own cultural patterns that they are almost always wrong. He expresses the notion that close proximity of geographical location, language, history, tradition, and even family ties may cause an observer to "be beguiled by the obvious similarities into overlooking important differences."[1] Although Moore has Canada's relationship to mainstream America in mind, his view is applicable to Black America's relationship to White America. To say Black theatre differs from White theatre is not to say they differ in all respects; the similarities far outnumber the differences. But those who are beguiled by obvious similarities and overlook important differences seem far more influential than those who are not. Often, a statement about differences between Black and White theatre motivates a litany of obvious similarities as though the similarities refute the assertion that differences exist. We try to refrain from reciting obvious similarities simply because they are obvious.

Afrocentric theatre is a highly complex organic whole. No instance of Afrocentric theatre is required to exhibit every characteristic we attribute to Afrocentric theatre, and some White theatre will undoubtedly contain characteristics we identify as attributes of Black theatre. Every work of art deserves to be regarded as an organic whole. To describe the nature of Afrocentric theatre is to describe sets of functions that are connected in a complex manner. The way things are connected often has value equal to or greater than the combination of the things. No single thing may be isolated from the organic whole and function as the determining factor in defining or identifying Afrocentric theatre, or differentiating Black theatre from White theatre. We describe the traditional and the prevalent in African American culture, values, and theatre art. We make generalizations to reduce those descriptions to a describable magnitude. To clarify those generalizations, we make similar generalizations about the dominant and influential in White culture, values, and theatre art.

In 1980, Molefi Kete Asante published a book entitled *Afrocentricity: The Theory of Social Change*. In the decades since, Afrocentricity has provided a linguistic and conceptual mechanism for many Black people to expand their understanding of themselves and the world. We use the terms "Afrocentric" and "Eurocentric" to describe ways of perceiving reality that place Africa and Europe, respectively, at the center. Asante believes, and we agree, that in a very broad sense, there are at least three broad views of cultural reality: Afrocentric, Eurocentric, and Asiocentric. He emphasizes that these categories are much too restrictive of the human personality; they only address the general thrust of each of the three cultural entities; and they are possibly oversimplifications. Within this context, Asante generalizes:

> The Afrocentric viewpoint holds that all modalities and realities are united and move in one grand manner. There can be no separation between material and spiritual, profane and sacred, form and substance . . . The human being, acting with personal power, can animate, activate, and galvanize the material or the spiritual. The continuity from material to spiritual is the reality of the Afrocentric viewpoint.

> Asiocentric viewpoints hold that the material is an illusion, that the real only comes from the spiritual. Therefore, Asian philosophical concepts are enamored with spirit-over-matter notions.
>
> The Eurocentric perspective on reality . . . holds that the material, the experiential, is real and that the spiritual is an illusion. Everything that is not within sense experiences is nonsense.[2]

Asante says each of these ways of perceiving reality is constrained by its culture, its mythology, ethos, creative motif, history, and its social, political, and economic systems. How one communicates with external entities is constrained by one's cultural identity, one's view of self, which in turn is determined and constrained by one's culture. Afrocentricism seeks to reinforce a view of self for Black people that is appropriate for Black people, a view that sees African people as subject rather than object, and locates African people and their traditional, contemporary, and evolving values at the center.[3]

A few centuries ago, many people believed the earth was the center of the universe, flat, and that one could fall off the edge. Although these people saw the universe in a highly limited context, their beliefs did not make them sinister or evil. Today, many people believe nearly everything on earth of importance or significance emanates from Europe. To describe such people as Eurocentric is not to say they are sinister or evil, but they see the universe in a highly limited context. They view data in a particular way because of the place from which they view it. Being Eurocentric only becomes negative or sinister or evil when Eurocentric people force others to accept their place or point of view as the universal one. The Eurocentric statement "Columbus discovered America" is not so much sinister or evil as it is narrow and Eurocentric. Such a view is as limiting as the view that the earth is the center of the universe and flat. Thinking about Afrocentric artists and art requires the kind of thinking that allowed people of an earlier era to question the view that the earth is flat and the center of the universe.

PREMISE

Just as dictionaries derive definitions from how influential people use words, our descriptions of Eurocentric culture derive from influential Eurocentric people's ideas and behaviors. We use these descriptions to relate how Eurocentric culture has expedited African Americans' miseducation to view others' best interests as their own. Relieving African Americans of the notion that Eurocentric culture is universal allows African Americans to appreciate the legitimacy of Eurocentric values for Eurocentric people. On the other hand, Eurocentric culture is not an entitlement to violate other people's civil and human rights. This concern for other people's rights is based on real instances of Eurocentric Christians claiming entitlement to murder large numbers of other people without guilt or shame, or punishment based on the ideology of manifest destiny, or the Nazis, or the Ku Klux Klan.

Carter G. Woodson's seminal work *The Mis-education of the Negro*, articulates several concepts that many African Americans endorse. One such concept is especially germane to this Premise.

> The same educational process which inspires and stimulates the oppressor with the thought that he is everything and has accomplished everything worthwhile, depresses and crushes at the same time the spark of genius in the Negro by making him feel that his race does not amount to much and never will measure up to the standards of other people.[4]

A case in point: one of us had an art teacher who regularly said, "African art is ugly." Although the teacher's physiognomy proclaimed African ancestry, he had been trained by a system he could be trusted to perpetuate. Dissemination of facts about Afrocentric theatre will not alleviate the erroneous notion that its standards are inherently inferior to Eurocentric standards. This Premise asserts that standards that grow out of African culture are legitimate, important, and valuable. Cognitive data about Black theatre is useful only to the extent it is acquired in concert with affective confidence that Afrocentric aesthetic standards are legitimate, important, and valuable. Deeper and more evaluative insight into Afrocentric theatre requires cognitive knowledge about African aesthetic standards that may be extracted from such sources as reading relevant books. But cognitive information alone will not generate sensibilities that are in harmony with Afrocentric culture. On the other hand, individuals from other ethnic backgrounds are as capable of appreciating Afrocentric theatre as people who are not Elizabethan or British are capable of appreciating Shakespeare.

Insightful evaluation of art requires a capacity to experience affective responses to it, whether it is art from one's own culture or from some other culture. Acquiring facts about art takes on an undeserved significance in formal educational settings because people who teach students to appreciate art must give tests and assign grades. Since a pencil-and-paper test that adequately measures the amount of sensitivity to art a student has recently acquired has yet to be devised, we measure the facts students have memorized instead. This practice leads many to incorrectly conclude one learns to appreciate art by memorizing lots of facts about it. While learning facts about art and the artists who create it has benefits, the practice is neither a substitute for experiencing affective responses to arts nor a significant contributor to the growth or development of affective capacity.

Sensitivity to art is optimally achieved by living in and acquiring the values of a culture from birth to adulthood, thereby accumulating a capacity to experience affective responses to that culture's arts. Every person who remains fully immersed in a culture from birth through adulthood does not develop an equal capability to experience affective responses to their culture's art or to articulate insightful evaluative responses to it. On the other hand, many if not most adults develop a depth of affective response and discernment to their culture's art that cannot be duplicated through the acquisition of facts and casual observation over a relatively short time span. Other processes for developing insightful evaluative responses to art are time-consuming and difficult, but not impossible.

PREMISE

Any activity that deserves to be called theatre will share some similar characteristics such as some form of presentation to an audience that communicates ideas and evokes emotions. Despite this similarity across cultural traditions, Asiocentric and Afrocentric theatre tends to place higher value on affective or emotional responses in contrast to Eurocentric rationalism, which devalues the emotional and places a higher value on rational responses. This Eurocentric perspective has evolved over the past several centuries with increasing disregard for anything and everything that cannot be experienced by the senses and quantified in some manner to the point that "materialism" is probably a more credible term to describe the point of view than "rationalism."

Afrocentric theatre places higher value on a presentation's ability to evoke emotions and lesser value on provoking rational responses. In what seems on the surface to be a contradiction, Afrocentric culture also places very high valuation on usefulness of theatre art. This seeming contradiction is not an actual one. Afrocentric culture values theatre's usefulness as a persuasive force while understanding that people are more likely to be persuaded by inciting emotions than by rational logical evidence.

Afrocentric presentations can include rituals, ceremonies, legends, myths, sermons, spontaneous responses, poems, and even the scripted imitations of actions regularly seen in Eurocentric realistic well-made plays. Afrocentric performers are dancers, storytellers, singers, instrumentalists, preachers, orators, actors performing imitations of actions, or all of the above. Audiences can be both passive and participatory. Presentations may take place in the opulence of a concert hall, the paucity of an urban storefront, or the unembellished spaciousness of an open field. Afrocentric theatre transcends the traditional Eurocentric division into disciplines and categories and encompasses artistic presentation of every form.

Four attributes of Afrocentric theatre were articulated by W. E. B. DuBois as early as 1926. He said "our" theatre must be "About us . . . By us . . . For us . . . Near us."[5] In contemporary America, changes in transportation and housing patterns demand a reassessment of the mandate for theatre "near us." In cities with large Black populations in the suburbs as well as in the core of the city, nearness is often unattainable and "accessible to us" is a more accurate way to describe this attribute. General agreement seems to prevail with regard to the notion that Afrocentric theatre is for, by, and about Black people. On the other hand, when "for," "by," or "about" becomes "integrated," the premise and presentation change to accommodate this diversity of culture and values. Changes occur when diverse priorities and assumptions are brought to the production. Since theatre's survival requires responsiveness to its audience, the differing priorities and assumptions of a more diverse audience can encourage Black theatre to adapt to its audience's diversity. Black theatre for a diverse audience may develop goals that take precedence over the reflection and perpetuation of Afrocentric values. While such a shift may be necessary to attract an audience, it will also tend to make the work less Afrocentric.

A. Peter Bailey has succinctly expressed this notion in more specific terms while revealing another of the concept's important ramifications.
> The difference between the man who wrote 'Slaveship' and the man who wrote 'Dutchman' is the difference between . . . Jones and Baraka. Baraka is talking directly to his people, whereas Jones is screaming: 'Acknowledge me! Hear me!' White critics have never given 'Slaveship' the praise that they gave 'Dutchman,' most likely because 'Slaveship' talks more to black folks.[6]

We use the term "Negro theatre" to describe an orientation that recognizes the realities of White power and privilege in our society that clarify the likelihood that White critics will not think a play about, by, for, and near Black people is worthy of serious attention. So one may decide to join the system rather than fight it. In the American theatre, that means choosing to speak to the people who dominate the world of theatre, the ticket purchasers, White people in the top 4 percent of income. Black theatre artists who make this choice also seem to favor the assimilation of Black

PREMISE

Americans into White American culture. Using the term "Negro theatre" in this manner does not infer these choices are wrong or right or better or worse strategies for success. Without seeking to make hierarchical rankings, we use the term "Negro theatre" to describe theatre by Black people that seems to presume or advocate cultural assimilation and speaking to the people who spend the most money on theatre tickets.

To suggest the terms "Black" and "Negro" have different connotative meanings does not place African Americans into two discreet groups. Instead, this terminology describes two, sometimes contradictory, sets of values and priorities that can exist within an individual. W. E. B. DuBois called this phenomenon "double consciousness."

> It is a peculiar sensation, this double consciousness, the sense of always looking at one's self through the eyes of others, of measuring one's soul by the tape of a world that looks on in amused contempt and pity. One ever feels his twoness, an American, a Negro, two souls, two thoughts, two unreconciled strivings . . . longing to attain self-conscious manhood.[7]

This statement represents DuBois' thinking at a relatively early stage in his adult life and he describes a phenomenon as it existed in the very early 1900s in his *The Souls of Black Folk,* which was first published in 1903. Despite more than a century of evolutionary progress, double consciousness remains a painfully persistent force in African American reality and in the art that reality inspires.

An optimal introductory exposure to Afrocentric theatre places primary emphasis on values and concepts and focuses on the nature of Afrocentric theatre. Although chronologically cataloging events and hierarchically organizing data into categories can lead to insights and promote societal well-being, these processes can also influence people to disrespect, disavow, and disconnect from their legitimate cultural heritage. Data becomes infused with meaning and significance when interpreted, and interpretation is constrained by the biases of the interpreter. An interpreter is most likely to derive useful insights from culturally-based data if the interpreter thoroughly understands and appreciates the cultural context that animates the data.

While our goal is to examine the nature of Afrocentric theatre from an Afrocentric point of view, we must confront an unavoidable dilemma. Sometimes, "the" Black point of view, or even "a" Black point of view may not be so clearly definable or even recognizable. Some Black points of view may turn out to be very similar to some White points of view. Some Black points of view may even bear a greater similarity to some White points of view than to some other Black points of view. To further complicate matters, Black people sometimes seem forced to choose between White points of view that range from unrelenting violent oppression to kinder more paternalistic oppression. In that context, African Americans may be beguiled into assuming the less objectionable point of view is "the Black" point of view.

Another set of often misinterpreted terms needs to be clarified, terms that describe oppressors and the people they oppress. Some people self-identify as members of the oppressor class often inaccurately described as "White People." We can only speculate that those who choose to self-identify in this manner are either oppressors or they aspire to be oppressors. Yet many who self-identify as White, European, or Eurocentric are victims of White oppression. Although a term like "Anglo-Saxon or Teutonic, upper-class male chauvinist imperialist elitist oppression" is more accurate than "White oppression," the term is also more cumbersome. Since many words in the English language began as acronyms, we propose a new acronym for wealthy, elite, powerful persons of European origin: WEPPEO. For centuries the WEPPEOs justified the Atlantic slave trade in the framework of Christian morality by creating a system that defined people of African origin as not fully human, therefore not entitled to the human rights demanded by Christian morality. Good people of various ethnic groups, including some White people, fought against the WEPPEOs, but their wealth and power and their ideology of White racial supremacy prevailed. After several centuries, the descendants of the original WEPPEOs continue to enjoy the massive benefits accrued by their ancestors during the slave trade. To continue reaping these benefits, each successive generation of WEPPEOs reinforce and reinvent and update their centuries-old systems based on an ideology of White supremacy.

African Americans are not the only oppressed people. Semitic people, Native American people, many other cultural or ethnic groups who consider themselves people of color, and the poor and uneducated generally, have been oppressed by the same or similar people as those who oppress Black people. However, we do not need to state that fact in conjunction with every reference to the oppression of Black people. Such terms as "White oppressors" and "White imperialists" refer to White people who are oppressors or imperialists, or who aspire to be oppressors or imperialists. Not all White people are oppressors or imperialists or wealthy or powerful or elite. The acronym WEPPEO applies only to the very few persons of European origin who are wealthy, elite, and powerful, or who seek to help the WEPPEOs keep their wealth and power because they fervently aspire to become WEPPEOs someday.

We have elected to capitalize the word "Black" when the word is used to describe people of African descent or their culture. This stylistic device allows us to differentiate between people of African descent, the visual sense perception black, and the negative connotations of that word in Eurocentric culture. This choice enables us to differentiate between, for example, Black comedy (a comedy that grows out of Black culture), and black comedy (comedy that has negative or sinister overtones). Dealing with the word "white" in a similar manner allows us to differentiate between White people (people of European heritage, Caucasians) and white people (people who, according to the dictionary, are chaste, pure, devoid of fault, etc.). Although we alternate the terms "Black," "African American," and

"Afrocentric," we recognize the existence of certain subtle differences in the meanings of these terms.

We also recognize that using the terms "actor" and "audience" creates a dilemma. The English language is based on a Eurocentric view of the world, and we are using these terms in an Afrocentric context. As an Afrocentric context is explicated, the subtle differences between the Afrocentric and Eurocentric meanings of the terms "actor" and "audience" will become clearer. We will undoubtedly use other terms with subtle connotative differences in Afrocentric and Eurocentric contexts as well. The way the terms are used here will become clearer as the Afrocentric context explicated here becomes clearer.

Black people are people of African descent wherever they are located now. African American people are people of African descent who are geographically, and in part culturally, located in the Americas. African people are people who reside on the continent of Africa. Most (but not nearly all) African people are visually Black. Most European people (but not nearly all) are visually White or Caucasian. Since there are Black people who live in Europe and White people who live in Africa, we oversimplify and generalize when we refer to Black people as "Africans" and White people as "Europeans."

Such terms as "Black," "White," "European," and "African" suggest to some that racial purity is a reality. There is only one race of people, the human race. Complex mixtures of what are traditionally called races have occurred in many parts of the world for many thousands of years. Either everyone is racially pure or nobody is. Since most people who speak English believe the term "race" has some particular meaning, we must use these ethnic, cultural, geographic descriptors, however vague and inadequate, to communicate here and now.

Afrocentric values that exist here and now are continuations of African culture passed down for thousands of years through generations of Africans who were brought to this hemisphere as a part of the slave trade and Africans who came both before and after on their own. Since an abundance of scholarly work documenting African cultural continuities in the visual and performing arts already exists, we will not try to duplicate it here. We recognize and accept the work of scholars who have offered ample evidence that slavery did not destroy all vestiges of African culture among the people who were subjected to its cruelties. African Americans have an African cultural heritage, and Afrocentric Americans will seek to analyze African American culture from inside the context of Afrocentric values and in a manner that conforms to accepted standards of scholarship. Other Americans need to be exposed to such an analysis as well. None of us is completely free of the pervasive impact of a miseducation process that denies significant information because it seems to be pro-Black. This miseducation process is detrimental to White people as well as to Black people. Hopefully, exposure to the various cultures that exist in the United States will eventually enable all to exist in an atmosphere of mutual respect.

Seeking to appreciate the history and literature of Afrocentric theatre without understanding the nature of Afrocentric theatre inevitably leads to incorrect conclusions. Organized, reasonable, analytical deliberations about the nature of Afrocentric theatre are optimally achieved by viewing Black theatre in the broader context of Afrocentric culture and values.

The arts often reveal truth by provoking personal visceral responses. If truths about Afrocentric arts are revealed, personal visceral responses will be provoked. Sometimes people are discomforted by truths they discover as a result of their personal visceral responses to Afrocentric artists and the arts they create. While our goal is not to cause discomfort, we believe a little discomfort is a small price to pay for enlightenment.

Chapter One

Culture and Values

"Reality is never experienced directly, but always through the cultural categories made available by a society." —Stuart Hall

Culture is a configuration of knowledge, whether explicit, implicit, rational, irrational, or nonrational, shared among members of an identifiable group. This shared knowledge shapes their values and perspectives, how they perceive and interpret symbols, artifacts, and behaviors. Culture manifests as learned patterns of behavior, cognitive constructs, and affective responses that both identify its members and differentiate them from other cultural groups.

As with culture, art begins with a presumption of prior knowledge and builds on knowledge that already exists among the people for whom the art is intended. People who share a culture can place an experience such as seeing a play into a context that is considered proper in that culture. People who share a culture recognize clichés, while people outside of that culture very well may not. If one expects to be accepted as a member of a group (cultural identity) one must acquire the group's culture, including the ability to communicate like other members of the group. For example, to be acceptable and accepted into a group comprised of individuals of a particular occupation that is presumed to leverage respect from the larger society, one must communicate like others in the group. To be included and understood, one must use the group's codes and vocabulary as well as the group's stylistic modes. Similarly, a culture's values determine which communication modes and messages are acceptable in that culture's art.

Art communicates and propagates a culture's values while functioning within the confines of that culture's values. Therefore, for an inquiry into the nature of Afrocentric theatre to be valid, it must take place within the confines of Afrocentric cultural values, including Afrocentric aesthetic values and Afrocentric modes of communication.

"Sankofa" is an Akan word meaning to return or go back for it, and is symbolized as a bird whose head is turned toward its tail. The West African symbol of a bird whose head is turned toward its tail represents a philosophy of cultural revivalism or renaissance and conveys the message: "Look to the past to be guided in the present and into the future." The practice of looking back is valued and the culture emphasizes respect for elderly people and traditional values.

Eurocentric classification presumes aesthetics, rhetoric, and the social sciences are separate disciplines with different modes of inquiry and ways of knowing. Eurocentric thought classifies theatre as a fine art; therefore, a Eurocentric point of view requires inquiry into the subject of theatre to methodologies appropriate for the study of aesthetics. To claim theatre must be analyzed by only one mode of inquiry and way of knowing creates a false division.[8] Eurocentric thought classifies the study of culture and values as social science, which is not considered an appropriate mode of inquiry or way of knowing about the arts. We contend, on the other hand, that inquiry into the nature of Afrocentric theatre is enhanced by using methodologies appropriate for the study of culture and values. Therefore, an Afrocentric study of Black theatre cannot take place within Eurocentric boundaries of scholarly inquiry.

While seeking to articulate an Afrocentric perspective about culture, we recognize that the phenomenon of double consciousness mitigates against achieving a totally Afrocentric point of view. Discourse about what to do with or about people of African descent has permeated national policy in the USA since the arrival of Europeans on this continent. However, the focus has shifted away from issues of race toward issues of culture. Two major responses to Afrocentric culture have emerged. The more liberal of the responses often seeks to do good by helping the "culturally deprived" and presume African Americans can and should learn to be Eurocentric in all cultural respects. This position presumes that becoming culturally White makes skin color irrelevant. This point of view further presumes African Americans and other "culturally deprived" people have been deprived, not of what makes them culturally White, but of what would make them civilized. Therefore, a "culturally deprived" individual can and will become more civilized by absorbing sufficient quantities of Eurocentric culture. This liberal view stresses the notion that cultural deprivation is usually not the fault of the culturally deprived, so the "culturally deprived" should not be blamed for being less civilized. The liberal view further holds that the "culturally deprived" can and should assimilate into mainstream culture by learning to be more culturally White, therefore more civilized.

A response to African American culture espoused by well-trained White racists who label themselves "conservative" only differs from the liberal response in that the conservative response is based in beliefs that: (1) culturally deprived people are responsible for their condition; (2) they deserve their plight; (3) the well-to-do bear no responsibility for extricating them from whatever difficulties they encounter; and (4) life was much better in the good old days when law and custom systematically excluded these others from the more genteel facets of Eurocentric society. This elitist, exclusionist response assumes people who are illiterate, jobless, homeless, or underemployed simply have not worked hard enough and deserve their unfortunate plight. This response excludes people who have not acquired at least a facade of Eurocentric culture and values from full participation in the American economy while holding the excluded responsible for their exclusion. This response further presumes most African Americans and most who belong to other "subcultures" cannot and should not be expected to assimilate fully into Eurocentric American society, nor do any of these others deserve the economic benefits that Eurocentric American society offers for its own. Each of these responses contains elements that, when taken out of context, many African Americans find attractive.

Some people of African descent in the USA, when required to choose between these two major responses to the question of what to do with or about them, select the conservative response because it seems on the surface to praise and reward hard work, diligence, thrift, and loyalty. This response is especially popular among individuals who are objects of praise and reward for "pulling themselves up by their own boot straps." Other African Americans select the liberal response since the conservative response appears to blame African Americans for simply being African American. Further, the liberal response recognizes that African Americans have the capacity to learn the things White people have learned and labeled "civilized." Whichever response an African American selects, the option selected is the less objectionable of two objectionable options and presumes no other options exist.

Culture

Our view of culture gratefully acknowledges Maulana Karenga,[9] one of the leading Black nationalist spokesmen and theorists of the 1960s, who often said "Culture is the basis of all ideas, images, and actions." Many of the advocates for the Black arts movement of the 1960s and 1970s agree with Karenga that seven elements comprise a culture, mythology, history, social organization, political organization, economic organization, creative motif, and ethos. This paradigm further asserts that all art consciously or unconsciously represents and promotes the values of its culture.

Since art grows out of a culture and reflects and perpetuates its culture's values, a work of art's underlying values are inextricably connected to the cultural identities of its creators. Culture transmits and propagates a value system that influences thoughts and behaviors and influences its members to act in ways that the culture regards as admirable. The same culture and value system that creates political, social, and economic systems also creates a mythology, a history, an ethos, and a creative motif. All seven elements of a viable culture are compatible with each other. Every viable culture is whole and must be examined holistically to gain an optimum understanding of it. To look at any art form as though it exists independent of its culture's other aspects is to do a disservice to that art form.

This effort at a holistic analysis requires that we focus, not only on Afrocentric theatre but also on the culture that spawns it. We will discuss some things that are not theatre in the Eurocentric sense of the term and we have provided a bibliography that surveys various aspects of Afrocentric culture in America in far greater depth and detail than could possibly be included in a single volume.

A dictionary definition of the term "culture" helps to substantiate some notions about culture that deserve consideration. The dictionary attributes meanings to words compiled from "important and influential people who write and publish in the English language."[10] Any presumptions of racial superiority and inferiority embedded in the word "culture" are not implanted, by the dictionary, but by people who the dictionary deems important and influential.

> culture,—n. 1 fineness of feelings, thoughts, tastes, or manners; refinement: . . . syn: breeding . . . 2 Anthropology. a the civilization of a given people or nation at a given time or over all time; its customs, its arts, and its conveniences: . . . b socially inherited artifacts. 3 the development of the mind or body by education or training

The first definition of culture suggests there are criteria that determine the absence or presence of refinement equally well without regard to race, culture, or nationality. Our observations indicate variations in what Eurocentric elitists generally describe as refinement are often alleged to be indistinguishable from the variations they perceive in race, culture, and nationality. The terms "fineness" and "refinement" imply purity, subtlety, the absence of coarseness, the presence of extreme care and accuracy, and superiority of quality, appearance, and conception. If one accepts the presupposition that Eurocentric criteria for fineness and refinement are the only valid criteria, it follows that criteria that vary from this standard are inferior. The dictionary's synonym "breeding" is even more blatantly racist in its assumptions. If breeding indicates fineness and refinement, then these qualities can only be passed on genetically. So if one has not genetically inherited these traits through breeding, they cannot possibly be acquired. In this Eurocentric paradigm, persons who do not have parents with breeding cannot possibly obtain breeding themselves, rendering them incapable of a high level of refinement or culture.

The anthropological definition of the word "culture" was devised to avoid the obvious prejudices in the most commonly accepted meaning of the word. On the other hand, the anthropological definition presents its own difficulty. The anthropological definition relies on the term "civilization" to express a qualitative valuation of a group's system of customs, arts, and conveniences. But *The World Book Dictionary* defines the word "civilize" as:
> 1 to change from being savage and ignorant to having good laws and customs and knowledge of the arts and sciences; train in culture, science, and art: . . . syn: enlighten, educate, humanize; 2 to improve in culture and good manners; refine. syn: polish

So the word "civilization" serves as a reminder of the notions of some sort of hierarchical arrangement of human groups ranging from "savage and ignorant to having good laws and customs and knowledge of the arts and sciences." When modern Eurocentric thought reveals such hierarchical arrangements of humankind, categories called races are inevitably used to differentiate the high from the low.

A discussion of the term "culture" that seeks to reflect an Afrocentric perspective must scrutinize some of the most commonly held notions about anthropology. These commonly held views are not necessarily those of the leading authorities in the field of anthropology. Rather, they are the concepts that trickle down to the Eurocentric Americans who comprise the general public. The most important commonly held notion about anthropology is that it is a science. The dictionary states anthropology is a science and defines science as "knowledge based on observed facts and tested truths arranged in an orderly system . . ." To the contrary, an expert in the field of anthropology has stated:

> It is still tremendously difficult to understand a culture different from our own.
>
> Anthropology is highly individualistic. One person goes to a place and writes an account and then later another scientist will see things differently.
>
> There is no final interpretation of another culture.[11]

The general public assumes that conclusions drawn by scientists using scientific methodology are "systematic; accurate; exact . . ."

Another notion, regarded by many in the general public as a scientific fact, posits that societies evolve from simple to complex. This view enables racism to shift its vocabulary, replacing old racist terms such as "heathen" and "savage" with such pseudoscientific terms as "preliterate" and "developing" while claiming the old vocabulary's disappearance chronicles the disappearance of racism itself.

Yet another factor in the anthropological definition of "culture" must be addressed. Anthropologists frequently fail to differentiate between the customs, arts, and artifacts they claim is evidence that validates their conclusions about a culture and the culture itself. The culture itself is the shared knowledge the culture's people use to create standards and make qualitative judgments about their customs, arts, and artifacts. But culture is also the behavioral style the culture's people use to transmit their society's values through their customs, arts, and artifacts as well as the standards the society uses to determine whether or not a particular example of their customs, arts, or artifacts is good. A foundation for understanding Afrocentric theatre requires information about the shared knowledge base, the stylistic features used to transmit Afrocentric values and the standards used to determine if a specific work is good.

Afrocentric values are inextricably connected to an African cultural heritage whose values are descended from the principles of Maat which were the basis for moral behavior in Kemet. Except when quoting someone else's work, we refer to what is traditionally called ancient Egypt as "Kemet" which means "black settlement" and is what the people who lived there called the place. We will also refer to the people traditionally called ancient Egyptians as Kemites," which means "the Black ones" in the Kemites' language.[12]

Diop noted that "the African is dominated by his social relations, because they reinforce his equilibrium, his personality, and his being."[13] The essence of Maat is summarized in a statement from Nefer-Seshem-Ra:

> I have spoken truly and done right. I spoke justly and repeated that which was just . . . I judged between two in such a way that would satisfy both of them. I rescued the weak from those who were stronger as much as was in my power. I gave bread to the hungry, clothes to the naked and brought the boatless to dry land. I buried those who had no children and built a boat for those [who] were without one. I respected my father, pleased my mother and raised my sisters and brothers.[14]

Kemites strove for truth, justice, and righteousness. The following lines are indicative of the essence of a life not of struggle, but of harmony.

> Do not terrorize people for if you do, God will punish you accordingly. If anyone lives by such means, God will take bread from his or her mouth . . . If one says I will rob another, he will end up being robbed himself . . . Therefore, one should live in peace with others and they will come and willingly give gifts which another would take from them through fear.[15]

In tune with the attitude expressed by Ptah-Hotep, the Kemites did not have a military aristocracy. Diop states "the soldiers play only an unobtrusive, if not nonexistent, political role."[16] In contrast, Eurocentric moral values are related to war and conflict and "Those who fall in battle or who died of their wounds were admitted to heaven, the dwelling place of the gods . . . where lived the Valkyries and where Fricka . . . received the heroes and presented them with the drinking horn."[17] These values were prevalent in early Greece and gave rise to the concept that conflict is an essential component of drama. Conversely, the Kemites' values spawned drama that fostered harmony by celebrating people and events considered deserving of veneration.

Recognizing individuals who deserve veneration remains an essential function of Black theatre as exemplified by Katori Hall's play entitled *Mountaintop*. Publicity preceding the 2012 Broadway premiere caused concern among many African Americans that the play focused on a facet of Martin Luther King, Jr.'s life that most people who admire his accomplishments consider both personal and irrelevant to his public good works. While the play portrays King as a human being who is not perfect, the human imperfections of the play's character enhance the significance of his accomplishments.

Values and How They are Acquired

A serious inquiry into the nature of Afrocentric theatre and the culture from which it emerges must also consider some aspects of Eurocentric American culture. These considerations are not made to denigrate the worth of Eurocentric values, but to ask whether or not instilling Eurocentric values in African Americans serves the best interests of African Americans. Before this concern can be addressed effectively, the term "values" must be understood. Our dictionary defines "values" as:
> values, - n . . . . Sociology. the established ideals of life; objects, customs, ways of acting, and the like, that the members of a given society regard as desirable: "Man lives by values; all his enterprises and

activities . . . make sense only in terms of some structure of purposes which are themselves values in action." (Will Herberg)

While this definition is helpful, it fails to emphasize important factors that lead to a useful understanding of the term in this context. Values are often confused with attitudes. While values are unconscious and virtually permanent, attitudes are external indications of such internal phenomena as thoughts, opinions, dispositions, moods, and emotions. Attitudes can be controlled to some extent with a combination of education, will power, and enforcement. But values are more basic, internal, and enduring than attitudes. They are learned during childhood and adults seldom experience significant changes, even when attitudes, the readily recognizable manifestations of one's values, are eradicated or at least stifled. The importance of environmental factors to the acquisition of values generally results in people with similar backgrounds developing similar values. Adults can, and often do, eliminate, reduce, or at least conceal racist attitudes. But despite these attitude shifts, an adult's racist values are virtually impossible to eliminate or reduce.

Morris Massey has made a career of explaining how values are acquired, how they impact a person's functioning in the workplace, and how an understanding of these phenomena enables managers to function more effectively. The following summary undoubtedly oversimplifies Massey's ideas as it focuses on how values impact Black theatre, so we recommend spending an hour or so viewing one of his video presentations.[18]

Values are acquired from the sum total of one's experiences during the so-called formative years. But certain major sources of information tend to impact more significantly on values formation, family, friends (and their families), church and other activities of organized religion, school and other activities of formal education, such as books and media (especially electronic media). Electronic media are relatively new but extremely powerful information sources in values formation. In the not-too-distant past, geographical region and family income contributed significantly to the values acquisition process. But these two factors have been greatly reduced and overwhelmingly replaced by electronic media, recorded music, and motion pictures.

Values are acquired individually, non-rationally, and at a very early age. Psychologists generally agree that within the first three or four years of our lives the basic personality is formed. This personality formation tends to remain intact for the rest of our lives. The first seven years of values acquisition are regarded as an *imprinting* process. We acquire the ability to eat, talk, and walk normally, and we develop other processes as well as more complex conceptual structures such as how to behave as an adult.

In the general age range of seven to thirteen, *modeling* is the principal mode of values acquisition. Heroes are identified and emulated. Heroes may be chosen from among those who are very close, such as parents, or from among those with whom there is no direct personal contact, such as sports and motion picture stars. Among the seven to thirteen age group, the critical nature of the electronic media in the modeling process is evident in the widespread hero identification with stars of electronic media, recorded music, and motion pictures. But hero identification is a symptom of a larger and more complex phenomenon. In addition to the impact of celebrities as heroes, the content of the material presented on electronic media, recorded music, and motion pictures has a significant effect on values acquisition. On scripted television programs, all problems are solved quickly and effortlessly. In commercials, all pains and anxieties can be quickly eliminated by using the right deodorant or toothpaste or taking the right pill, or driving the right automobile. The most complex entanglements are regularly resolved within the standard one-hour timeframe. And the people who solve the problems always survive, usually without even working up a sweat. In the face of these media-generated modeling examples, such values as self-discipline, delayed gratification, and work ethic become more difficult to instill through such traditional sources as family, church, and school.

In the general age range of fourteen to twenty, the dominant urge is toward *socialization*. People in this age range want to be like everyone else in every detail. In this age range, the most significant information for values acquisition comes from others who are like us in terms of interests, age, and the other major factors that shape our values. People intuitively recognized this phenomenon long before it was described in scientific terms. Segregation with race or religion or gender as its basis has most often focused on persons between the ages of fourteen and twenty. In this age range, the importance of family decreases and the importance of friends increases in the values-acquisition process. So societies seeking to maintain their values have often established rules that prohibit or at least limit access to people of different age range or gender or religion or race.

From birth until approximately age twenty-one, we continuously acquire information. In addition to rational information, we acquire nonrational information about what is pleasant and what is not, and about various and sundry prejudices. A great deal of this information is tested during the socialization process. One might receive a long list of thou-shalt-not's accompanied by an indication of horrendous consequences for violating them. But if an individual tests one thou-shalt-not and it turns out to be fun, a shift occurs in the values that are forming. On the other hand, if the testing process verifies the information, then the information eventually becomes locked into that individual's values.

Social systems sometimes help to ensure survival of prejudices inculcated by a family or a larger society when such values are tested during the socialization process. If a White social structure inculcates in its children the value that Black people tend to be poorer because they do not have the discipline or intelligence to be more successful, then White children must be discouraged from testing that value's validity. If the White children attend school with Black children and discover some of them have more discipline and intelligence than many White children, the White children's values may shift in a direction their parents and the larger society find undesirable. If on the other hand a child only comes in contact with others who are visually and culturally similar, their parents' and the larger society's values will probably remain intact until adulthood when the values are locked in. At approximately age twenty-one, an individual's values are locked in. Each person's basic gut level responses to the stimuli the world provides have been set for life. Only a major emotional upheaval can generate a change in one's established system of values thereafter.

An example of such an upheaval occurred in the life of the first White student at a historically Black university where we once worked. When the student was in the age range for testing the racial prejudices inculcated by his parents and the larger society, he worked to register Black voters in a rural parish in Louisiana. While engaged in that activity, he was attacked and left in a ditch to die. Instead, he was discovered by some Black farmers who hid him and nursed him back to health. Motivated by the values shift that resulted from this trauma, he refused to attend a predominantly White college in the south, and on occasion indicated that he was uncomfortable or did not feel safe around White people.

Values operate on a subconscious level and on a continuing basis. They provide individuals with instant programmed responses to the constant stream of stimuli with which we are all bombarded. These instant programmed responses inform individuals that each given stimulus is right or wrong, good or bad, normal or not normal. And the information that forms a person's values is received almost totally before the age of twenty-one. Any analysis and interpretation of art is impossible except within the context of the values of the person making the analysis and interpretation. When one encounters a work of art or an analysis or interpretation of art, an optimum understanding and appreciation requires as much awareness as possible of the work's creator's values. When we examine White people's responses to Black theatre, the time and place of their response is less indicative of the values that control their response than how African American people and their culture were regarded in the time span and environments in which the responder spent her or his first twenty-one years.

Many White people who exhibit relatively subtle forms of racial prejudice object to having their behavior described as racist. These individuals generally define racism as hatred and racist behavior as inflicting deliberate physical harm and vituperative communication on another human being because of race. On the other hand, Black people and other targets of racism in the USA tend to regard less violent behavior as racist as well. In order to avoid protracted debates about what the word "racist" means, we sometimes use the terms "Afrophobia" and "Afrophobic" describe nonbelligerent behavior that grows out of fear, discomfort, or uneasiness with proximity to or interaction with Black people and their culture.

Individuals who suffer from Afrophobia often avoid facing their fear, discomfort, or uneasiness by ignoring African people and their culture. This process of denying things African has become institutionalized. When planning a trip, we called an airline to ask if they had flights to Africa. We were told they did not. But when we read the airline's brochures, we discovered they had scheduled flights to one of the African countries we were interested in visiting, Egypt. A director of an outstanding museum in a major city once publicly lamented his museum did not have an African art collection while boasting of their collection of Ancient Egyptian art. Somehow the nation of Egypt has been removed from the continent of Africa and put in a place called the "Middle East." In 1970, give or take a year, NBC did a special program in primetime about Ethiopia. The program opened with the statement, "The Ethiopians are a dark-skinned Caucasian people." That statement is the only detail about the program we remember. Ethiopians were characterized as a good and proud people who are descended from an important ancient civilization. These credentials empowered an American television network to override skin color and hair texture and declare Ethiopians *Caucasian*, thereby separating them from their Africanness. Afrophobia distorts geography, history, and aesthetics, encouraging its victims to be blinded by their fear or discomfort or uneasiness over proximity to things African or to disassociate anything they regard as good or important from its Africanness.

Most influential historical analysis and interpretation of Afrocentric theatre is created by White males who work at authoritative media outlets, respected scholarly journals, prestigious universities, and the largest and best funded theatres. Individuals whose values were locked in over thirty years ago shape the public's perspectives about Black theatre. But values are heavily influenced by parents, other older family and friends, and former teachers and professors whose values reflect an even earlier era. So these people's values regarding such things as a Black person's "place" (as in "stay in your place") may reflect what was regarded as normal or acceptable more than sixty years ago.

Some persons have been inculcated with values that regard people who do not belong to their racial and religious groups as heathen and pagan. Many people regularly use words that refer to people or things of a different culture or nationality in a demeaning manner. These words exemplify attitudes based on values. We may change our attitudes by training ourselves to avoid using words that some other group finds offensive. But learning to avoid politically incorrect words does not alter the values that caused those words to be used in the first place.

Thorny issues cannot be resolved by avoiding such difficult questions as, "Can a White person analyze Afrocentric culture or theatre as well as an African American can?" The question's complexity is exacerbated when the specter of genetic transfer of cultural attributes is present. While we will not cause agreement about this question, we recognize the phenomenon of racism exists and assert that it is the pivotal factor in a complex set of factors. Whether African Americans can or should sing European opera would hold no interest as a question were it not for the presence of racism. By the same token, "can or should White people analyze Afrocentric culture and Black theatre" would hold no interest as a question were it not for racism. So a more relevant question might be, "Can a specific individual overcome racism in responding to Afrocentric theatre?"

Another aspect of this issue is the reality that a society as diverse as the USA's needs people who can interpret life across cultures. Just as we need people who can teach others to understand and appreciate the cultures of earlier times and other places, we need people who can teach people who are not culturally Afrocentric to understand and appreciate Afrocentric culture and the art it creates. But this society remains so focused on race that it insists on asking the question: "Who is better qualified to perform this task, someone who is totally grounded in the culture being interpreted or someone who is totally grounded in the culture of those receiving the information?" While we have expressed the view that an optimal analysis of the art of any culture will most likely emerge from a grounding in and familiarity with that culture, we also recognize the possibility that a person who is born and raised in culture A might be a better interpreter of culture B to culture A than someone born and raised in the culture B.

Another factor must be addressed even though it may seem to contradict a previously stated idea. American culture exists. Overrated as it is, the melting pot myth has some validity. African culture has influenced European culture more than most Eurocentric people will admit, and European culture has influenced African American culture. While there is no one conglomerate American culture, several hyphenated American cultures profoundly influence each other, causing many cherished beliefs of European Americans to also be cherished beliefs of African Americans, even when the beliefs are not in African Americans' best interest. Eurocentric schools teach Black children that Greece is the cradle of civilization when the cradle of civilization is actually the Nile valley in Africa. Children are taught to parrot phrases like "Columbus discovered America," as though nobody already lived here when Columbus arrived. By and large, African Americans get their formal education in Eurocentric schools and much of their informal education is subject to Eurocentric American influences as well. The result is a cultural fusion that is extremely complex and getting more so as time goes on.

Chapter Two

Race is a Social Construction

"There is no black racism because there is no centuries-old system of racialized subordination and discrimination designed by African Americans to exclude white Americans from full participation in the rights, privileges, and benefits of this society."[19] —Feagin and Vera, *White Racism,* 1995

Although debate about whether certain human characteristics are inherited or learned will no doubt continue for decades, if not centuries to come, in recent decades the idea that race is a social construction continues to gain acceptance. The American Anthropological Association explains this idea about the nature of race on its website.

> Race shapes how one sees and is seen by others. Yet, many people poorly understand what race is and isn't.
> To help promote a broad understanding of race and human variation, the American Anthropological Association . . . produced an award-winning public education program entitled RACE: are We so Different?
> The program explains how human variation differs from race, when and why the idea of race was invented, and how race and racism affects everyday life.
> The program conveys three overall messages:
> Race is a recent human invention.
> Race is about culture, not biology.
> Race and racism are embedded in institutions and everyday life.[20]

RACE IS A SOCIAL CONSTRUCTION

To know race is a social construction is to know Afrocentric, Eurocentric, and Asiocentric behaviors and points of view are not biologically or genetically inherited. Many believe race is not only socially constructed, it is fluid, capricious, whimsical and non-rational, while others remain totally committed to the idea that race is biological, permanent, and visually determinable. Nevertheless, race and racism remain so institutionally embedded in our everyday lives that many who have learned to recite the words "race is a social construction" continue to believe some people are mulatto and others are racially pure and that they can visually identify individuals who, in their view, belong to these categories.

The affirmation that race is a social construction raises questions about why we continue to use racial labels. Although words that describe cultural identities or physical attributes are not inherently objectionable, racism has ingrained the idea that any description of an "other" race presumes a hierarchal arrangement. What makes racism offensive is not the words that describe differences or the actual differences the words describe. The offensive aspect of racism is the assumption of an inherent hierarchal arrangement, that people who look different or behave differently are necessarily better or worse. Some seem to believe the offensive aspects of racial labeling can be alleviated by refusing to speak about differences or pretending differences do not exist in the belief that racism will go away if we refuse to acknowledge these obvious human differences.

Acknowledging White Racism

White racism exists. It promotes massive power and privilege for a few who will not allow their power and privilege to diminish just because good people of diverse backgrounds wish it so. White racism has and continues to provide a moral imperative for cultural imperialism, an insidious system that forces the culture of one group on others of a different culture. The group that forces its culture on others must have both the desire and the power to establish dominance over another group and coerce the other group to reject their own culture in favor of the dominant group's culture.

Some beliefs about culture advanced by leaders of Nazi Germany shed light on how racism has been used to justify cultural imperialism. Despite contentions of others to the contrary, Nazi science proclaimed many characteristics of other groups result from biological (genetic) imprinting, proving one race (theirs) was superior, rendering all other races inferior to varying degrees. The idea that science supports a hierarchical view of race permeates the ideology of Western rationalism. While most societies reject the barbarism that allowed these ideas to justify the Holocaust, the propaganda strategy designed to make the Holocaust seem appropriate continues to divert other societies from asking the obvious question: do differences in appearance and behavior, even genetic ones, inevitably signify a hierarchical structure of racial superiority and inferiority?

Nazi propaganda's core concept claims planet earth is populated by people of scientifically determinable, recognizably different races. The horrendous magnitude of Hitler's crimes has left an ironic legacy. Nazi propaganda's core concept remains alive and well in Europe and the USA. Further, Eurocentric cultural imperialism has imbedded it in many other societies of the world. As a result, debate continues over such questions as "do races differ in such respects as moral compass, work ethic, intelligence, and the like?" The residue of this ironic legacy is evidenced by political leaders who leverage preconceived notions of racial hierarchy by using code words such as "welfare queen," "illegal immigrant," and "food stamp president" to generate fear and distrust, which in turn enhances their political status. But the discussion about race remains focused on how we treat people of other races without questioning the assertion that other races exist.

Another ironic legacy of Nazi propaganda's core concept is our continuing inability to engage in civil discourse over such questions as whether or not traits of personality, character, intelligence, physical strengths, or weaknesses and the like are biological traits that can be passed on genetically. Common sense suggests that some shared visually observable traits within a family are biologically inherited. So some hypothesize that other more difficult-to-observe traits in larger groups are also passed on genetically. Sadly, this hypothesis foments a controversy in which nearly everyone defends a predetermined side while regarding anything that remotely resembles the other side's position out of the question. This issue will not be resolved so long as either side remains devoted to the idea that groups of human beings with different physiognomies constitute different races. If most Americans believed the only race is the human race, this deeply divisive dispute would not exist. Conversely, so long as the belief prevails that there are several races of people, racism will prevail.

To appreciate the arts that emerge from Afrocentric culture, one must acknowledge the most pervasive external force affecting (whether consciously or not) African American artists' cultural perspectives: White racism. White racism's core concept is that the world is populated by people of different races, which enables a concurrent belief that races exist in a hierarchy, which enables a pattern of advantage based on a deeply held belief that those with power and privilege deserve and are entitled to it while others neither deserve nor are entitled to it.

White racism presumes races exist in a predestined hierarchical pattern in which differences inherently range from inferior (primitive) to superior (civilized or developed). Darwin's theory of evolution provides a seemingly scientific foundation for inferring: (1) societies evolve linearly through time from primitive (simple) to civilized (complex); (2) technologies are never lost and have been cumulative through humankind's life on earth; (3) societies with written codes and histories are more civilized than those whose codes and histories are not written. Further, the more detailed, complex, and voluminous the written laws and prohibitions, the more civilized the society; (4) separation of and clear distinction between the religious and the secular is indicative of significant societal advancement.

Not only Black people but also people of diverse backgrounds, even the majority of White people, are adversely affected by White racism. While White racism's nonrational nature seems to support the idea that it is a product of ignorance and hatred, the ignorant, hate-filled people whose negative actions are often touted as exemplars of racism are not the real racists. They are actually pawns of racism's real perpetrators and beneficiaries: WEPPEOs (wealthy, elite, powerful persons of European origin). Blaming ignorant, hate-filled people diminishes the problem's magnitude and shifts focus away from those who deserve the blame.

White racism is not a byproduct of ignorance. Therefore, supplying people with information will not cure it. Instead, White racism is an assertion of entitlement. But entitlement is meaningless unless those claiming it wield unbridled power as exemplified in a ruling by the U.S. Supreme Court that said in essence, "a Negro has no rights that a White man is bound to respect." The Dred Scott decision of 1857 is the quintessence of racism because it carries the formidable authority of the U.S. Supreme Court. Ability to exert unbridled power enables those in power to define not only themselves, but also others with less power. The powerful make the rules and change them whenever the rules no longer suit their purposes. But contemporary times have encouraged the wealthy and powerful to seek a benevolent self-image by creating two illusions: first, America is a meritocracy in which those who have wealth and power deserve it and have earned it; and second, more wealth for the wealthy will automatically create more jobs and a better life for ordinary Americans.

White racial supremacy as an ideology depends on a doctrine that presumes differences in systems of knowledge among large groups of human beings (cultures) are related to genetic differences or different evolutionary stages of human development as evidenced by differences in observable features. This fundamental premise of racism is so solidly ingrained that every mention of a differing characteristic is presumed to be an assertion that the difference makes one human being good or better, and the other bad or worse.

RACE IS A SOCIAL CONSTRUCTION

For several hundred years, WEPPEOs justified the Atlantic slave trade in the framework of Christian morality by creating an elaborate system that defined people of African origin as less than human, therefore not entitled to the human rights Christian morality demands. Good people of various ethnic groups, including many White people, fought against these wealthy, powerful men of European origin, but wealth, power, and the ideology of White racial supremacy prevailed. Several centuries later, the descendants of these wealthy, powerful men continue to enjoy the massive benefits accrued by their ancestors during the slave trade. To continue reaping the benefits they enjoy, these wealthy, powerful men maintain their centuries-old ideology of White supremacy and the institutional systems it spawned.

All White people do not derive equal benefits from these systems, nor do all White people endorse these systems with equal vigor. Many White people oppose many aspects of these systems. Nevertheless, racism was built into the society's structure by the White people who control the society for their benefit. This system of White advantage is enabled by a vast array of wealth and power generated by White racial supremacy as an ideology. The system does not require White people to ask for each advantage they receive, or even realize they are receiving advantages. Many White people who readily accept the system's advantages claim they oppose the system. Most White people are so accustomed to their automatic advantage that they only notice the system exists when some glitch interrupts the delivery of their advantages. Further, the system's ideology of White supremacy enables some White people to feel obliged to commit individual bad acts to punish any Black person who, in their view, fails to respect the system that places White people at the top and Black people far beneath. Arguably, the term "White racism" is a more appropriate term than just "racism." On the other hand, American racism is White racism. So to constantly modify the terms "race" and "racist" with the term "White" seems an unneeded belaboring of an obvious point.

Although one does not need to know or acknowledge one's power and privilege to benefit from it, those with power and privilege seldom exhibit a predilection to relinquish it. Racism, by definition and design, aids in maintaining power and privilege for those who already possess it. Racism is not the same as bigotry, which can involve a person of one race behaving badly toward a person of a different race. Bigotry is fueled by racism, but bigotry is an individual phenomenon while racism is a societal phenomenon. Since bigotry has no direct connection to real wealth or power, a person of any race or societal strata can be a bigot. Bigots despise, distrust, or disapprove of other people simply because they are other. Often bigots are frustrated over their inability to wield power over the people they despise. This frustration sometimes escalates to the level of hate crime. While there are undoubtedly some Black bigots, there are no Black racists. The often-used terms "reverse discrimination" and "Black racism" describe concepts that only exist in theory, never in actuality. Only persons with power and privilege can practice racism.

By defining racism as hatred of people of some other race, the true beneficiaries and strongest advocates of racism exempt themselves from being identified as racist. The people with the most power and privilege create an environment in which their lackeys feel either honor-bound to commit horrendous acts under the guise of hatred or they feel afraid of some fabricated threat from another race. Both of these strategies encourage White men with very little wealth, power, training, or intelligence to acquire guns and use them to defend White honor or protect White people from some perceived fear. However, the real racists, the ones with real wealth, power, and privilege, do not need to commit acts of violence themselves. They only need to create an environment that encourages the other classes of White men to keep the other races in line.

America's "Stand Your Ground" laws are clear examples of how racism works. The Florida "Stand Your Ground" law went into effect in 2005. Five years later, it had been invoked in ninety-three cases that caused sixty-five deaths statewide. There are at least twenty-three other states with similar laws. In Florida, the law states:

> A person who is not engaged in an unlawful activity and who is attacked in any other place where he or she has a right to be has no duty to retreat and has the right to stand his or her ground and meet force with force, including deadly force if he or she reasonably believes it is necessary to do so to prevent death or great bodily harm to himself or herself or another or to prevent the commission of a forcible felony.

Events following Trayvon Martin's murder show racism empowering less fortunate White men to do the racists' dirty work. Such laws exist in at least twenty-four states, including Florida, where George Zimmerman admittedly shot and killed Martin on February 26, 2012. The Trayvon Martin case sparked national outrage only because Martin was a "clean-cut" middle-class teenager (seventeen), unarmed, and en route on foot to his father's home inside a gated community, and only after the release of 911 audio recorded just prior to Martin's death and video of Zimmerman's deferential treatment by police. Only then was the case removed from local jurisdiction and assigned by the state attorney's office to a special prosecutor, and only then was Zimmerman charged with second-degree murder.

Zimmerman longed for a career in law enforcement and to follow in the footsteps of his father, a retired magistrate judge. But according to a mistakenly released email, he failed algebra twice and earned a D in intro to criminal justice at Seminole State College. This information, while irrelevant to the murder case, strengthens the contention that racism encourages and empowers bigoted White men with very little wealth, power, training, or intelligence to acquire guns and use them to protect "White honor."

In contrast, there was no national outrage on June 30, 2008, when Joe Horn of Pasadena, Texas (a suburb of Houston) was cleared of any wrongdoing by a Harris County grand jury. News reports agreed that on November 14, 2007, Horn noticed his neighbor's home was being burglarized and called 911. The operator explicitly told Horn to stay inside his house; the police were on the way. Instead, Horn got his shotgun, told the operator he was going to kill the robbers, went outside, and shouted, "Move, you're dead!" Three gunshots are heard on the 911 tape, and about eighty seconds later the police arrived. The two unarmed burglars were shot in the back and killed, and there is no indication they threatened Horn.

While Horn is undoubtedly a bigot, he is not the racist in this incident. The law that literally gave him permission to do what he did is the racist. Horn told the 911 operator, "I'm going to shoot." After the operator admonished him not to go outside with a gun, Horn replied, "The laws have been changed in this country since September the first, and you know it." The operator says, "You're going to get yourself shot." And Horn replies, "You want to make a bet? I'm going to kill them." Horn went outside and killed them knowing the system would not punish him for killing two Black men who appeared to have robbed his neighbor's house. Although Horn was adamant about killing the burglars, he never mentioned they were Black. The new strategy for new millennium lynching is to feign color-blindness.

For several decades, American theatre has proffered a panacea for the well-documented lack of employment opportunity for Black actors. This panacea is called "color-blind casting." But color-blindness has a negative side that seems to outweigh its potential benefits. This negative side of color-blindness is succinctly described by Derald Wing Sue in an article entitled "Dismantling the Myth of a Color-Blind Society."

> Color-blindness . . . uses "whiteness" as the default key to mimic the norms of fairness, justice and equity by 'whiting' out differences and perpetuating the belief in sameness.
> The pretense by some White Americans of not seeing color is motivated by the need to appear free of bias and prejudice, fears that what they say or do may appear racist, or an attempt to cover up hidden biases.
> To be color-blind . . . allows the White person to deny how his or her whiteness intrudes upon the person of color.

> White teachers [may admonish] African American students to 'leave your cultural baggage at home and don't bring it into the classroom.' They have little awareness that they bring their whiteness into the classroom and operate from a predominantly White ethnocentric perspective. How would they react if one were to say, 'Why don't you leave your White cultural baggage at home?' The invisible veil of whiteness inundates the definitions of a 'human being,' being just a 'person' and being an 'American.'[21]

When Prof. William Julius Wilson published a book entitled *The Declining Significance of Race: Blacks and Changing American Institutions* in 1978, it stimulated condemnation and praise with nearly equal amounts of exuberance. Sociological data used to support such theses as Wilson's *The Declining Significance of Race* and Daniel Patrick Moynihan's 1965 *Report* from the U.S. Department of Labor is generated by methods to seek truth (gathering and interpreting statistical data) that are significantly different from those typically used by artists (imagining and creating). Artists expect their truths to be experienced viscerally and directly by their audience, whereas social science truths are often articulated by some intermediary who interprets the work, thereby filtering it through an interpreter's biases. Very few people have read either *The Declining Significance of Race* or the Moynihan *Report*, deferring instead to summary interpretations filtered through the biases of spin doctors and radio and television pundits whose audiences expect to be told what to think. Whether or not the significance of race is declining is more likely to be exposed through a form that focuses on feelings than through a form that makes a concerted effort to only consider objective data.

People who believe in the declining significance of race or a post-racial America often cite data that allegedly support their position. But as social science data gathering techniques strive to be objective, they deliberately avoid emotional involvement with subjects whose lives they reduce to fit a statistical model. Artists, on the other hand, generally place a higher value on emotional aspects of the truths they seek to articulate. Artists are more likely to seriously consider people's intuitive and emotional responses to issues of race, and are therefore more likely to articulate a truth that includes, for example, how a specific White character in a play feels about a Black character with whom she or he interacts. Issues of how someone feels about someone else who is racially different are articulated in theatre and other art in far more forceful ways than statistical data enables. Since bigotry is a feeling that often defies statistical measurement or rational explanation, it can be more effectively expressed and addressed through theatre than through statistical data.

In fairness, statistical data has enabled the enactment of laws, official definitions, and policies regarding racial discrimination that have helped to achieve statistically measurable shifts toward racial equity. But statistics often fail to indicate subtle complexities such as the price one may be required to pay for an employment opportunity. In our allegedly post-racial society, a Black person may have a job that used to be denied on the basis of race, but the statistics do not reveal how that Black person is treated in the workplace or how culturally White that Black person is required to appear in order to remain on the job, or how such behavior modification effects that person's sense of identity and wellbeing. While visually observable racial characteristics may not matter as much as they used to, cultural and economic Whiteness matters as much as ever.

Location and Agency

To discuss race means to tackle white racial supremacy as an ideology, conscious or unconscious, in the American psyche; it is to discuss the issue of "African agency," that is, an America in which African Americans do not have to abandon their cultural heritage in order to be Americans.[22]—Molefi K. Asante, *Erasing Racism*

To appreciate the experience of an African American artist, one must understand the concept of "African agency." African American artists express this concept in a variety of ways, but it boils down to the question:

Do I have to abandon my cultural heritage in order to get a job, to be an American, to be an artist?

Playwright August Wilson expressed the concept of "African agency" in more poetic terms.

> The African who arrived chained and malnourished in the hold of a 350-ton Portuguese vessel has not disappeared . . . has not vanished off the face of the earth. He, in effect, still continues to live . . . within myself . . . within every Black person in America . . . there is at least one heartbeat that is fueled by the blood of Africa. We find ourselves in a world that did not recognize our language, our customs, did not recognize our gods, and ultimately, did not recognize our humanity. Once you understand that you have an intrinsic sense of self-worth and the way your ideas of morality, your concept of justice and beauty, your eating habits, your ideas of pleasure and pain . . . All these things go into your mythology, your history. All these things go into the making of a culture. And I think it's crucial that we, as Black Americans, keep that alive. Now, what the society has told us is that, if you are willing to deny that . . . if you are willing to deny the fact that you are African . . . if you are willing to give up your culture and adopt the cultural values of the dominant society, you can go to school, and you can get a decent job and have decent housing, et cetera. But that is at tremendous cost. That is at the loss of self. And I think the vast majority of the 35 million Blacks in America have rejected that social contract. They want another social contract that will allow them to participate in society as African people with their culture intact.[23]

If one presumes race is biological, permanent, and visually determinable, most of what we seek to convey here will be misunderstood. Often, scholars who subscribe to Asante's Afrocentric paradigm are met with the retort, "Afrocentricism is racism in reverse." Asante has frequently and fervently explained that Afrocentricism is a description of location or place.

Asante's seminal work *The Afrocentric Idea*, published in 1987, describes this concept in detail. A more succinct description appears in his essay, "Location Theory and African Aesthetics," published in *African Aesthetics: Keeper of the Traditions*, edited by Kariamu Welsh-Asante.

> The primary view held by Afrocentrists is that the most rewarding results of any analysis of culture derive from a centered position, usually defined as the *place* from which all concepts, ideas, purposes, and vision radiate.[24]

To visualize a concrete example of location, imagine a complex piece of three-dimensional sculpture surrounded by four people who stand to the precise north, south, east, and west of the sculpture. Each person may get as close or as far away as they wish to view the sculpture, but each person must remain in line with their assigned angle to the piece. After adequate observation time, each person turns 180 degrees, walks away, and writes a description of the same sculpture. If each person's description is accurate, each description will be different. But each description will also be correct from the point of view of each writer.

As we describe contrasts between Afrocentric and Eurocentric thought, values, behavior, etc., we know that while each location is different, each is undoubtedly legitimate and correct from its own perspective. But persons whose location embraces Western rationalism sometimes insist that if their position is right, then any differing position must be wrong. Western rationalism encourages a method of analyzing people or things that arranges them into categories and tends to encourage thinking about them in terms of dichotomy (dividing into two opposed parts) and hierarchy (arranging by rank from good to bad or high to low). We recognize that many people believe this approach is the natural or normal or preferred way to think about things. On the other hand, our descriptions of differences in Afrocentric and Eurocentric thought, values, behavior, etc., do not presume or infer that either location is opposed to the other or is better or worse or higher or lower than the other. But race and racism are so thoroughly embedded in institutions and everyday life that some will unconsciously presume the terms Afrocentric and Eurocentric are really descriptors of race and any allegation of a difference between Afrocentric and Eurocentric people or things infers that the differing attributes are either inherently opposed to each other or that one is inherently superior to the other.

These unconscious patterns of thought and behavior are difficult to recognize and even more difficult to overcome. We do not claim to be immune to the pervasive impact of racism. Our society overwhelms us with the idea that Eurocentric patterns of thought and behavior are human nature. To actually change one's location is not simple or easy or comfortable. A subtle but crucially important difference between Afrocentric and Eurocentric theatre has to do with the location from which a play is conceived by the playwright(s), interpreted for production, and observed by audience and critic(s). The location from which the playwright conceives the play and the artists collaborate to produce the play must be a vantage point from which critics and audience members agree to observe the play. When Black plays are produced in nonracial or color-blind (meaning White) American theatres, differences of opinion about location are often as disregarded as dirt swept under the rug. Pretense that race (meaning cultural identity) is an insignificant factor discourages honest conversation among collaborators. Black theatre artists are generally left with a choice: create your work from a nonracial or color-blind (meaning White) location, or in the words of that eminent philosopher, Ray Charles: "Hit the road, Jack."

From Mr. Brown's African Grove Theatre in 1816, to the American Negro Theatre in the 1930s and '40s, to the Black Arts Movement of the 1960s and '70s, to the Black theatre companies that have survived in the new millennium, the consistent goal has been to empower Black theatre artists to create alternative definitions of success, to encourage African agency. To paraphrase Molefi Asanti, to establish a theatre in which African Americans do not have to abandon their cultural heritage in order to create theatre. So instead of (White) critical acclaim and box office revenue serving as the only arbiters of success, acceptance of their work by Black audiences and Black community support become creditable standards of accomplishment. This type of empowerment can only occur after the supposition that a Eurocentric vantage point as a worldview has been rejected. On the other hand, failure to create a vantage point from which White critics or ticket purchasers or wealthy contributors are willing to view a play virtually guarantees two things: (1) failure by their standards and (2) both fame and fortune are out of the question (despite examples to the contrary, ranging from Spike Lee to Tyler Perry).

As the concept of location is useful in understanding Afrocentricism, the concept of tipping is useful in understanding the subtle nature of location. Tipping refers to the change that tips the balance when using scales that place weights on one side until they equal the weight of the object being weighed on the other side. When both sides contain equal amounts of weight, the scale is balanced. But a minuscule amount of weight added to either side will throw the scale out of balance and tip the scale. In the real estate business, tipping describes a perceived shift that throws White racial comfort out of balance. Farai Chideya, author of *Don't Believe the Hype*,[25] says tipping the racial balance in what used to be an all-White neighborhood occurs when the Black population reaches 8 percent. Subsequently, White homeowners and potential home purchasers perceive the neighborhood as too Black. White people no longer want to buy homes in the neighborhood, and White homeowners want to sell their homes for reasons they do not wish to explain. A few grains of sand will cause a delicately balanced scale to tip. Aesthetic factors frequently envisioned as a White/Black dichotomy may be envisioned more accurately as a grain of sand that tips the scale. Rhetorical strategies that belittle Afrocentric concepts tend to attribute false dichotomies between Eurocentric and Afrocentric positions when the magnitude of difference between the locations is often more aptly understood by using the concept of tipping.

While the distance between Afrocentric and Eurocentric locations may be so similar that shifting from one to the other can be described as tipping, the effort required to overcome double-consciousness is an arduous and ongoing task. An opportunity to confront our own double-consciousness presented itself in 1997 as an invitation to workshop our play entitled *Fortunes of the Moor* with Abibigromma (the National Theatre Company of Ghana) and later present the play at the University of Ghana in Legon, Ghana's National Theatre in Accra, and at Panafest '97 in Cape Coast. The process enabled us to recognize the extent to which early iterations of the script were shaped by the pervasive impact of Eurocentricism and shift the play's location while working in a truly Afrocentric environment.

We did not begin work on *Fortunes of the Moor* until 1993, although some twenty years earlier we discussed the idea of a play that addressed the question: "What if Othello and Desdemona had a son?" Following a reading at the 1995 National Black Theatre Festival, the play premiered at the Frank Silvera Writers' Workshop in New York, with additional productions at Western Michigan University and the Connecticut Repertory Theatre. The Ohio State University had scheduled a production for 1998 when we were invited to develop a production for Abibigromma during the summer of 1997.

We were familiar with Molefi Asante's concept of location when we began to think about *Fortunes of the Moor* for Abibigromma, but developing the play for Ghana forced us to consider location in practical behavioral terms. After decades of earnest endeavor to write from an Afrocentric location, we were forced to admit the place from which we envisioned *Fortunes of the Moor* was more Eurocentric than we had realized or intended. As we began to think about creating the play in Ghana with a Ghanaian cast, we started to conceptually (unconsciously) relocate the play. While in Ghana, we were surrounded by constant reminders that a Eurocentric view is not a worldview. Our physical location stimulated our mental and spiritual relocation and enabled us to relocate the play to a more African place.

AFROCENTRIC THEATRE

This summary of *Fortunes of the Moor* as we initially conceived it will enable us to explain the changes we made in Ghana. As Shakespeare's *Othello* concludes, Desdemona and Othello are dead and Desdemona's cousin Lodovico urges his uncle Gratiano to "seize upon the fortunes of the Moor." Later, Gratiano learns Desdemona secretly gave birth to a baby boy who resides at a Venetian convent. The baby is heir to two fortunes: Othello's and Desdemona's father Brabantio's. With the baby out of the picture, Brabantio's younger brother Gratiano stands to inherit the fortunes. Gratiano's greed motivates him to send Lodovico to Africa to find Othello's family and convince them to claim the child. In anticipation of his elderly brother's demise, Gratiano has purloined money from Brabantio to invest in a slave ship. Brabantio discovers the child's existence and declares his intent to claim the child and make him his heir. Gratiano uses racist references to the child's heritage to persuade Brabantio to abandon his desire to keep the child, but to no avail. Hassan, Othello's uncle, arrives to claim the child and Gratiano decides the only way he is certain to inherit the fortunes is to murder the child. He plots with Lodovico to have some thugs kidnap the child from the convent and murder him. Lodovico bungles the job and Gratiano's web of murder and deceit unravels. Ultimately, Hassan and Brabantio each believe they have seized the best of Othello's legacy.

Since the advent of realism, a pervasive convention of Eurocentric theatre has been the illusion of eavesdropping. The location for both the playwright's conception and the audience's view offers direct observation of events unfolding in a linear time narrative. Originally, *Fortunes of the Moor* was conceived in this Eurocentric convention, which allowed the audience to look directly into Venice in 1565. The action moved in linear time. The audience eavesdrops as Gratiano discusses the investment he plans to make in a slave ship with his brother's money. The play's representational style seemed to emerge from Gratiano's perspective and focus on his dilemma. In anticipation of our work in Ghana, we began to revise the script for a company of Ghanaian actors, whose appearance did not offer the phenotype differences earlier iterations of the script assumed. As we restructured the play for a Ghanaian cast and audience, we began to discover the Eurocentricism inherent in earlier assumptions about the play's location. Conversations with Mohammed Ben Abdallah, PhD, former minister of culture and founder of Abbibigromma, enhanced this discovery process and generated a series of changes.

The pivotal change relocates the play's action to Africa. Hassan is a *griot* (storyteller) who tells the story of Hassan who goes to Venice to claim his grandson. The story is told in Abibigoro, an African style that is presentational and interactive, combining narrative story telling and dramatic portrayal of the action. Changing the locale to Africa facilitated changing the concept of costumes, scenery, and props from direct observation to one that presumes the artifacts used in the play come from Hassan's hometown. Venice and Venetian characters are seen through Hassan's eyes as portrayed by Hassan's townspeople. In the tradition of Abibigoro, we created a voice for the community. This communal voice periodically comments on the action, but with its own internal conflicts, sometimes taking opposing sides of issues.

Traditionally, Abibigoro stories are structured with circular plots. The story begins at the end and circles to the beginning and around and back to the end. Storytellers announce they will explain a certain phenomenon, such as "how spider obtained the sky god's stories." Since the audience already knows how the story ends, they accept the storyteller as a conveyor of truth, and focus on how well the story is told. Abibigoro tradition also allows the play to shift back and forth between narrative and action.

The Abibigromma *Fortunes of the Moor* contains narrative, singing, and dancing. The *griot* tells a story that begins as Hassan returns to his home and explains what happened in Venice. As the production was staged, the audience cannot be certain if Othello's kin have returned with the baby or not. The community asks if they were successful; to which Hassan replies, "We will tell the story." In the Abibigoro tradition, the audience observes the story from the *griot's* point of view. Hassan's, Elissa's, and Somaia's return become the play's enveloping action. The play begins and ends with the same welcoming ceremony, except the baby is present at the end.

Since we were with Abibigromma for ten weeks, we were able to develop some of the play's new attributes through company participation. We described a scenario for the beginning of the play that involved the return of Hassan, Elissa, and Somaia to their home and asked, "What kind of welcome would their village provide?" The company created music and dance for the occasion. The play begins with actors entering the stage and announcing they are going to do a play. They talk about the premise of the play and justify its enactment. Hassan, as the *griot*, pours a libation to request that the act of storytelling be blessed. He asks the townspeople to play the roles of the Venetian characters. They agree, and as they don masks to portray the Venetians, they sing and dance to bid Hassan and his family a safe journey to Venice. We accommodate American (including African American) sensibilities and create suspense by having the action unfold in a linear sequence. The actors wear African costumes and use African artifacts for props. The play's locale is Hassan's African hometown. The focus is on Hassan, who introduces himself and his family and explains his goal. Hassan occasionally steps out of the scene, and as the *griot*, comments on the action to the townspeople and to the audience.

Chapter Three

Foundations of Interpretation

"A great many people think they are thinking when they are merely rearranging their prejudices." —William James (1842-1910)

Black theatre has existed in the Americas since the first performance in the Americas by people who came from Africa. Since context and environment have a profound effect on performance, the first Black performances in America were not exactly what they would have been had they taken place in Africa. They were not African performances in America, but African American performances. Black theatre in America evolved as African culture evolved into African American culture and Afrocentric cultural values are reflected and perpetuated by Black theatre.

Some Eurocentric theatre experts have used the term Black theatre to describe only the theatre of the Black arts movement of the 1960s. To suggest that Black theatre only dates back to the 1960s is misleading and demeaning. The Black theatre movement of the 1960s was a significant milestone that helped repopularize the term Black and had a number of other positive effects on the cultural awareness of African Americans and others in the African diaspora including a reawakening of pride in African cultural identity among African Americans. To suggest the Black theatre movement of the 1960s created a new culture or a new theatre denigrates the accomplishments of our ancestors. Afrocentric theatre and culture are older than recorded history. Evidence that Black theatre existed over four thousand years ago is readily available but ignored by many Eurocentric theatre history experts. On the other hand, at least two early authors of American books that examine theatre as a worldwide phenomenon, Vera Mowry Roberts and Oscar G. Brockett, discuss the theatre of Kemet (which they call ancient Egypt).

On Stage, a History of Theatre by Vera Mowry Roberts was published in 1962 and was the first serious discussion of theatre in Kemet that we ever read in a theatre history book. *History of the Theatre* by Oscar G. Brockett, first published in 1968, contains a short section entitled "Ritual Drama in Egypt and the Near East." Brockett's *History of the Theatre* is widely regarded as the standard theatre history textbook in the United States, with many subsequent editions. Each successive edition of the book seems to have expanded and improved its coverage of African theatre on the African continent and in the diaspora, and an eleventh edition of *History of Theatre* by Oscar G. Brockett and Franklin J. Hildy was published in 2012.

Having garnered a sense of how values function, we may reasonably posit the idea that analysis and interpretation of the arts is controlled by the analyst's or interpreter's values. Comparing Eurocentric and Afrocentric analyses and interpretations of the same data may illustrate how analysts' or interpreters' values shape opinions that come to be regarded as facts. This comparison may also explain how well-intentioned people in this multicultural society can examine some Afrocentric theatre event from a Eurocentric location and see something markedly different from what is seen when the same event is viewed from an Afrocentric location.

We will consider data about the first theatre, the oldest extant African American script, the first African American theatre, and the minstrel tradition.

The First Theatre

In 1968, Brockett's sixth edition of *History of the Theatre* asserts:
> Although the influence of Egypt on Greece apparently was considerable, one important difference remains between their performance traditions. The Egyptians maintained an advanced

civilization for some three thousand years (a period longer than the one that separates us from the beginnings of Greek drama) and never developed theatrically beyond ritualized performances, repeating the same ceremonies year after year for centuries. Theirs was a relatively static society which resisted changes that might have led to an autonomous theatre, whereas the Greeks went on to develop a theatre in which new plays were presented each year. Thus, despite the achievements of the Egyptians, it is Greece that took the decisive step toward an autonomous theatre.[26]

This passage illustrates at least two fundamental differences between contemporary Afrocentric and Eurocentric theatre interpreters. First, Brockett's Eurocentric location seems to assume Greek theatre's shift from religious-based ritual theatre to autonomous (meaning secular) theatre constitutes progress. Afrocentric philosophy as codified by the Kemites contends there is no differentiation between the religious and the secular because religion permeates every aspect of human existence. In contrast, Brockett's Eurocentric location sees this separation as not only possible but as preferable. Moreover, Brockett's location sees the development of institutionalized secular art as progress in the evolutionary development of civilization. Second, Brockett's Eurocentric location seems to assume competition, a fundamental characteristic of Greek theatre, fosters excellence. In contrast, competition held no value for the Kemites, who were more concerned with abiding by the guiding principles of Maat: truth, justice, and righteousness. These governing moral values "stemmed from a collective, sedentary, relatively easy, peaceful life, once it had been regulated by a few social laws."[27]

The Greek idea of the dramatic contest seems to presuppose it is better to perform new scripts every year than it is to do a better job of performing the same old scripts year after year after year. The Kemites, by virtue of their behavior, would obviously disagree with this supposition. A continuation of the Kemites' philosophical view can be seen in current

Afrocentric aesthetic ideals and will be described in the section of this book that deals with Afrocentric ritual theatre. Here, it is sufficient to note that the Eurocentric aesthetic ideal places a greater value on the presentation of new content than the continuation of traditional values through ritual. In African ritual, there are internal and external motivations to perform a ritual well, possibly to perform the ritual better than it has ever been performed before. However, since there is no contest, there is no need to proclaim winners and losers.

Ancient Greek drama, on the other hand, evolved into an annual competition in which winners and losers were declared. The competitive nature of Greek drama, along with its secularization, undoubtedly fostered the development of new theatrical content. However, the unanswerable question remains to what extent did the shift from religious ritual to a secular competition reduce Greek drama's effectiveness in instilling the values of truth, justice, and righteousness in its audience?

Brockett indicates there are more than fifty surviving pyramid texts from the period 2800 to 2400 BC, and that certain passages may have been traditional by that time and may have originated 1,000 years earlier. These texts generally portray the values and beliefs that governed the Kemites' lives. Brockett also says some scholars contend these texts were scripts to be performed while others "disagree violently over the degree to which these texts should be considered dramatic," arguing they were not intended for performance.[28] In addition to the pyramid texts, Brockett mentions there are texts related to the coronation of pharaohs; a text called the "Memphite Drama," which was performed on the first day of spring, dating back to 2500 BC; and a text that some scholars call the "Abydos Passion Play" that was performed annually from about 2500 until about 550 BC[29] The "Memphite Drama" was composed during the first dynasty and rewritten by Shabako about 700 BC on a stone, which now resides in the British Museum. The "Memphite Drama" commemorated the unification of upper and lower Kemet by Menes about 5500 BC and "is in reality the libretto of a drama or stage-play which was probably acted when certain important festivals were celebrated at Memphis."[30] The Abydos Passion Play is based on the myth of Osiris and Horus. The term "passion play" is traditionally used to describe a type of medieval Christian drama that focuses on the death and resurrection of Jesus. The myth of Osiris and Horus is considerably more than 2,000 years older than the similar Greek myths that deal with death and resurrection or rebirth. According to the Greek historian Herodotus:

> Almost all the names of the gods came into Greece from Egypt. My inquiries prove that they were all derived from a foreign source, and my opinion is that Egypt furnished the greater number.[31]

Brockett points out that Herodotus visited Kemet in about 450 BC, "noted two performances there," and thought the Greek god Dionysus was a "disguised version of the Egyptian god Osiris."

Brockett recognizes that some scholars consider these Kemite texts the earliest recorded theatrical productions while others "have vigorously objected."[32] Brockett's *History of the Theatre* contains a photograph of a relief sculpture from a tomb at Saqqara [or *Sakkara*] that clearly illustrates some individuals performing a dance while others "seem to be providing a clapping accompaniment."[33] There are paintings that depict ritual dancing; there are texts that describe dramatic action; and there are highly respected scholars who have validated the conclusion that the texts were enacted in the form of dramatic ceremonial rituals.

Most of the widely disseminated information that recognizes the theatre and drama of Kemet implies that the Kemites were committed to their religious beliefs and practices to the extent that they seem to have been a humorless people. Yet a scholar of considerable Eurocentric respectability, E. A. Wallis Budge, indicates that what he calls ancient Egyptian drama and theatre was not limited to serious plays. Budge states, "The lapses of the gods and goddesses, moral or otherwise, did not stir men to anger, but did provoke men to regard them with a sort of kindly and good-humoured ridicule."[34]

He uses the hieratic text, "The Contendings of Horus and Set," translated by Alan Gardiner to illustrate the point. Budge writes:

> This contains what I believe to be the 'book of words' of a play, . . . which may rightly be described as 'a Mythological Drama.' The narrative is slight, but the speeches of all the actors are given at length, and a connected story can be constructed. This play represents the gods assembled as a Court of Justice with Ra as chairman, and they have to decide a simple issue, viz. whether the son of Osiris, the youthful cripple Horus, is to succeed to his father's office, or whether it is to be given to his bold, handsome and free-living uncle (or brother) Set. Ra is in favour of Set, but many of the gods are not. They lose their tempers, contradict and insult each other, and wrangle together like the members of a local or municipal Miglis in Egypt at the present day. The delay of the law is laughed at, and the indecision and vacillation of the gods is made clear. The gross social customs of a bygone age are pilloried in the story of the criminal assault which Set made on Horus whilst they were occupying the same couch, and in the account of the obscene relations which existed between Isis and her son Horus. The ribaldry of Neith, the whorish behavior of Hathor, the daughter of Ra, the lasciviousness of Set, the quarrel of Set with the gods when he threatened to slay them one by one, the quarrel of Horus with Isis when he cut off her head, . . . are all lightly but clearly brought out. The gods adjourn and change the site of their court, but come to no decision, for they ignore the advice of the old gods, and the evidence which they ask for and obtain from them and snub their referees. Finally, forgetting their precarious position, they address disparaging words in their letters to Osiris, but his reply is so menacing that they fulfil straightway his command to make Horus his successor, and give Set a position in the sky where he can act as the god of thunder. This play makes good reading and is a thoroughly 'human document', but

it is difficult to think that those who saw it played would find their reverence for the gods increased.[35]

The "kindly and good-humoured ridicule" presented in a performance of "The Contendings of Horus and Set" is comedy. The existence of comedy in Kemetic theatre is significant because it contradicts the widely held view that the Kemites were humorless people inclined to take themselves too seriously, as evidenced by their religious zeal. The Kemites left further evidence that the extant scripts were actually performed by indicating who the performers were. Diop supports the contention that these works were performed. In *Civilization or Barbarism*, he observes:

> Up to the first Tanite dynasty, the royal family itself acted in Osiris' drama, . . . Then later, only the priests would act, before the royal family, in the passion of Osiris, the mystery of his death, and resurrection.[36]

One approach that theatre scholars use to aid in determining whether or not a work was performed in its historical context is to perform the work. The assumption is that texts that were not intended to be performed usually do not result in a polished performance without modification, while a work that was intended to be performed usually has undergone whatever modification is necessary to enable a polished performance. Further evidence that these texts were performed is provided by Diop:

> The British School of Egyptology has translated one of these plays written in hieroglyphics; a team of disguised British actors performed it, following the texts faithfully. The film that was made of this unique document was shown by the dramatist and poet G.M. Tsegaye, during the 1973 Pan-African Congress in Addis-Ababa.[37]

In the face of this evidence, the proof that theatre art existed in Kemet by 2500 BC and continued for at least 2,000 years would seem to be substantial, but many scholars still reject this notion. The Kemites constructed a stone performance space with scenery in 2778 BC in Sakkara, the same location as the relief sculpture depicting a performance that is reproduced in Brockett's *History of the Theatre*. And this performance space still exists. In 1896, Sir Banister Fletcher published the first edition of his seminal work, *A History of Architecture on the Comparative Method*. Since Fletcher's death in 1953, the work continues to be revised and reprinted. Although we owned the book for many years, we did not realize Fletcher was describing a performance space until we visited the Step Pyramid in 1988.

> The Step Pyramid of Zoser, Sakkara (2778 B.C., beginning of Third Dynasty) is remarkable as being the world's first large-scale monument in stone. King Zoser's architect, Imhotep, was greatly revered both in his own and later times, and in the Twenty-sixth Dynasty was deified.[38]

From the perspective of theatre history, the iconoclastic information comes in the following quote (italics ours).

> Surrounding the pyramid was a vast rectangular enclosure, 1790 ft from north to south and 912 ft wide, with a massive Tura limestone wall, 35 ft high . . . . Around the walls were bastions, fourteen in all, and each had *stone false doors*. The only entrance was in a broader bastion near the southern end of the eastern face . . . . *all the rest of the structures . . . . are dummy representations of the palace of Zoser and the buildings used in connection with the celebration of his jubilee in his lifetime. Most of them therefore are solid, or almost so, comprised of earth or debris faced with Tura limestone* . . . . Just inside the enclosure entrance a narrow corridor runs deviously northwards to the Heb-sed Court, the principal scene of this festival lined with *sham chapels*, each with its small forecourt, those on the western side representing the provinces or "nomes" of Upper Egypt and those on the eastern, of Lower Egypt. These *virtually solid structures* . . . might have symbolized the two kingdoms.[39]

These "dummy representations" were not usable in the traditional architectural sense as there was no space inside them to permit human occupancy. The only plausible use for these structures is to evoke a sense of place for a performance in this "vast rectangular enclosure." Based on these facts, we postulate that these structures are what we currently call stage scenery, and the first known designer and builder of stage scenery was Imhotep in approximately 2778 BC in Sakkara, Kemet. Diop lends further credence to this idea:

> In Egypt, it is the Pharaoh Zoser who seems to have inaugurated the ceremony of the symbolic death of the king, of his regeneration.[40]

As one seeks answers about the origins of theatre art in Africa, an interesting pattern in Eurocentric scholarship becomes evident. Recent scholarship has rediscovered and recent technology has enabled wider dissemination of seemingly obvious evidence that theatre art achieved a remarkable level of sophistication in the Nile valley on the continent of Africa 2,000 years prior to the golden age of Greek drama. As this evidence becomes more readily available to a broader segment of the population, Eurocentric scholarship seems determined to classify the people of this ancient African civilization as Caucasian. Brockett acknowledges that:

> Archeological discoveries in recent years seem to establish that human beings evolved first in the Rift Valley of eastern Africa. Thus, the oldest humans and the first rulers of Egypt may have been black, information which some recent scholars see as having been de-emphasized because of racial prejudice.[41]

The examples of dark brown skin color in the paintings and facial features and hair texture that is represented in considerable detail in the sculpture produced by these people over a span of more than three thousand years, provide obvious and ample evidence that the people of the Nile valley's ancient civilization exhibited physical characteristics that the USA has traditionally defined as "Negro" or "Colored," and in more recent years, as "Black" or "African American."

> Negro, *n., pl.*—groes, *adj.- n.* 1a a person belonging to any of the black races of Africa, characterized by brown or black skin, coarse, woolly hair, and a broad, flat nose; b a member of any other dark-skinned

people; 2 a person having some black ancestors (subject to precise definition by law in certain states and countries)

The ancient Nile valley civilization located where the current nation of Egypt is located called itself Kemet, which means "Black settlement" in their language and the people called themselves Kemites, which means "the Black ones" in their language. Descendants of these people, who now call themselves "Nubian," still live in the Nile valley along with many other groups who have migrated there over the millennia. Further, the root of the word "Kemet" is also the word for the color of "charcoal" in their language.[42] These are the people who built the great pyramids at Giza, the temples at Abu Simbel, the two great temples at Thebes with their connecting avenue of sphinxes, and many other astounding architectural achievements. One of their early architectural achievements was the step pyramid at Sakkara and the surrounding structures. The people of Kemet: (1) are Africans with brown or black skin and coarse woolly hair, the characteristics of people the USA defines as Colored, Negro, Black, or African; (2) built the first known structures for the performance of theatre; and (3) wrote and performed the earliest known dramas and the oldest extant drama.

Since we say race is a social construction, we need to explain that the Kemites' brown or black skin and coarse woolly hair is significant because many Eurocentric scholars insist the Kemites were Caucasian. This insistence has been unrelenting, even in the face of massive scholarship to the contrary by an imminent White scholar at an Ivy League university. Since so many Eurocentric scholars have attacked Martin Bernal's scholarship, we encourage all to read *Black Athena: The Afroasiatic Roots of Classical Civilization*. The facts he has amassed speak for themselves.

In 2778 BC, the step pyramid at Sakkara was constructed. In 1492 AD, Columbus discovered what he thought was a sea route to India. In the 4,270 years between the two events, scholars have documented a southwesternly migration by inhabitants of the Nile river valley. By the time the capture and transport of Africans to the Americas became a significant factor in the European economy, the culture of West Africa had been heavily influenced by the ancient Nile River valley culture. Hence, there is a direct cultural connection between Kemites and African Americans.[43]

The First African American Theatre

In 1816 or 1817, a man known as Mr. Brown opened a tea garden in what was then a thriving community of free African Americans in New York. Although this Mr. Brown's full name was most likely William Alexander Brown, there has been considerable disagreement about his full name.[44] This Mr. Brown and William Wells Brown who wrote *The Escape: or A Leap for Freedom* are not the same person. William Wells Brown could not have been more than two or three years of age when this Mr. Brown began the first professional African American theatre company in the city of New York.[45] Mr. Brown gave up his job as a steward on a ship that sailed between New York and Liverpool, England to open a tea garden in New York. Among the tea garden's early entertainers was a man named James Hewlett, who was known for portraying the roles of several different characters in one performance. By 1821, Mr. Brown had organized the African Company to perform at a theatre he had built to accommodate three or four hundred people, and later at other venues where they might attract larger audiences.[46] One member of the company, Ira Aldridge, went on to become one of the most renowned actors of nineteenth-century Europe.[47]

Playbills of the African Company's performances indicate they may have performed as regularly and definitely charged as much as the other professional theatres operating in New York at the time.[48] An African Company playbill dated June 7, year unspecified but probably from 1822 or 1823, announces their production of *Tom and Jerry, or Life in London*. They undoubtedly drew heavily on the original (1821) Pierce Egan script, but the African Company added a scene entitled, "On the Slave Market." The playbill lists Mr. Smith as the auctioneer, and slaves are portrayed by the Company.[49] One may reasonably assume this scene was added to galvanize existing antislavery sentiment among the audience members who were among the few free people of African origin in the United States at the time. Since the scene was added to a popular British melodrama, there is a strong probability that the means of achieving this antislavery theme was through the use of comic irony.

Mr. Brown's African company was among the first American theatres to produce Pierce Egan's *Tom and Jerry, or Life in London*, a play that "began a trend toward the melodramas of contemporary life and local color."[50] The play was adapted by other groups and became *Life in Philadelphia or Life in New York*. One can reasonably conclude the African Company was among the pioneer American theatre groups in the movement to appreciate the urban folk hero who did not emerge into full popularity until the 1840s.

A later playbill and newspaper article announced on June 20 and 21, 1823, the African Company would present, for the second time, a play called *King Shotaway or The Insurrection of the Caribs*.[51] The play was billed as portraying a struggle by free Black people on the island of St. Vincent written from actual experiences of Mr. Brown, who was both playwright and manager of the company. The newspaper statement that Mr. Brown actually took part in the insurrection could very well be a fabrication aimed at selling tickets. Such marketing techniques were as commonplace then as now. On the other hand, how could anyone conclude a play written and produced by an African American in 1823 about free Black men fighting to keep control of their land was not a significant mark on the history of the theatre?[52] Although the available information about the play is limited to the playbill announcing its presentation for a second time, the implications are clear. The play made a statement in opposition to the institution of slavery. The title character is a hero because he was the leader of people who fought the British to retain control of St. Vincent.

Current research about events portrayed in the play[53] tell us that the Black Caribs of St. Vincent [also known as *Garifuna*], led by their paramount chief, Joseph Chatoyer, fought to retain political and economic control of their land. After the British defeated the Garifuna in 1796, the British officer credited with Chief Chatoyer's death was considered a hero for nearly two centuries. Official recognition and designation of Chief Joseph Chatoyer as the "first national hero of St. Vincent and the Grenadines" took place on March 14, 2002.

After the British defeated the Garifuna in 1796, they attempted to round up the remaining "dissidents" and exile them to an island in the Grenadines that is visible from nearby St. Vincent but remains uninhabitable to this day because there is no apparent water supply. After many managed to survive for over a year, the British removed over 5,000 Garifuna in March of 1798 to an area that now straddles the border between Belize and Honduras—the area from which Mr. Brown immigrated to the United States. In 1795, not long after the United States gained freedom from British domination, these free Black Caribs fought to retain freedom from domination by the British and control of their small island nation. Undoubtedly, the play *King Shotaway* expressed the thematic assumption that for Black people to engage in such an effort was appropriate.

Although neither *King Shotaway* nor *On the Slave Market* is extant as a script, their historical significance as theatrical productions is evident. But their significance may have a negative tone from a Eurocentric perspective. The issues Mr. Brown presents in these plays could very well have led Eurocentric analysts of an earlier time to conclude the principal characters in both plays were insane. Joseph Baldwin, national president of the Association of Black Psychologists was quoted in an Associated Press article saying, "Samuel Cartwright, a white psychologist who worked while slavery existed in the United States . . . identified two disorders suffered by blacks . . . 'Drapetomania' was the desire to run away from slavery, and 'dysathesia aethopica' was a form of rascality where slaves broke hoes or walked over cotton plants or poisoned cows to get out of work." Baldwin further explains that although Whites regarded such behavior as crazy, African Americans considered it the logical thing to do.[54]

Undoubtedly, many White people in New York in 1823 would have regarded a public statement by African Americans in favor of any armed resistance to White domination as insane or criminal, or both. Even before they presented *King Shotaway*, the African Company had its share of troubles with the New York Police Department. The Company had been harassed repeatedly and on more than one occasion, members of the company were arrested and jailed.[55] After the African Company's June 1823 performances of *King Shotaway*, details of the theatre's demise are complicated and difficult to fathom. The hostility of an influential segment of New York's White community as reflected in newspaper coverage of the African Company's encounters with the police, suggests a possible explanation.

Herbert Marshall and Mildred Stock have provided an outstanding example of thorough scholarship in their book entitled *Ira Aldridge: The Negro Tragedian*. Chapter four of the book is devoted to Mr. Brown's African Company. Marshall and Stock cite a number of contemporary newspaper accounts of The African Company. Their quote from an article in the *National Advocate* of September 21, 1821, cites at least two occasions when the New York police interfered with the operation of the African Grove, the place that housed both Mr. Brown's tea garden and his African Company. On one occasion the police apparently closed the place altogether and on another occasion they arrested the actors portraying Richard III and Catesby following a performance of Shakespeare's *Richard III*. The values expressed in the *National Advocate* newspaper, with regard to whether or not it is acceptable for Shakespeare to be performed by a company of African American actors, seem rather transparent and in concert with the police. The *National Advocate* refers to the African Company at one point as "These imitative inmates of the kitchen and pantries . . ." and the actor who portrayed Richard III as "a dapper, woolly-headed waiter . . ." The *National*

Advocate later describes the same actor as "a fellow as black as the ace of spades." The role of Richard III was undoubtedly played by James Hewlett, who is described in a different newspaper as "of lighter color than ordinary mulattoes." The latter (lighter) description is also corroborated by a drawing of Hewlett that is reproduced in *Ira Aldridge: The Negro Tragedian*.[56]

Marshall and Stock cite still another newspaper account of police harassment several months later in the *American* of January 10, 1822.[57] A portion of that article is quoted here to give a sense of how many White people felt about the African Company, or at least how one newspaper wanted them to feel.

HUNG BE THE HEAVENS WITH BLACK
—Shakespeare

We have heretofore noticed the performances of a black corps dramatique in this city, at their theatre, the corner of Bleecker and Mercer streets. It appears that the sable managers, not satisfied with a small share of the profit and a great portion of fame, determined to rival the great Park Theatre, belonging to Messrs. Beekman and Astor, and accordingly hired the Hotel next door . . . where they announced their performances . . . . The ebony-colored wags were notified by the police that they must announce their last performance, but they, defying the public authority, went on and acted nightly. It was at length considered necessary to interpose the arm of authority, and on Monday evening a dozen watchmen made part of the audience . . . .

Several . . . ascended the stage and arrested His Majesty. "Where am I going?" says he. "To de tower?"

"No, to the watch house," said the Knight of the Lantern. Henry, Queen Elizabeth, and the two young princes were escorted in their tinselled robes, to the watch house, into which they marched with royal contempt and defiance.

"Come, come," said the watch, "none of your playacting airs; into the black hole with you." The sable corps were thrust in one green room together where, for some time, they were loud and theatrical; ever and anon, one would thrust his head through a circular hole to survey the grim visages of the watchmen. Finally they plead so hard in blank verse, and promised never to act Shakespeare again, that the Police Magistrates released them at a very late hour.

James Hewlett, who played the title roles in both *King Shotaway* and *Richard III*, managed to continue his acting career. In December of l825, Hewlett appeared at the Spruce Street Theater in New York, apparently in his one-man show in which he played several different characters in one performance and did imitations of the better known White actors of his day. There is some indication that Hewlett performed his one-man show in England in 1825 as well. February 3, 1826, was announced as his last appearance in the United States (at Military Garden) prior to his return to London, where he was allegedly scheduled to appear at the Royal Coburg Theatre, the theatre that eventually became known as the Old Vic. There are no records of Hewlett's appearance at the Royal Coburg to substantiate the announcement. Hewlett's appearances in England were, in all likelihood, made at a theatre of lesser importance or possibly in a major theatre (maybe even the Royal Coburg) but in a minor role. However, Hewlett performed in New York as late as September 22, 1831.[58] James Hewlett was an actor of note in the New York theatre beginning with his rise to prominence with The African Company and lasting for at least a decade. The only known reference to his apparently sudden departure from the spotlight is in a letter from Ira Aldridge to a mutual friend, in which Aldridge refers to Hewlett as "poor Jim Hewlett."[59]

Ira Aldridge made a uniquely successful sojourn from the African Company in New York to London and eventually to the Royal Coburg Theatre. In October of 1825, Aldridge launched a European career that led to his being recognized as one of the leading actors in the Eurocentric world. Despite the significance of Aldridge's success, recognition during his lifetime occurred only in Europe and in strictly Eurocentric terms. Despite White America's desire to love and imitate things European, recognition of Aldridge's excellence as an actor came to America begrudgingly and a century late. In Eurocentric terms, Aldridge succeeded and Hewlett did not. In Afrocentric terms, both were influenced to abandon the venue of artistic expression they had initially chosen. With the African Company's demise, neither Hewlett nor Aldridge would again have an opportunity to appear professionally in a play written by an African American, for an African American audience, with an African American acting company managed by an African American.

The African Company's early nineteenth century exploits do not fully expose the beginnings of Afrocentric theatre in America. These beginnings occur as Black people's life circumstances impact on African art forms. This process occurred with relative rapidity because of the oppressive conditions experienced by both free and enslaved Black people in America. Although conditions were certainly better for free African Americans, their circumstances were far from ideal.

The fate of two schools established by New England abolitionists in the 1830s to educate free African Americans illustrates the oppressive conditions free African Americans faced as far north as New England. The Noyes Academy in Canaan, New Hampshire was attacked by local citizens who used ninety yoke of oxen to drag the schoolhouse from its foundation into a swamp about a half mile from its original site. After Prudence Crandall established an Academy for young women of color in Canterbury, Connecticut, a state law was enacted for the sole purpose of destroying the academy. After Crandall was arrested, jailed, and tried, the school's influential enemies realized abolitionists planned to appeal the case to the U.S. Supreme Court, so the case was thrown out on a technicality. An attempt to destroy the building by arson failed. Late one night as the boarding students slept, the building was invaded and vandalized. The school's board decided they could not guarantee the young women's safety, closed the school, and Prudence Crandall moved out of the state.

When enslaved African Americans used traditional African modes of communication, the result was brutal punishment of various kinds: whipping, mutilation, or even the severing of various extremities. Survival demanded that African American art forms evolve within certain rigidly enforced specifications. For instance, the language used had to be English; African languages were generally not allowed. In addition, the use of drums was almost always prohibited.

The Oldest Extant African American Script

When historians apply Eurocentric values to African American theatre history, they either conclude African American theatre did not exist and ignore it, or they misinterpret it in some significant way. We do not question motives or cast blame on theatre historians who have ignored or misinterpreted African American theatre history. People can only respond to the evidence they perceive according to the dictates of their values. Whether deliberately or unconsciously, Eurocentric historians have generally managed to forestall the dissemination of information about significant achievements by African Americans in a context of Afrocentric culture. When Eurocentric historians have congratulated achievements by Black people, they have often done so in a way that either praises Black people for mimicking Eurocentric culture or strengthens preconceived notions about Black people's inherent inferiority. Praising Black people for mimicking Eurocentric culture often leads to defining Black theatre as an effort to conform to Eurocentric standards and please Eurocentric audiences, thereby achieving greater financial success than attracting only a Black audience could achieve. Using money-driven Eurocentric criteria to define quality tends to focus consideration on plays produced in New York that attract predominately White audiences.

FOUNDATIONS OF INTERPRETATION

In the 1990s, the National Conference on African American Theatre created a committee to address the issue of who and how a canon of Black theatre ought to be established. [NCAAT was later subsumed by a larger organization, Black Theatre Network.] Since most people who seek information about a subject tend to rely on people who are regarded as experts on that subject, both NCAAT and BTN have undertaken the responsibility of creating a short list of plays that form an exemplary body of work by Black dramatists. The NCAAT Canon Committee released the following list in 1997:

Dutchman by Amiri Baraka
The Purple Flower by Marita Bonner
The Escape: or a Leap for Freedom by William Wells Brown
Natural Man by Theodore Browne
Clara's Ol' Man by Ed Bullins
Trouble in Mind by Alice Childress
The Star of Ethiopia by W. E. B. DuBois
Old Man Pete and *Nat Turner* by S. Randolph Edmonds
Ceremonies in Dark Old Men by Lonne Elder
The Brownsville Raid by Charles Fuller
Rachel by Angelina Grimke
A Raisin in the Sun by Lorraine Hansberry
On Strivers Row by Abram Hill
The Confession Stone by Owen Dodson
Mulatto by Langston Hughes
A Sunday Morning in the South by Georgia Douglas Johnson
Funnyhouse of a Negro by Adrienne Kennedy
Graven Images by May Miller
The Chip Woman's Fortune by Willis Richardson
For Colored Girls Who have Considered Suicide/When the Rainbow is Enuf by Ntozake Shange
Contributions (three plays *Contribution*, *Shoes*, and *Plantation*) by Ted Shine
Day of Absence by Douglas Turner Ward
Our Lan' by Theodore Ward
The Talented Tenth by Richard Wesley

AFROCENTRIC THEATRE

Joe Turner's Come and Gone by August Wilson
The Colored Museum by George C. Wolfe

Of the twenty-six plays on the canon list, several have been produced in New York at a venue that attracts mostly White audiences, but most have not. When money-driven standards define quality in Black theatre, many historically significant and artistically competent plays and playwrights are excluded. NCAAT's Canon Committee had a mandate to limit their list to twenty-five plays. They limited it to twenty-six. Making lists like this is always dangerous. The process is bound to omit someone who obviously belongs. There are notable names we would like to see on the list. But all the plays and playwrights on the list deserve to be there. Expanding the list to more than fifty playwrights makes room for Eulalie Spence, Zora Neale Hurston, Sonia Sanchez, P. J. Gibson, Pearl Cleage, Judi Ann Mason, John Ross, James Butcher, Thomas Pawley, Melvin Tolson, Loften Mitchell, Louis Peterson, William Branch, Ray McIver, Ossie Davis, Steve Carter, Gus Edwards, Joseph Walker, Rob Penney, Don Evans, Oyamo, Laurence Holder, Daniel Owens, Kalamu ya Salaam, Samm-Art Williams, Phillip Hayes Dean, Leslie Lee, Paul Carter Harrison, and others. And this list does not include playwrights who have emerged in the new millennium. Some of the playwrights on both lists have had successful Broadway productions. Many have not. All of these historically significant and artistically competent playwrights have had plays produced for enthusiastically appreciative audiences. But money collected at the box office is not the measure of historical significance or artistic competence.

Doris Abramson laments the fact that "Between 1925 and 1959 only eighteen plays by fifteen Negro playwrights were produced in the New York Professional theatre."[60] But her definition of a play enables her to dismiss the work of William Alexander Brown as not plays at all and to call *The Escape: or a Leap for Freedom* by William Wells Brown, published in 1858,[61] and *Caleb, the Degenerate*, written by Joseph S. Cotter in 1903, "examples of crude art . . . really tracts, meant for the library or the platform." According to the dictionary, *crude* means *uncultured*. But whose culture? Because the pervasive Eurocentric definition views the term *play* as literature, what theatre people call the script, even a work of the stature of John Hope Franklin's *From Slavery to Freedom* asserts that *The Escape: or a Leap for Freedom* was the first African American play.[62]

Although *The Escape: or a Leap for Freedom* is not really the first African American play, its accessibility as a script enables examination for its significance as history, as literature, and as presentable theatre art. Clearly, *The Escape: or a Leap for Freedom* offers significant insights into antebellum plantation life from the point of view of a formerly enslaved African American. William Wells Brown's comic irony presents a view of White and Black people in the antebellum South that no White writer of the period could have created. Walker, a slave trader, says to Dr. Gaines, who considers himself a kinder, gentler plantation owner:

> The price of niggers is up, and I em gwine to take advantage of the times. Now, doctor, ef you've got any niggers that you wants to sell, I em your man. I am paying the highest price of anybody in the market. I pay cash down, and no grumblin'.

DR. GAINES: I don't know that I want to sell any of my people now. Still, I've got to make up a little money next month, to pay in bank; and another thing, the doctors say that we are likely to have a touch of the cholera this summer, and if that's the case, I suppose I had better turn as many of my slaves into cash as I can.

WALKER: Yes, doctor, that is very true. The cholera is death on slaves, and a thousand dollars in your pocket is a great deal better than a nigger in the field, with cholera at his heels . . .

The Reverend Mr. Pinchen, while this discussion is going on, proclaims:
> I tell you, Mr. Walker, I've been in the gospel ministry these thirteen years, and I am satisfied that the heart of man is full of sin and

desperately wicked. This is a wicked world, Mr. Walker, a wicked world, and we ought all of us to have religion. Religion is a good thing to live by, and we all want it when we die. Yes, sir, when the great trumpet blows, we ought to be ready. And a man in your business of buying and selling slaves needs religion more than anybody else, for it makes you treat your people as you should. Now, there is Mr. Haskins, he is a slave-trader, like yourself. Well, I converted him. Before he got religion, he was one of the worst men to his niggers I ever saw; his heart was as hard as stone. But religion has made his heart as soft as a piece of cotton. Before I converted him, he would sell husbands from their wives, and seem to take delight in it; but now he won't sell a man from his wife, if he can get anyone to buy both of them together.

Later, as Walker is about to depart with the slaves he has purchased from Dr. Gaines, Rev. Pinchen asks:

What kind of niggers sells best in the Orleans market, Mr. Walker?

WALKER: Why, field hands. Did you think of goin' in the trade?

REV. PINCHEN: Oh, no; only it's a long ways down to Natchez, and I thought I'd just buy five or six niggers, and take 'em down and sell 'em to pay my travellin' expenses. I only want to clear my way.[63]

A playwright's style is bound to be influenced by the theatre practices of his time and place, and William Wells Brown's use of language is stylistically mid-nineteenth century. Therefore, the play's language sounds stilted to twenty-first-century ears, whether Eurocentric or Afrocentric. But so does the language of Brown's White contemporaries. However, there is one aspect of mid-nineteenth-century Eurocentric theatre practice that William Wells Brown did not adhere to. He addressed a subject that his White counterparts generally avoided. He exposed the hypocrisy of sexual behavior on antebellum plantations with frankness and insight in a time when candid public communication about sex was rare, and public mention of interracial sex was forbidden.

Walker, the slave trader, asks Mr. Wildmarsh, Dr. Gaines' neighbor, if he has "any niggers to sell." Wildmarsh says he does not, having just sold "the smartest gal I've ever raised . . ." Walker then inquires:
Then she was of your own raising, was she?

WILDMARSH: Oh, yes; she was raised on my place, and if I could have kept her three or four years longer, and taken her to the market myself, I am sure I could have sold her for three thousand dollars. But you see, Mr. Walker, my wife got a little jealous, and you know jealousy sets the women's heads a teetering, and so I had to sell the gal. She's got straight hair, blue eyes, prominent features, and is almost white . . . .

WALKER: Why, Squire, was she that pretty little gal that I saw on your knee the day that your wife was gone, when I was at your place three years ago?

WILDMARSH: Yes, the same.

WALKER: Well now, Squire, I thought that was your daughter; she looked mightily like you. She was your daughter, wasn't she? You need not be ashamed to own it to me, for I am mum upon such matters.

While attempting to decide which slaves to sell, Dr. Gaines tells his wife:
My dear, I'll sell any servant from the place to suit you, except Melinda. I can't think of selling her; I can't think of it.

MRS. GAINES: I tell you that Melinda shall leave this house, or I'll go. There, now you have it. I've had my life tormented out of me by the presence of that yellow wench, and I'll stand it no longer. I know you love her more than you do me, and I'll . . . I'll . . . I'll write . . . write to my father (weeps).

Dr. Gaines later tells his wife he has sold Melinda. Mrs. Gaines is certain her husband is having sex with "the yellow wench." Actually, Dr. Gaines keeps Melinda in a cottage some ten miles away from the plantation house. When he visits Melinda, he tells her:

I will set you free, let you live in this cottage, and be your own mistress, and I'll dress you like a lady. Come now, be reasonable!

MELINDA: Sir, let me warn you that if you compass my ruin, a woman's bitterest curse will be laid upon your head, with all the crushing, withering weight that my soul can impart to it; a curse that shall cling to you throughout the remainder of your wretched life; a curse that shall haunt you like a spectre in your dreams by night, and attend upon you by day; a curse, too, that shall embody itself in the ghastly form of the woman whose chastity you will have outraged. Command me to bury myself in yonder stream, and I will obey you. Bid me do anything else, but I beseech you not to commit a double crime, outrage a woman, and make her false to her husband.[64]

Although Melinda's speech sounds stilted to contemporary ears, Brown was able to present a taboo subject in a manner that was permissible in polite public performance in mid-nineteenth-century America.

For us to say *The Escape: or a Leap for Freedom* is viable as a fully staged play is not an untested opinion. We produced an adaptation of the play by Barbara Molette in 1976 as Texas Southern University Theatre's bicentennial offering. Although some contemporary theatregoers undoubtedly find the play's nineteenth century language difficult to navigate, theatregoers who regularly attend plays written before 1900 will not find this play's language unusual or difficult.

Eurocentric analysts and interpreters who believe their culture and values are universal and therefore should be imposed on the artistic creations of other cultures will undoubtedly continue to reach incorrect conclusions. The reverse of this assertion may be applicable in theory, but not in reality since Black Americans are educated in Eurocentric schools where they are taught to value Eurocentric culture to a degree that few White Americans ever learn to value Black culture.

The Minstrel Tradition

The slave experience mandated a survival technique that employs double meaning. Things were almost never what they seemed to be when heard and seen by White folks. The use of double meaning was a common characteristic among the practitioners of the early forms of communication art from which African American theatre developed: minstrel performers, singers of spirituals, storytellers, and preachers.

Historians who have erroneously described the beginnings of the Negro minstrel have made the kind of misinterpretations that Black minstrel performers intended for White people to make. During the early days of the minstrel, performances were by Black people for the entertainment of Black people. White people had to be misled in order to assure the survival of the Black people who were involved as both performers and audience. This deception was necessary because the minstrel entertainments invariably included some rather caustic satire on the subject of the ineptness of White folks.

A quote from Loften Mitchell's play *Star of the Morning* is included in his book about Black theatre in New York entitled *Black Drama*. He uses dialogue from the play to explain what minstrel entertainment meant to Black Americans before White people coopted it. The character who speaks is Oliver, an elderly ex-slave and minstrel man. Oliver tells the leading character in the play that, when he was a slave, minstrels performed on plantations deliberately sought "to poke fun at Old Master." Oliver stresses the importance of getting a house Negro to be the interlocutor. Oliver explains:

> We used to take off on that house Negro 'cause he was the Master up and down.
>
> (Imitating Tams)
>
> Tams would say: "Mistah Stafford, do darkies go to heaven?"
>
> (Moves over, imitates Bones)
>
> Old Bones would say: "Yes suh, Mistah Stafford. Do us darkies go to Heaven?"
>
> (Moves back, imitates the house Negro)
>
> House Negro would say: "Now, why would you darkies be going to heaven? That's for white folks!"
>
> (Imitates Tams)
>
> Tams would say: "We just wanted to know who opens them Pearly Gates for white folks to get inside?"
>
> (All laugh. Oliver becomes serious now)
>
> That's how it was. Them white folks come from up North and copied what we was doing. They made me a fool, and now I got to go out there and make money laughing at me![65]

The focus of comic irony in this early African American minstrel routine is clearly intended to provoke Black people to laugh at the White slaveholder who presumes he is superior to Black people despite his obvious dependence on Black people to perform many of the simplest and most basic tasks required for human survival.

Then a White man named Thomas Rice added a large dose of buffoonery to his vaudeville imitation of a Black man. Rice's Jim Crow routine was such a huge success that the entire process of demeaning discrimination came to be known as "Jim Crow". Rice made money by making White Americans laugh at his demeaning portrayal of a Black man. His success led other White performers to take advantage of the financial opportunity he exposed and the commercial product called "Negro minstrel" was born. Unlike the earlier African American minstrel where Black people entertained other Black people, throngs of White people paid to pack theatres all across America and laugh at White men who smeared their faces with burnt cork and painted enormous lips in what became a time-honored tradition called "blackface." The outrageous makeup and buffoonery was, without a doubt, crucial to the Negro minstrel's immense financial success. Black people were portrayed with a preposterous array of stereotypical characteristics. Negro minstrel characters had to be physically inept, lazy, and stupid. They inevitably failed at nearly any task they were expected to perform unless they were under the constant scrutiny of a White supervisor.

In contrast, the entertainment Black people performed for other Black people remains largely unknown and undocumented in American theatre history although these entertainments continued well into the 1950s. The Negro minstrel that many Americans, White and Black, find so demeaning today was, no doubt, an accurate reflection of what White Americans' values allowed them to see and hear from their location. And the Negro minstrel was clearly something White audiences gladly paid to see. The Negro minstrel remained a basic entertainment commodity for White Americans with major White stars putting on blackface makeup in motion pictures and on television as well as in live performance venues at least into the early 1950s. But this White invention represented a reversal of the African American minstrel performances' values. These Black American minstrels were presented for the entertainment of Black Americans and reflected and perpetuated their values.

Describing some elements of the original Black American minstrel form sheds light on goals and functions of Black performance: first, the physical arrangement of the performers: the "master" in the middle, the "darkies" on the ends; second, the obsession with calling the interlocutor "mister" with such frequency as to become ludicrous and trite, unless we assume the practice was a lampoon of how Whites expected to be treated by African Americans; and third, the tradition of using a light-skinned African American who could "talk like White folks" as the interlocutor. The original African American minstrel performances not only entertained African American people but made life tolerable for African American slaves in the USA by ridiculing, through the use of comic irony, the White slave owner, the key figure in the system that caused their oppression. Of course, the ridicule had to be presented in a manner to ensure that while African American people were certain to understand and appreciate it, White people were certain to misunderstand. The successful functioning of this type of African American theatre was a significant factor in the mental health and physical survival of African American people within the slave experience and far beyond.

These historical examples reveal functions of Afrocentric theatre that reflect the values of both artist and audience. Although the style of language and other such surface characteristics have changed, the intended goals and functions of theatre for African American audiences have not changed. Goals converge around physical survival and mental health in an environment of systematic oppression and demeaning ridicule. Functions include the combined use of double meaning and comic irony, and the galvanizing of existing antislavery sentiment. If some of the more contemporary meanings of the term "slavery" are recognized, these functions continue as important manifestations of the values of African American theatre artists and their audiences. These values, as transmitted by African American culture and the African antecedents to African American culture, comprise the Premise of Afrocentric theatre.

Chapter Four

Foundations of Evaluation

To paraphrase Howard Gardiner, education is not so much about addressing unanswered questions as addressing unquestioned answers.

Valid evaluations of any culture's theatre require prior understanding and appreciation of the aesthetic foundations of the culture being evaluated. Yet Eurocentric theatre critics and historians have often evaluated African American theatre without first learning what constitutes success from the points of view of Afrocentric theatre artists or the intended recipients of their art. Such a process disrespects the cultural location of the art's creators and its intended recipients and would not warrant serious attention were it not for its widespread and frequent occurrence among those who are regarded as expert evaluators and the widely held presumption that the work of these Eurocentric evaluators is valid across cultures and deserves to be taken seriously.

Most Afrocentric theatre artists desire the simple social contract August Wilson described as: "to participate in society as African people with their culture intact." But these Afrocentric theatre artists also recognize their dilemma: failure to establish a vantage point from which Eurocentric critics and ticket purchasers are comfortable with a Black play virtually assures its artistic failure by Eurocentric criteria. By Eurocentric criteria, a play is an artistic success when it makes money at the box office. Commercial success is the standard for artistic success. Failure of Eurocentric critics and ticket purchasers to like an African American play prohibits or at the very least deters its commercial success. Eurocentric critics explain or excuse commercial success of Tyler Perry's magnitude as a unique exception that proves the rule. Despite the commercial success routinely regarded as proof of artistic success when White folks buy the tickets, a work is considered artistically inferior when just as many tickets are purchased by Black folks. The cognitive dissonance of such racially based standards is revealed when Eurocentric critics proclaim Jerry Lewis is a comic genius while disrespecting or ignoring Tyler Perry.

Ironically, America's regional theatres are noncommercial, not-for-profit institutions that depend on tax exempt charitable contributions for their survival, and as such are not designed to achieve commercial success. By turning the Tyler Perry explanation upside down, they say not-for-profit institutions, unfettered by pressure to achieve commercial success, enables them to achieve a higher level of artistic success. Somehow the lack of commercial success enables artistic superiority. Yet not-for-profit theatres with the highest levels of charitable contributions contradict the rhetoric that chasing commercial success reduces the likelihood of artistic quality when they endeavor to garner commercial profit and critical acclaim by moving their most financially successful productions to Broadway venues.

Recipients and evaluators of art can only process what they perceive from inside the parameters of their values. As Eurocentric evaluators often assume their values are the only valid ones, they tend to presume any divergence from their values is proof of inferiority by a set of standards they regard as universal. And yet some clearly Afrocentric theatre has been judged good, even great, by Eurocentric evaluators who do not fully understand or appreciate Afrocentric values. While the judgments they make across cultures will often be inaccurate, they may occasionally reach the right conclusions for the wrong reasons.

Empowered by the belief that their standards are universal, some Eurocentric theatre historians and drama critics conclusively proclaim Black playwrights have made few, if any, significant contributions to theatre arts in America, at least not until *A Raisin in the Sun* appeared on Broadway. On the other hand, one might safely assume nearly everyone with sufficient interest, desire, and access to the requisite financial resources to produce a Broadway play is White, male, and over fifty years of age; and rare is the Broadway producer who will gamble a small fortune and their reputation as a producer on the artistic and ticket-selling potential of a Black playwright. Further, providing the opportunity to a Black playwright is *de facto* denial of that opportunity to a White playwright. In light of these assertions: (1) the production of even one Black play on Broadway is a remarkable occurrence; and (2) Broadway production or the length of a Broadway run is completely irrelevant as a standard for determining the quality of a Black play.

The use of negative Black stereotypes in plays and motion pictures has been a highly successful device for selling tickets to White audiences. According to Donald Bogle, D. W. Griffith's film, *The Birth of a Nation* (1915), "altered the entire course and concept of American moviemaking, developing the close-up, cross-cutting, rapid-fire editing, the iris, the split-screen shot, and realistic and impressionistic lighting . . . . the film's magnitude and epic grandeur swept audiences off their feet. At a private White House screening President Woodrow Wilson exclaimed, 'It's like writing history with lightning!'"[66] *The Birth of a Nation* remains one of the highest grossing films ever. Bogle posits, "Griffith's film had succeeded because of its director's artistry and technical virtuosity."[67] But this artistry and technical virtuosity also enabled the film to establish Black stereotypes that persist today as the staple of motion pictures, television, and theatre. Therefore, *The Birth of a Nation* cannot be regarded as anything but a morally reprehensible disaster.

Black stereotypes in Broadway plays tend to be far more sophisticated than the blatantly racist images in *The Birth of a Nation*. But in many respects, more sophisticated stereotypes from *Porgy* and *The Emperor Jones* to *Ain't Misbehavin'* and *Dreamgirls*, to *The Scotsboro Boys* are more effective in provoking negative perceptions of Black people because they seem on the surface to portray Black people as more fully developed characters. In these Black-cast Broadway productions, the acting and (when relevant) the singing and dancing were superb. Although we are genuinely happy whenever Black performers collect a Broadway paycheck, many Black-cast Broadway productions have perpetuated negative Black stereotypes. Typically, these productions' success relies on ticket sales to White theatregoers. On the other hand, a few plays by African American playwrights have appeared on the Great White Way since the Broadway opening of *Simply Heavenly* in the late 1950s, and deservedly acquired support from Black ticket purchasers. While the number of such plays is far fewer than it should be, there have been too many in sixty years to list here, and we would inevitably insult an outstanding playwright and production team by omitting one or two. These examples demonstrate that acclaim by White critics and financial success on Broadway neither confirms nor denies a play's worth from a Black perspective.

One of our favorite nontheatre examples of a lack of familiarity with Afrocentric values leading to inaccurate evaluation of Afrocentric art has to do with evaluation of African sculpture and sculptors. White art experts determined that some human figures sculpted in Africa are out of proportion; for instance, the figures have heads that are larger in proportion to the bodies than those of actual human beings. Until recently, almost all of the White art experts who wrote about this subject concluded these disproportionate human figures were indicative of the primitive state of African art and African artists. The Eurocentric art experts said the African artists in question were not culturally and intellectually advanced enough to get the proportions right. Of course, these art experts were assuming the universal goal of all sculptors is to accurately reproduce external surface characteristics and details. They failed to ask an African sculptor what he was trying to achieve or why. The African sculptors in question considered accurate reproduction of a human figure's surface details unseemly and were accomplishing precisely what they intended to accomplish, as well as what their people valued and considered proper, right, and beautiful.

Inevitably, inaccurate evaluations of Afrocentric art occur when the evaluator fails to ascertain the artist's values and take that information into account in the evaluation process. A number of Afrocentric analysts of African American art have suggested that few, if any, White critics have any business attempting to evaluate Afrocentric art, basing their conclusion on the influence of the ideology of racial and cultural superiority, which leads to such obvious errors as the one just mentioned. In contrast, Eurocentric critics frequently articulate their racist values through such statements as "When evaluating works of art from their own culture, Black folks are unable to maintain objectivity. They get emotionally involved. They do not analyze; they support, defend and apologize." Yet these Eurocentric critics are confident of their ability to dispassionately analyze their culture's art without indulging in apologetic rhetoric. Although they claim they are objective, examples to the contrary are so abundant that to cite a few might imply there are not thousands of other equally valid examples.

Creators and Imitators of Art

Afrocentric aesthetic location sees a major distinction between creators and imitators of art. Perceiving such distinctions requires, among other things, a historical frame of reference. Characteristically, adolescents do not possess the experiential frame of reference to determine whether or not some work of art is new and innovative or old and trite. While this inability to differentiate between innovation and cliché is a reasonable expectation in an adolescent, it is unforgivable in a society's expert evaluators of an art form. Yet highly respected drama critics have proclaimed in respected major metropolitan newspapers that Lorraine Hansberry is "the first Black female playwright."

Ironically, experts who have articulated a negative evaluation of a Black original often praise a subsequent White copy of the Black original. This practice is not based on the Black artist's skin color or hair texture, but on differences between the Black artist's culture, values, and location and the White evaluator's. Although many aspects of Afrocentric culture are being assimilated into Eurocentric culture, the process typically filters out Afrocentric elements that conflict with Eurocentric values. American popular music offers numerous examples of sanitizing Afrocentric culture for Eurocentric consumption. For over fifty years, much of the most popular recorded music among White American young people has been European and White American *covers* (the music industry term for recordings by an artist other than the original) of Black performers. White acceptance has generally required White covers of Black records to be so sanitized that Black Americans consider them an aesthetic failure, as exemplified by such artists as Bill Haley and the Comets, Pat Boone, and Nancy Sinatra. Although Elvis Presley's cover of Willie Mae "Big Mama" Thornton's *Hound Dog* caused some to be uncertain about whether the relatively new singer was Black or White, Black Americans who knew and loved the 1953 "Big Mama" Thornton original that zoomed to number one on the rhythm and blues chart were not susceptible to this uncertainty.

The popular appeal of White musicians from Elvis Presley, Tom Jones, Englebert Humperdink, and Janis Joplin, to Vanilla Ice, Eminem, Robin Thicke, and Teena Marie is a result of their ability to mimic Black artists. The feature film *Blues Brothers* uses this irony to comic effect by flipping the actuality so the genuine blues singers of the title are White. But even when a Black artist is credited by White experts with some innovation, the credit's validity must be questioned. Chubby Checker recorded a cover of The Midnighters' original, *The Twist*. The Midnighters' song and the dance named for it were popular among young Black people several years before Chubby Checker's cover popularized the song and dance among young White people. In this instance both the artistic innovation and the sanitized cover for White consumption were created by Black performers.

The judgment to credit Chubby Checker with an innovation actually made by the Midnighters is not altogether due to a lack of awareness among expert evaluators of recorded music. Selection of the Chubby

Checker cover over the Midnighters' original is probably more of a moral response to the Midnighters' front-to-back undulating pelvic motions in their original version of the twist, which was considered suggestive and unacceptable by 1950s Eurocentric standards. Chubby Checker's version kept the spinal column nearly straight and rotated the torso from side to side. Movement of the arms was of little consequence in the Midnighters' version, but movement of the arms while held away from the torso was an important element in Chubby Checker's version. Chubby Checker's movements were Whiter—that is, more in keeping with Eurocentric American values—than were Elvis Presley's and much more Eurocentric than the Midnighters' version.

Most Midnighters fans were Black, and a large portion of Chubby Checker's fan base was White. This fact undoubtedly contributed to Chubby Checker receiving credit for inventing the twist. The logic that allows one to conclude that Chubby Checker invented the twist is similar to the logic that allows one to conclude Columbus discovered America. The people who were Midnighters fans and the people who greeted Columbus on his arrival in this hemisphere are defined as nonpersons by the arbiters of Eurocentric evaluative standards.

Ray Charles, Chuck Berry, Muddy Waters, Little Richard, and many other Black performers developed musical concepts and popularized them with Black audiences while more Eurocentric performers received greater financial rewards and greater status for imitating the Black originals for European and Eurocentric American audiences. A few of the recipients of Eurocentric approbation have been Black. However, the far more significant fact is that whether the recipient of recognition and financial reward is Black or White, the bestowing authority and the determining standards are always Eurocentric. The bestowing of praise by Eurocentric experts is generally accepted as proof of universal artistic quality. Most Americans assume experts objectively analyze the objects being considered and bestow praise based solely on merit. Despite the similarity in their conclusions, we do not believe these experts are involved in a conspiracy. Most of these experts are far too self-centered to collaborate in a conspiracy. While each evaluative response can only come from within the parameters of the evaluator's prior experiences, their experiences are so remarkably similar that their conclusions may seem conspiratorial to people with experiences that are markedly different from those of the evaluators.

While negative appraisal of Afrocentric art by White critics is not a dependable standard, their disapproval is not a certain sign that a work of Afrocentric art is praiseworthy. Public acclamation is largely a function of leveraging power or influence or money. Acclamation for artists is largely determined by such White-controlled processes as the acquisition of media exposure and bookings into facilities that provide optimum access. Recognition and acclamation for artistic achievement is not directly related to artistic quality, not even in Eurocentric terms. This assertion does not mean that poor quality always triumphs among Eurocentric people. Rather, an artist of poorer quality is more likely to triumph when accorded effective marketing than one of higher quality who has less effective marketing. The relationship of Afrocentric art to Eurocentric recognition and acclamation has even less to do with Afrocentric standards of quality. Power, influence, and money are used to market art and artists in much the same manner that America markets other consumer products. Those who can bestow public recognition, acclaim, and status usually expect to either turn a profit or increase their status and power. On the rare occasion when a Eurocentric entrepreneur decides to present a work of Afrocentric art, the entrepreneur generally assumes the work needs to be altered to "give it more universal appeal," meaning "make it more palatable for Eurocentric consumers."

Several decades ago, we happened to see a thirty-minute television documentary about the marriage of England's Anne and Mark Phillips. One of this country's best known and most highly paid television news commentators went to England to cover the wedding. During the program, she frequently referred to England as "the most enduring monarchy of them all." We do not champion monarchy as a political system, but what about Ethiopia? Apparently Ethiopia is not in the universe; at least, not the Eurocentric universe. At the time the documentary was made, the world's most enduring monarchy was Ethiopia; the Ethiopian monarchy dated back, in a continuous line, to a time when England was inhabited by primitive barbarians who had not yet evolved a concept of nationalism.

We recognize our use of the terms "primitive" and "nationalism" contradicts a cherished belief of Eurocentric American culture. When Eurocentric Americans speak of African people, nationalism is called *tribalism*. Ironically, a centuries-old tribal conflict persists in Ireland between the Celtic and Anglo-Saxon tribes. Tribal conflicts in and around Germany have precipitated two world wars. Tribal conflicts caused the Union of Soviet Socialist Republics to dissolve. Yet, the term "tribe" is diligently avoided when referring to White people. The term "tribe" devalues Africans and other people of color as primitive; and primitive societies are not as "evolved" as Eurocentric societies.

Distinguishing between creators and imitators of art should not be confused with several other recognizable differences between artists. Creative artists and interpretative artists perform different functions. Both kinds of artists are necessary to create some forms of performing art. Among creative artists, some adhere to a classical form such as ballet, sonnet, symphony, or the blues, while others are more innovative and seek to move beyond traditional forms or ways of arranging works of art. In addition to these different kinds of artists, there are those who simply copy or imitate others. In an effort to illuminate this concept, we will quote from a newspaper commentary that was inspired by the massive outpouring of grief by White Americans following the death of Elvis Presley in August of 1977.[68]

Rip-off King

Forty million Americans remain largely unaffected by the death of white America's favorite singer, Elvis Presley. Most Black Americans cannot fathom the hysteria and mania that surrounded Presley's live stage appearances. The publicity and the mass demonstration of public sentiment about his demise exceed that which has occurred following the deaths of recent American presidents. How is it that a boy born and bred in Mississippi and who later called Memphis his home, was catapulted into such prominence? Was it his voice? Or was it his guitar virtuosity? The answer is obviously negative to both questions. Perhaps, the one valid answer to the question of his success would be Thomas Andrew Parker, Elvis' manager. "Colonel" Parker, as he is usually called, deftly guided Elvis' climb to fame and fortune. Parker cleverly orchestrated the recording aspects of Elvis' career so that, in later years, public appearances were held to a minimum. Through Parker's maneuvering, Elvis was proclaimed by a rabid public as "the King of Rock and Roll."

An example of Parker's business acumen can be seen in the story surrounding Elvis' recording of "Hound Dog." The lyrics for "Hound Dog" were written by two white adolescents, Jerry Liber and Mich Stoller. Johnny Otis, a white R and B musician, and Otis Rene, a black songwriter who wrote the music for "Sleepy Time Down South," collaborated on the tune. The song was recorded by Willie Mae "Big Mama" Thornton on the Peacock label . . . . Black folks were humming "Hound Dog" all over the USA long before Elvis made his recording . . . . The song is not a masterpiece, but [it] was a success among black record buyers [primarily] because of the monumental voice of "Big Mama" Thornton.

The column further explains that by the time he recorded "Hound Dog," Elvis owned the publisher's rights, even though the song had been previously published. The publisher controls permission to record and garners a major share of royalties for recordings, public performances, and sheet music. Although Don Robey is alleged to have negotiated a better deal than Black Americans usually received in those days, Elvis acquired a greater share of the revenues from record sales than one would reasonably expect a singer to get for a fairly successful previously recorded song. The Afrocentric aesthetic issue is that Elvis' record was a blatant, though mediocre, imitation of "Big Mama" Thornton's earlier recording of "Hound Dog."

Since Presley's death, a story has emerged describing a more organized imitativeness on Presley's part than most had previously suspected. An African American named Otis Blackwell has offered plausible evidence that he created the sound of such Elvis Presley hits as "Don't Be Cruel" and "Fever." Admitting he never met Elvis face to face, he says he recorded audiotapes of every rendition he created for Elvis and Elvis mimicked the tapes. We are unable to conceive of any other plausible scenario that explains Elvis' suddenly acquired ability to achieve both a vocal production quality and an articulation pattern that were such exclusively Negro characteristics in the mid-1950s. After hearing Otis Blackwell sing, it is apparent that either Elvis imitated Otis, or Otis learned to imitate Elvis with great precision.

African Americans' widespread dislike for Elvis is not altogether an aesthetic judgment based on his mediocre imitativeness. There is a quote attributed to Elvis Presley. Whether Elvis actually said it or not, many Black people believe he said, "The only things a 'boot' can do for me is to buy my records and shine my shoes."

Anecdotes implying Presley was a bigot or confirming his imitativeness do not diminish his status in American popular culture. He became an icon and the African Americans who created the music he imitated did not. He was White and marketed effectively, and they were neither. Some have attributed Presley's success, at least in part, to a widely felt concern that a Black male singer might emerge as a popular sex symbol among young White females. Adult-Americans of that era were not receptive to such an occurrence. Most Americans think Elvis was chosen by the musical tastes of the general populace functioning in an unfettered market. But the general populace chooses from among artists who receive massive public exposure. Since the marketing of Elvis Presley, post-Internet technology has slightly diminished the control WEPPEOs [wealthy, elite, powerful persons of European origin] are able to exert over public exposure. Then and now, music industry marketing departments determine which artists are available as options from which the general populace gets to choose.

Chubby Checker was neither the first nor the only African American imitator of African American musical creators. In 1981, William Cockerham of the *Hartford Courant* wrote an article about Joe Boatner who claimed to be the only surviving member of the original Ink Spots. All the original Ink Spots had been dead for several years by the time Cockerham wrote the article in 1981. Boatner says he joined the original group when Hoppy Jones died in 1943. With as many as fourteen groups called the Ink Spots performing all over the world, Cockerham asked the rhetorical question: Were the Ink Spots, except for the first seven or eight years, "one of the biggest frauds in history?" Cockerham quotes Boatner as saying:

> The public didn't know. All they saw were four black faces and four white suits. The only member of the group whose name they did recognize was Bill Kenny's, the distinctively high tenor with the "good diction," and if anyone ever asked about him, they'd say he was sick, that he had a sore throat or something.[69]

The Ink Spots were, as Boatner puts it:

> a black group, but a white act. Ninety-nine percent of the clubs we played were white. Black people didn't come to the clubs to hear us sing. Black people were into rhythm and blues back then.[70]

Cockerham portrays Boatner as an intelligent, sensitive man who "worked his way through Atlanta University and later the Cleveland School of Music." Why would he wait until long after the Ink Spots were in demand in the record and nightclub businesses to expose the fact that there were as many as fourteen groups claiming to be the Ink Spots? Boatner suggests the singers who were billed as the Ink Spots simply wanted an opportunity to work at their chosen profession. He further suggests that African Americans were powerless to prevent the seemingly fraudulent practice. Boatner explained:

> You have to understand the segregation patterns back in those days. No one did business with a black person. You did business with the White agents. They controlled you and your money, and this went on right up until the late 1960s.

Did the White businessmen who were booking fourteen different groups touring all over the world assume no one would notice there was more than one group claiming to be the Ink Spots? Boatner claims, on one occasion, the Ink Spots were advertised at two different Manhattan clubs on the same street at the same time. This incident seems to indicate some people must have known the group they paid to see was not the only group called the Ink Spots. Although the Ink Spots' promoters may have pioneered the practice, they are not the only promoters who booked multiple groups with the same name. If a fraud was perpetrated, White promoters were swindling White audiences. There were only two options for the fifty-six or so Black singers calling themselves members of a quartet called the Ink Spots, either get paid for performing or find another line of work.

Boatner said the myth of how the Ink Spots came up with their name was perpetuated by theatrical agents who attributed the name to an accident during a record contract session when a member of the group took out his fountain pen to sign the contract and it leaked ink spots all over the legal form. But according to Boatner:

> The name didn't come by any accident.... The white public was clamoring for a black singing group and they needed a name that would let everyone know they were black. Originally, they wanted to call us the Sambos. If we were called the Four Niggers, it would have been the biggest act in the country.[71]

An African American group that performed almost totally for White audiences was certainly in no position to change the way White folks do business with other White folks.

Cherished Beliefs

To view any humanistic issue from an Afrocentric location requires one to examine some cherished beliefs of an elite group of White males who believe it is their ethical responsibility to impose their standards of taste and judgment on others. A real dilemma is created for African Americans by the constant repetition of an overwhelming mantra, of such statements as "Columbus discovered America," "Africans are primitive," and "England is the most enduring monarchy of them all." These statements are so totally without substance as to make sensible, reasonable argument against them virtually impossible. One of Europe's most influential twentieth-century leaders, Adolf Hitler, nearly parlayed the rhetorical technique known as "the big lie" into an empire. One of the key components of the big lie technique is never ever engage in reasonable or logical or polite discourse. Techniques for defending a big lie against reasonable rebuttal include shouting the lie louder and more stridently, and *ad hominem* attacks on the person who argues against the lie. In America, effective names to call challengers of big lies have included *terrorist, Communist, socialist, atheist, traitor,* and *un-American,* as well as invoking names of real enemies such a Hitler and Stalin. Other *ad hominem* enemies are fabricated from whichever religious or ethnic identities are most likely to generate fear at a particular time and place. These *ad hominem* attacks can take an ironic twist when, for example, a real racial bigot calls an enemy a racist, thereby neutralizing any factual evidence of their own bigotry.

Another cherished idea in White American culture is *bigger is better*. Although there are so many examples of this cultural affinity for bigness that to mention a few specific instances might diminish the statement's impact, we will, nevertheless, mention two examples. One example, "big automobiles are better than small ones," is an idea that many Americans of diverse cultures have traditionally cherished. But as recent decades have seen the cost of gasoline escalate, Americans of diverse cultures have reevaluated their attraction to large automobiles. Georgia's Stone Mountain is a more permanent example of the bigger is better ideology. Stone Mountain is alleged to be the world's largest exposed piece of solid granite. Also, Stone Mountain has, carved on it, the world's largest sculpture. We have never heard a serious claim that it is the best sculpture or even a pretty good sculpture, just big. The Mount Rushmore fans may want to question this claim, but the folks in Georgia explain Stone Mountain is a single sculpture, while Mount Rushmore has several different sculptures, each of which is smaller than the Stone Mountain sculpture. But the significant issue is that both Stone Mountain and Mount Rushmore emphasize the attribute of size and diminish concerns for aesthetic qualities that might otherwise be determining factors in an evaluative judgment.

Freedom is among the most cherished ideas promoted by White American culture and generally accepted by other American cultures. Democratic institutions are allegedly traceable back to the Greeks, who also embraced the institution of slavery and did not regard women as citizens. A very small percentage of the people who lived in what is now Greece in the Fifth century BC enjoyed democracy. The alleged democracy that, by implication, was the national government of Greece was actually the municipal government of Athens. Whatever the origins of the Eurocentric idea of freedom, one must not question the idea that the best freedom ever is present-day United States freedom. An African playwright named Chiek N'dao pointed out to us that freedom in the American frame of reference includes the individual's freedom not to help his brother. In some cultures, a person does not have the right, the freedom, to stand by and watch his brother or sister drown, or get robbed, or go hungry or homeless.

Dianna English, a faculty colleague's daughter, emailed from South Africa while in the Peace Corps about the concept of *ubuntu*, which means "people are people through other people." This Afrocentric idea regards the need to connect with other people and take responsibility for each other's wellbeing as a fundamental aspect of humanness. Every individual is responsible for family and community members, as well as family and community units that are components of a larger society for which one also has responsibility. The Black vernacular expression "represent" is current acknowledgment that an individual is never just an individual but represents family and community as well. Eurocentric American individualism, in contrast, often moves beyond the idea of self-reliance into isolation as exemplified by the allegedly constitutional right to privacy. In America, the desire for isolated personal space is even apparent within the family unit. Not only in Africa, but even in most of the industrialized nations of Europe and the Americas, children do not have a right to isolate themselves from others in their immediate family. Where else but America can a teenager living in a comfortable middle-class home with two parents acquire and learn to use firearms, take them to a public place, and kill people at random?

In the United States, the ideal of individualism has morphed into rugged individualism. This ideal promotes the point of view that the individual is more important than the community and romanticizes the ruggedness of settling the West as portrayed in motion pictures starring the likes of John Wayne, and romanticizes rugged individualism in modern law enforcement in motion pictures starring the likes of Clint Eastwood. The motion pictures that idealize and romanticize rugged individualism often have a component that shows the hero taking overtly violent action to keep some person of color in a subservient place. This ideal of rugged individualism is quite apparent in the aesthetic position that promotes individuality of characterization in European and American works of art and in the ethical position that makes heroes of criminals such as Achilles, Robin Hood, Billy the Kid, Jesse James, Al Capone, and more recent criminals who have used economic and political power instead of guns. This ethical position is even supported by Eurocentric science. Darwin, Freud, and their contemporary acolytes tell us hatred and avarice are natural human instincts and that only the fittest will survive. Others have lauded these concepts as scientific facts and interpreted them to justify hoarding natural resources for the powerful and to the exclusion of others; withholding basic supplies from the sick, wounded, and starving; and the violent overthrow of those who are either unwilling to commit acts of violence or not powerful enough to hold on to what is rightfully theirs. If your brother is homeless or hungry, that is the way life is, only the fittest survive. This concept is in direct contradiction to the Bible's assertion that the meek will inherit the earth.

Ironically, the same ethical position that grants freedom to withhold the essentials to sustain life from one's brother permits one to offer that brother unsolicited advice. African Americans call this practice "meddling in other people's business." Further, the standards of taste in American popular culture are shaped in large degree by the society's adolescents. What could possibly cause people of such a society to assume they have the competence, the right, even the responsibility, to pass judgment on the creative products of other people's cultures? We interpolated the following definition of cultural imperialism from the words' dictionary definitions: the act, fact, or policy of dominating another people's structure or system of what is good in feelings, thoughts, tastes, manners, conveniences, customs, arts, socially inherited artifacts, and development of the mind or body by education or training, especially when such domination occurs without taking physical or governmental control of the dominated society.

The Eurocentric missionary view makes nearly identical assumptions to those used to justify cultural imperialism. Some contend evangelism is simply a form of cultural imperialism that focuses on religion while many advocates of evangelism believe cultural imperialism is unacceptable and unwarranted. The term imperialism usually describes someone else's effort to seize political, military, and economic control of another people who usually have fewer expendable resources than the imperialist. Most Americans are predisposed to cheer for the underdog, and most oppose the idea of imperialism so long as the power accused of imperialism is not America. Conversely, most Americans support the concept of evangelism so long as it is aimed at others. So people who are annoyed when an evangelist rings their doorbell readily donate money to support their church's evangelical efforts in "underdeveloped" places like Africa.

The difference between evangelism and cultural imperialism seems to be that most Christians regard evangelism as unequivocally good. Some argue that failure to participate in evangelical activity constitutes failure to do good, and is therefore bad. Evangelists consider themselves duty bound to convert all of humankind to the one right religion which is theirs. Evangelists do not consider whether or not objects of their attention want to be converted or would prefer to continue their traditional ways a valid concern and they often justify this view by calling both the person they want to convert and that person's religion "primitive" or "uncivilized."

"Imperialism" is a term that describes someone else's behavior. When White Americans have wanted to acquire political, military, and economic control, they have generally used a rhetorical device to describe what they were doing that implies a far more positive mode of behavior than the word "imperialism" implies. The USA is allegedly opposed to colonialism, so the USA has no colonies. But what is a "protectorate"? If Samoa, Guam, and Puerto Rico are not sovereign nations, what are they? The term "manifest destiny" has been America's most effective rhetorical device for turning imperialism into an altruistic ideal. Arthur Schlesinger, Jr. attributes the term to John L. O'Sullivan, a proponent of the westward expansionist movement of the 1840s. O'Sullivan is credited with writing the credo in the *Democratic Review* in 1839 that was the justification cited by the territorial expansionists. According to Schlesinger, O'Sullivan said the "mission of

America" . . . was to spread the four freedoms through the world, "freedom of conscience, freedom of person, freedom of trade and business pursuits, universality of freedom and equality." Schlesinger refers to this view as "the new imperialism." The phrase "manifest destiny" was used by O'Sullivan in an article supporting the United States' right to claim Oregon . . . "by the right of our manifest destiny to overspread and to possess the whole of the continent which Providence has given us for the . . . great experiment of liberty."[72]

"Manifest destiny" was also a rallying cry of poet, essayist, and journalist Walt Whitman, who wrote: "It is for the interest of mankind . . . that its power and territory should be extended; the farther the better."[73] Manifest destiny was the new imperialism of the 1840s. Once established, it lasted throughout the twentieth century. Its values remain today and are exemplified in the rhetoric that sought to justify continued U.S. ownership of the Panama Canal. In the new millennium, the rhetoric of manifest destiny was used to justify sending U.S. armed forces into Iraq and Afghanistan. After manifest destiny provided philosophical justification for territorial imperialism for over a century, overt political and economic control over ever-increasing territory no longer seems feasible to many Americans who currently seek to supplant territorial imperialism with cultural imperialism.

Objectivity and Universality

The primary definition of "objective" is "a goal or aim." But the uses of the word that foster the mythology of Eurocentric objectivity are:
> n. 2 something real and observable. adj. 2 existing outside the mind as an actual object and not merely in the mind as an idea; real. Buildings and actions are objective; ideas are subjective. 3 about outward things, not about the thoughts and feelings of the speaker, writer, or painter; giving facts as they are without a bias toward either side; impersonal: an objective analysis of a poem or painting. An "objective test" is often true or false or multiple choice. A scientist must be objective

in his experiments. The policeman gave an objective report of the accident.

Wealthy, elite, powerful persons of European origin [WEPPEOs] created and disseminated the idea that objectivity and universality are valued attributes. Not surprisingly, WEPPEOs possess relatively large amounts of the traits that demonstrate objectivity and universality. WEPPEOs also developed mythological structures that make the traits associated with objectivity and universality the standard criteria for ascertaining who is qualified to make substantive societal decisions and who is not. WEPPEOs thereby established a basis for rejecting the views of others as neither objective nor universal.

The myth of objectivity is embodied in the concept that all which is real is observable by WEPPEOs. Therefore, they assert, phenomena not observable by them are not real. Most Americans who are not WEPPEOs believe the myth to some degree. From our point of view, objectivity is a condition commonly found among WEPPEOs that is characterized by a near absence of spirituality, imagination, and creativity. WEPPEOs hold objectivity in high esteem. Each succeeding generation of WEPPEOs is taught to systematically stifle behaviors that exhibit spirituality, imagination, or creativity. They believe such behaviors are emotional and ought to be eliminated, or at least stifled and hidden. They further believe this view is an extension of Greek culture. Actually, the city-state of Sparta is generally regarded to have been the exemplar of this view.

Developing the traits associated with objectivity is a prerequisite step in the process that empowers WEPPEOs to impose their will on others through objectivity's interdependent relationship with universality. Objectivity is founded on the myth that what is not observable by WEPPEOs is not real. But the myth of objectivity depends on the accompanying myth of universality. Without the myth of universality, non-WEPPEOs would recognize the WEPPEOs' failure to perceive something the rest of us perceive is a problem with their perception. Hence, WEPPEOs' need the myth of universality to support the myth of objectivity. Combining the two myths allows WEPPEOs to convince most of the rest of us that what they observe is observed by all who know how to observe well. Non-WEPPEOs must learn to observe what WEPPEOs observe in order to be regarded by them as civilized. When WEPPEOs observe a thing and pronounce it universal, the rest of us must claim we observed it too. The compulsion to make such a claim is inherent in how the term "universal" is defined.

>adj. 1a of all; belonging to all; concerning all; shared by all: Food is a universal need; b coming from all; shared in by all: a universal protest; c understood or used by all: the universal language of love

Most who are not WEPPEOs but live in a Eurocentric environment are reluctant to be viewed as one who does not share in what is "shared by all" or understand what is "understood by all" or use what is "used by all" or comprehend "the universal language of love."

Drama critics and professors of dramatic literature often attribute the quality of universality to a play, or character in a play. They believe their analysis is objective when they conclude the Eurocentric American theatre's most highly valued characteristics are universal while ignoring the cultural traditions of three-fourths of the world's population. *Universal* is a very weighty term to be so lightly bestowed.

Various Asiocentric and Afrocentric societies, nationalities, or ethnic groups have views that are fundamental to their cultural identity that differ from some Eurocentric society's concept of reality. Such views include: filial piety; reincarnation after death; real property belongs to the community; each individual is responsible for the entire community's wellbeing; and polygamy is the optimum foundation for family structure. Many Eurocentric Americans consider these other views quaint, picturesque, primitive, naive, or worse. The myths of objectivity and universality establish a framework that requires all such ideas to be objectively determined to be universally right or wrong. This process fundamentally opposes the ideal of cultural diversity.

The modes of communication vary enough from one culture to another to make the label of universality for any work of theatre art disputable. Works originally written in another language must be translated, and even works from a different time or place in the same language often require extensive explanation. Further, the specific characteristics of the human condition that are most frequently extolled as universal by Eurocentric Americans operate in a rather paradoxical fashion as they relate to standards of excellence in the art of theatre.

Jealousy as illuminated by Shakespeare's *Othello* is an allegedly universal characteristic. Even if jealously in general is a universal element of the human condition, jealousy in the framework of a monogamous marriage in which a husband murders his wife because he has been bamboozled into believing her chastity has been violated is not universal. Neither monogamy nor chastity is a valued ideal in all societies; and many societies that value monogamy and chastity do not believe their alleged violation justifies murder. The foundation for the play's plot, the idea of romantic love, was only a few hundred years old when Shakespeare wrote *Othello*. Jealousy in a context of romantic love does not function independently of the play's overall quality. Witness television soap operas and murder mysteries that thrive on such jealousy, yet are condemned by critics who praise *Othello*. Many people see the play as having more to do with the title character's gullibility than his jealousy. Despite these issues to the contrary, something causes *Othello* to be considered universal by Eurocentric critics. We have asked several Eurocentric drama experts to explain exactly what makes this play universal and we have not received an explicit answer. Although *Othello* may well be an excellent example of Eurocentric dramatic art, to claim it is universal is an exaggeration.

Laura Bohannan wrote an article in *Natural History* magazine in 1966 that generated a fan base among proponents of respect for cultural differences. Bohannan, an anthropologist living in an isolated African village, was asked by the village elders to tell a story from her home.

Here was my chance to prove *Hamlet* universally intelligible . . . . I began in the proper style, "Not yesterday, not yesterday, but long ago, a thing occurred. One night three men were keeping watch outside the homestead of the great chief, when suddenly they saw the former chief approach them."

Bohannan gets to the part of the story where,
"The dead chief's younger brother had become the great chief. He had also married his elder brother's widow only about a month after the funeral."

One of the elders responds,
"He did well . . . . In our country, also . . . the younger brother marries the elder brother's widow and becomes the father of his children."

Bohannan explains "our custom" requires a much longer period for the widow to mourn, and the elder's wife objects to the longer period of mourning and pointedly inquires,
"Who will hoe your farms for you while you have no husband?"

As Bohannan ponders the dilemma created by,
"an audience convinced that Claudius and Gertrude had behaved in the best possible manner, one of the younger men asked . . . who had married the other wives of the dead chief.

When she explained the dead chief had no other wives, her audience responded,
"But a chief must have many wives! How else can he brew beer and prepare food for all his guests?"

Bohannan explained that in her country even chiefs have only one wife, and the elders responded,

> It was better . . . for a chief to have many wives and sons who would help him hoe his farms and feed his people.

Bohannan faced another dilemma when discussing Hamlet's second encounter with his father's ghost. This ethnic group does not believe in anything that conceptually resembles a ghost. Failing to convince anyone that such a thing as a ghost exists, Bohannan continued efforts to convey Hamlet's "universal truths" across cultures and inspired various elders to respond.

> "You tell the story well, and we are listening. But it is clear that the elders of your country have never told you what the story really means . . . . We believe you when you say your marriage customs are different, or your clothes and weapons. But people are the same everywhere.

> "Polonius knew his son would get into trouble, and so he did. [In order to get money] . . . to pay for fighting, and debts from gambling . . . [he wanted] to marry off his sister at once, but it is difficult to find a man who will marry a woman desired by the son of a chief. For if the chief's heir commits adultery with your wife, what can you do? Only a fool calls a case against a man who will someday be his judge."

The elders seem to believe the difficulties with her story arise, not from cultural differences, but from her inexperience. They are certain the elders of her culture see the world very much as they do. This idea seems to infer that many, if not all, cultures tend to regard their most cherished beliefs as universal. But not everyone who thinks the most cherished attributes of their culture are universal forces others outside their culture to acquiesce to their behavior and thought patterns.

The term "universality" is often used to praise a work of art when a more accurate term is "longevity." A work's longevity is at least as dependent on such nonaesthetic phenomena as war and climatic conditions as the work's quality. Eurocentric works that "stand the test of time" are mostly held in high esteem by WEPPEOs who have the "refined taste" to appreciate antiques and the ability to require others to learn or pretend to learn that these works are masterpieces. Others who must learn about these Eurocentric masterpieces often memorize the data to pass an exam and move on without actually learning to appreciate the alleged masterpieces. The *Mona Lisa*, *Hamlet,* and *Oedipus Rex* deserve to be recognized as Eurocentric masterpieces, but are they masterpieces from other cultural perspectives? Many Eurocentric scholars seem unaware that African and Asian cultures have masterpieces as well and seem to feel their lack of awareness constitutes proof that these other masterpieces do not exist. Ignorance of the best works of art from other civilizations in Africa or Asia thereby becomes evidence of other societies' inferiority.

What remains from antiquity is not determined by aesthetic quality alone but by complex sets of circumstances. A culture's remaining artifacts may not be the best of that culture, especially when descendants of a culture discover their ancestral treasures are being shipped to European and Eurocentric American museums. One may reasonably assume the best and most sacred works of art might be hidden or even destroyed to keep them from being stolen by a nation that takes pride in the artifacts they have "collected" from other places. Some of the most important art treasures, not only from the African continent but also from other nations such as Greece and Mexico, were forcibly removed and now reside in European and Eurocentric American museums. Whether these art treasures were collected or stolen is essentially a question of one's perspective. From our perspective, these art treasures were stolen.

Many people at different times and places have chosen not to focus energy and intelligence on preserving artifacts for posterity. We cannot conclude a society produced no masterpieces simply because it did not preserve them for examination and evaluation several centuries later. Eurocentric scholars may be unaware of the achievements of societies who concealed their icons from powerful outsiders who blatantly disrespect their culture for fear their icons would be desecrated if they were found.

Memphite drama is inscribed on a stone called the Memphite stele. This religious icon provides an important example of the consequences of a work of great cultural significance falling into alien hands. The Memphite stele, inscribed in around 700 BC, has been in the British Museum since 1805. It was nearly destroyed by various invading powers in the centuries prior to its "rescue" by the British. Whereas the British undoubtedly regard their theft of this artifact as a rescue, the Kemites probably would not. If practitioners of the Kemites' religious doctrines were here today, they would undoubtedly object to the current location and use their sacred icon.

The quality of a work of art is subject to variables that have little, if anything, to do with objectivity or universality, even when the work is Eurocentric. But the mythological attributes of objectivity and universality have become virtually self-perpetuating. Since denying these myths is tantamount to denying one's humanity, the rest of us voluntarily perpetuate the myths and the elite group that is responsible for perpetuating the myths no longer needs to force their acceptance. In addition to being White and male, those who control the economic resources and the dissemination of ideas tend to be similar in dress, speech, other observable behavior patterns such as the recreational activities they enjoy, and the certainty they are objective. When they proclaim a thing has some universal quality, they do so without concern that their position will face significant opposition. To contradict the elite group's affirmation of universality is to risk being labeled less sophisticated, less knowledgeable, and less refined than other human beings. If this elite group says some universal response should occur as a result of viewing the *Mona Lisa*, to admit to not having that response is to admit failing to achieve a level of refinement that most other human beings achieve. To admit to the absence of several allegedly universal responses would undoubtedly cause one to be labeled less than civilized, possibly even less than human.

The interdependent ideologies of objectivity and universality fabricate vague and misleading justifications for political and economic oppression, cultural imperialism, manifest destiny, and evangelism.

Chapter Five

Evaluation of Art

"Each play is an act of aggression against the *status quo* . . . I think all my plays are political. I think all art is corrective in showing us how to lead our lives more fully."[74] —Edward Albee

Aesthetics

Although values in general affect the outcome of any adjudication process, aesthetic values are the primary source of evaluative assessments about art.
> aesthetic, adj., n.—adj.1 having to do with the beautiful, as distinguished from the useful, scientific, or moral; based on or determined by beauty rather than by practical or moral considerations: . . . 2 (of persons) having or showing an appreciation of beauty in nature and art. 3 (of things) showing good taste; artistic; pleasing . . . aesthetics, n. the study of beauty in art and nature; philosophy of beauty or taste; theory of fine arts . . .

The classic questions raised by aesthetics are: What is beauty? Is some specific thing beautiful? If so, what are the characteristics that make it beautiful? Answers to those questions have been many and varied in different times and at different places. Standards of what constitutes good and beauty will be as different as cultures and values are different. Aesthetic values determine the qualitative standards by which the art of any culture is judged. One can only regard as beautiful that which one's values allow to be regarded as beautiful. Most people have very strong views about what is beautiful and what is not, what is valuable and what is not, and what makes their art better or worse than other people's art. Although cultures usually allow for some variation in individual taste, cultures inevitably impose parameters for what may or may not be considered beautiful. Those parameters differ from culture to culture. Therefore, aesthetic standards vary as the cultural context in which art occurs varies.

Aesthetics ponders both general and specific questions about what beauty is and the creation, evaluation, and uses of beauty. Who in a given society determines and controls standards of beauty? Who decides what constitutes good taste? How is art created, perceived, evaluated and used? When can it be said, with validity, that a work of art is good? What does a group of people expect of its art?

In every society, some especially influential segment is invested with the authority to dictate taste and define art. In America, that authority belongs to WEPPEOs. Their values filter all concepts of beauty and art as well as other cultural phenomena. Their filters allow some things to pass while preventing or drastically reducing the passage of others. In America, all cultural traditions, the values on which they are based, and their works of art are filtered by criteria created and implemented by the WEPPEOs, who control the information dissemination process. Their filter system is so effective, pervasive, and well connected to rhetoric about democracy and the American Dream that others often believe they have embraced some work of art of their own free will based on their own evaluative conclusions. One obvious example of this phenomenon is the music choices made by various segments of America's youth culture. Younger Americans generally believe they select the music they prefer of their own free will while music product is marketed just like every other commodity that generates profits.

Fine vs. Applied Art

Eurocentric culture distinguishes between fine and applied art, at least in part, to reinforce class differences between people who create or find beauty in things that are useful to them and people who are wealthy enough to purchase things that have no immediate use. These latter individuals enhance their status through conspicuous consumption of goods and services. Ironically, conspicuous display of expensive automobiles has become so widespread among persons of relatively low socioeconomic status that the practice no longer functions as a status symbol among the wealthy. A few automobiles (mostly antiques and European imports) cost enough to retain their value as status symbols; but automobiles, no matter how expensive, provide pragmatic transportation. Except for those who own a yacht to attract paying passengers, few people find any truly pragmatic use for a yacht. As a result, yachts carry a much higher status value than automobiles.

The highest degree of status is achieved by purchase and conspicuous display of items that, in addition to their beauty and high purchase price, have little or no pragmatic value. For example, reading seems to have a pragmatic outcome, even when none is deliberately intended. Although some people buy books to read, books may overtly avoid the appearance of pragmatism by functioning more as expensive, elegant decor than as reading material. Such books are displayed for status and advertised for the elegance of their matching covers (genuine leather with gold lettering, hand sewn, etc.), often with only a vague mention that the contents of the books are "classic" or "great."

Eurocentric highbrow arts provide opportunities to be seen at high status events and have one's name included on lists of patrons of the arts. The most elite of the arts patrons have their names carved in the stone walls of the expensively appointed buildings dedicated to the preservation and dissemination of Eurocentric fine arts. The wealthiest of the WEPPEOs donate enough money to have the buildings in which the arts are housed named for them. Memberships on boards of directors of arts institutions provide another kind of status symbolism. These are only examples of the many factors that create the Eurocentric concept that true appreciation of fine art requires leisure time and a highbrow education. This Eurocentric concept conversely infers that persons who do not have a highbrow education, leisure time, financial resources, and social status cannot fully appreciate the finer things in life, especially the fine arts. Although purveyors of Eurocentric arts frequently acquire a modicum of financial security and status for their artists and respect for the art they create, the status and security the arts patrons provide for artists in no way approximates their own status and wealth. These arts patrons endorse an array of products (the arts) with significant financial contributions, attendance at events, and service on boards. The presumed return on investment is the tacit understanding that the content of the art they sponsor will not generate discomfort for them and their cohort. When art causes discomfort for its patrons, the purveyors of art for art's sake invoke it as an ideology to proclaim the offending work is not really art. The impact of this tactic is clearly evident when some member of the U.S. Congress zealously claims to be in favor of less government controls while assertively seeking to micromanage the National Endowment for the Arts. Things created by human beings and pronounced beautiful by Eurocentric standards are called fine art. Cultural and educational institutions, most of which receive public funding and all of which claim tax exempt status, accentuate class and status differences by separating fine arts from other arts. For more about how this process functions, we recommend Thorstein Veblen's *Theory of the Leisure Class*.[75] This definitive work provides a detailed and appropriately Eurocentric American analysis. WEPPEO-endorsed critics use the term "fine art" to describe art they consider superior to un-fine art, applied art, or craft. Such visual art as quilts, embroidery, and wood carving created by White people and exhibited at such vernacular venues as fairs is, by their definition, un-fine art. They also define White vernacular music (music created by White people who are not trained in the Eurocentric classical tradition) as un-fine art. It should not be surprising that WEPPEO-endorsed critics define most African American art as un-fine.

Labeling art of other cultures primitive, vernacular, coarse, crude, or uncivilized enables Eurocentric critics to demean and denigrate it without actually considering the art itself. Eurocentric visual art critics use the term "primitive" to describe artists not trained in Eurocentric academic institutions and the art they create. Eurocentric music critics use the term "vernacular" to describe music created by musicians not trained in Eurocentric academic institutions.

An influential African American scholar repopularized the term "chitlin circuit"[76] to describe Black theatre's equivalent to "vernacular music" and "primitive art." The term "chitlin circuit" originated in the 1920s as a wry self-deprecating description of venues across America where Black performers entertained Black audiences. The term was sanctioned by Black people in an America so segregated by race that one could reasonably assume no White people would hear the term being used. Calling this contemporary Black theatre genre "chitlin circuit" rhetorically demeans a diverse group of plays in performance without bothering to consider the work itself. This rhetorical device is reminiscent of the practice that demeaned jazz because it was performed in places where the monetary income came from alcohol consumption, gambling, and prostitution.

When Eurocentric critics attempt to justify why some work of un-fine art deserves a lesser status, the invariable essence of their rationale is that un-fine art consciously serves some useful purpose. Fine art is, by definition, useless. Art for art's sake and the concept of fine art are inextricably connected. These connected ideologies assume art, and even the act of creating art, has intrinsic significance, meaning, and value. In this ideological context, a chair, a door, anything overtly and intentionally useful to ordinary people, is not fine art. A chair that is actually used to sit in is not fine art, no matter how beautiful. But a painting of a chair, which has no function except to be contemplated for its intrinsic beauty, is fine art. In this ideological context, theatre is expected to eschew usefulness to ordinary members of society.

The cost of theatre as calculated by admission prices, ease of accessibility, and availability of leisure time encourages the financial and educational elite to attend. By inference, nonelite individuals are encouraged to stay away. Most nonelite individuals are further enticed to stay away because they perceive no significant benefit in absorbing the art these fine arts institutions offer. Theatre in this fine arts context discourages participation by nonelite White people and culturally and ethnically different others. How WEPPEO-endorsed critics define things they do not appreciate would not matter a great deal except that they have sufficient influence to cause their hierarchical view of the arts to impact the whole society.

An Afrocentric place contends the value of any work of art is, in part, related to its usefulness; that is, art for people's use. The term "fine art" is inappropriate for describing Afrocentric arts since intentional usefulness is a positive factor by Afrocentric aesthetic standards. Playwrights who disseminate ideas that help African Americans shape their lives for their own betterment on their own terms foster aesthetic goals that may materialize as political reality, causing such playwrights to be bombarded with such slogans as "art and politics don't mix." These slogans only have credibility for those who subscribe to the ideology of art for art's sake and therefore believe fine art must not be of any significant use.

These contrasting views about what a culture should expect from its arts have caused interesting behavior patterns as American society moves very slowly but inexorably toward its founding democratic and egalitarian ideals. Although appreciation of fine arts serves as a status symbol for WEPPEOs, the need to seem to promote democratic and egalitarian ideals has caused WEPPEOs to encourage fine arts outreach programs whose stated purpose is to encourage nonelite individuals to participate in the fine arts institutions supported by the WEPPEOs. These outreach programs encourage a small number of persons of other ethnic backgrounds and economic classes (and to some extent, even regional locations) to mingle with the WEPPEOs.

Two major determinants keep outreach participants' numbers relatively small. First, outsiders' access to experiences that lead to acquisition of the values and income requisite for ongoing participation in these fine arts institutions remains limited. Second, some outsiders discontinue when they feel pressured to either reject or pretend to reject much of their cultural heritage; in other words, the program either prohibits or stifles African agency. Many who have participated in these outreach programs feel they were enticed to cherish values they do not accept. Although the WEPPEOs tend to think most of the outsiders in the outreach programs lack sufficient refinement to appreciate the fine arts, they welcome the rare exception who seems to assimilate their values and strives to approximate their financial status. These rare exceptions enable them to seem color-blind.

Although the new criteria appear to focus more on economic class than race, White elites continue to encourage nonelite Whites to regard themselves as superior to non-White token elites. This hierarchical racial construction encourages nonelite White people to believe WEPPEOs hold them in higher esteem than people of color. We do not know and will not speculate about whether or not WEPPEOs actually hold race in higher esteem than educational, social, or economic status, or the ability to appreciate fine arts. Just as nonelite White people need to believe they are superior in the WEPPEOs hierarchy, ethnic diversity tokens need to believe WEPPEOs hold democratic and egalitarian ideals in higher esteem than race. By convincing each group of opposite hierarchical arrangements, fine arts institutions obtain a constant but very small supply of tokens who exemplify the egalitarian myth that both nonelite Caucasians and people of color can become acceptable if they learn to mimic WEPPEOs.

Predictably, the most effective way for African American artists to gain acceptability among American WEPPEOs is to spend time in Europe, achieve a modicum of acceptability there, and return to the USA able to love Europe and its arts with greater fervor and more specificity than most White Americans. This description of how some Black artists have gained respect among Eurocentric arts patrons is not intended to demean any Black artist who has chosen to pursue career goals in Europe. Most who have done so seem to have been motivated by the desire to practice their art without abandoning their cultural identity.

In the economic theory of capitalism, when desire for a thing is greater than a society's supply, the thing's value increases. Mere scarcity does not increase value. The law of supply and demand says demand must exceed supply for a thing's value to increase. Eurocentric American culture places a high value on people with blond hair and blue eyes. While this category of people is comparatively small, scarcity may not be the only factor contributing to the high valuation of blondness. This construction of blondness exists in concert with Nazi propaganda about Aryan superiority and may benefit from it. On the other hand, White American culture has pushed back against the Aryan superiority myth with a genre of humor called the "blonde joke." While the Aryan superiority myth says blonde women are the most beautiful and desirable, the push back generates jokes that stereotype blonde women, especially those with large bosoms, as incredibly stupid.

The supply-and-demand phenomenon seldom, if ever, creates value for a thing that is totally absent in a society. People with blond hair and blue eyes would probably not be highly valued in America if these traits were completely absent from the American experience. Blond hair and blue eyes among brown-skinned people who by Eurocentric definition are Black, Negro, or Colored is not a naturally occurring characteristic. Yet some brown-skinned people elect to chemically induce blondness and cosmetically change their eye color to blue. While we do not question any adult American's right to induce these changes, the decision to make such choices raises questions about the societal forces that motivate some brown-skinned Americans to believe their appearance is improved by inducing these changes. Did some Black Americans not get the memo that Black is beautiful? Do some brown-skinned Americans believe mythic attributes of beauty can be assimilated by chemically inducing blondness?

These admittedly shallow questions lead to deeper questions: What factors exist in the institutional process of transmitting culture in the USA that promote and enhance the values expressed in the advertising slogan "Is it true blondes have more fun?" What are the ramifications of indoctrinating African American children with such values? Does the system that indoctrinates children to place a higher aesthetic value on blonde hair that is straight than in black hair that is curly create deeper issues? Does this indoctrination benefit anyone in such a diverse society, regardless of their physiognomy?

Psychological studies over fifty years ago found that when asked to select the prettiest doll from among dolls with diverse ethnic characteristics, a significant percentage of Black children selected a White doll. These data were presented to the U.S. Supreme Court in the landmark 1954 school desegregation case. Many were surprised when a half-century later a significant percentage of Black children still found the White doll prettier. When Black children are taught aesthetic values that lead them to consider themselves ugly, or at least less beautiful than others, what must they think about the beauty of a work of art that portrays Black people? What kinds of value assumptions will they tend to make about both African American art and African American artists? And much more importantly, how will they evaluate their own worth as human beings?

Artists and Responders to Art

The study of aesthetics also raises questions about the nature of the artist. There must be an artist before there is art. While human beings observe and appreciate the beauty of nature, that beauty is not art. Art is, by definition, a human creation. So we ask: Who is an artist? How does the artist fit into the society? What are the artist's responsibilities to the society? What are the society's responsibilities to the artist? Do we identify and differentiate between creators, interpreters, and imitators of art? If so, how? Another aspect of aesthetics raises a set of questions about the people who observe and respond to art: How do people respond to art? Can their responses be measured objectively? Do people from different times and places respond in a universal manner to a given work of art, or do responses differ? What factors, whether genetic or experiential, incite these differences?

Afrocentric aesthetics is concerned with the previously stated generally phrased aesthetics questions as they specifically relate to African American artists, art, and responders to that art. Afrocentric aesthetics asks: What do African Americans perceive as beautiful? What are the characteristics, criteria, and standards of beauty among African Americans? What do African Americans consider to be good art? In what specific ways do African Americans respond to things beautiful and to art? What kinds of expectations do African Americans have of their artists? What kind of an effect should African American artists have on other people? Since these questions impact several groups of African Americans, the questions must also focus more narrowly to reveal possible differences between African Americans in general, African American art theorists, and African American artists. These questions must also focus more narrowly to examine the specific art form of theatre.

Each of these questions raises a concurrent question: How does one know a particular answer is valid, correct, or true? Epistemology raises questions about how we know what we know. How do we know we know something about Afrocentric aesthetics? How do we determine that a given concept or theory about Afrocentric aesthetics is valid, correct, or true? How do we derive knowledge about the subject of aesthetics? In very general terms, two approaches to such questions have been widely used: one is a contemplative approach, and the other, a perceptual approach. The contemplative approach turns inward to inspiration or insight, or both, to gain transcendental knowledge, knowledge that transcends data. The perceptual approach takes data that can be perceived by the senses and analyzes it by organizing and measuring it in some way. Although many assume one approach is superior to the other, we believe both are necessary and neither achieves optimal results without the other.

Examples abound of valid knowledge gained through both the contemplative approach—inspiration, creative vision, insight, and the like—and the perceptual approach, the organization and analysis of data that has been perceived and measured in some way. While we believe both methods are valid ways to gain knowledge, in Eurocentric academic settings, knowledge gained through the contemplative approach tends to be more lightly regarded. The two approaches have been viewed by some in the Eurocentric American academic community as mutually exclusive opposing positions, but they are not. The depth of understanding a good artist must possess demands the use of both faculties in a holistic manner.

Our intention is to study the nature of Afrocentric theatre from a descriptive rather than a prescriptive approach. Of course, we must be concerned, at various levels, with what ought to be. However, we believe that preliminary to a concern with what ought to be, we must discover to some reasonable degree what is, as well as what the group generally agrees ought to be. Our approach to an analysis of Afrocentric aesthetics includes the study of at least four aspects of aesthetics: (1) works of art, the finished product, methods and materials of achieving the finished work; (2) the persons who create art; (3) the intended audience and its responses to art as well as its behavior generally; and (4) other people's theory and analysis of art and people's responses to art. In observing these four aspects of aesthetics as they function in African American culture, we will not assume that everything in our environment is beautiful simply because it is there.

Other Factors that Influence Evaluation

Some African American scholars express concern that many Black aesthetic concepts are fundamentally byproducts of White oppression and therefore should not be revered. Some scholars have taken the position that Black art forms, which are byproducts of White oppression, should be rejected. How White oppression has limited Black folks' choices regarding what is beautiful is exemplified by such soul food delicacies as chitterlings. Black folks decided chitterlings were a delicacy without the opportunity to compare chitterlings to broiled beef steak, lobster tails, escargot, or other Eurocentric delicacies. Enslaved people who ate chitterlings on Southern plantations prior to the Confederate Rebellion were able to obtain chitterlings and some other soul food ingredients only because White people did not consider them fit to eat. Arguably, hip-hop, blues, spirituals, jazz, and every other Black American music and dance genre, as well as soul food cooking, was created as a reaction to oppression. Scientific evidence of health issues aside, should soul food cooking be discarded because it came about, at least partially, in response to oppressive conditions? Should Black people eschew Black American music and dance because it came about, at least partially, in response to oppressive conditions?

All cultures develop a concept of beauty from the materials available to them. The architects and sculptors of Kemet worked with stone because, among other things, timber in sufficient quantity and size was not readily available. Greek architects and sculptors of the fifth century BC, building on the legacy of the Kemites, made similar choices for similar reasons more than two thousand years later. If the abundant supply of hardwood that was available in equatorial Africa had been available to the Kemites or the Greeks, their architecture might not have survived for thousands of years.

Martin Luther King, Jr. often said unwarranted suffering is redemptive. Without theorizing about the ethical or the theological desirability of unwarranted suffering, we contend unwarranted suffering due to racial oppression has encouraged depths and subtleties of artistic expression that might not be present in such large measure otherwise. For example, the subtle meaning in a spiritual's lyrics is directly attributable to this phenomenon. Systematic oppression of an entire group may actually increase the tendency of its members to be creative. Any behavior that is truly creative changes some aspect of the status quo, no matter how minute. Oppressed people are usually sufficiently dissatisfied with their condition to want to change it.

On the other hand, some social scientists who focus on African American studies have postulated that oppression manifests itself through rage, impotence, and fantasy. While these characteristics have their negative manifestations, they may also provide the ingredients for creativity. One of the useful functions of Afrocentric art is to counteract or overcome these manifestations of oppression. African Americans use art (the acts of producing and reacting to beauty) to forestall individual and community self-destruction by reducing levels of rage, impotence, and fantasy.

In seeking to answer the fundamental questions aesthetics raises, one may presuppose, as Plato did, that beauty is eternal and universal. That is, a study of beauty involves a search for elements of beauty (assuming that there are some) that transcend time and place. The traditional Eurocentric method of analyzing beauty presupposes, as Plato did, that eternal, ideal, prototypical characteristics of beauty exist. On the other hand, we presume some characteristics of beauty exist only within a cultural framework. This presumption permits some broad general aspects of beauty to be regarded as universal while recognizing more specific characteristics of beauty will vary as cultures vary. While all cultures undoubtedly regard something as beautiful, a specific object or characteristic thought to be beautiful in one cultural framework may very well be considered ugly in a different one. Music is often alleged to be more universal than other art forms that depend on language. Yet the melodic beauty of Chinese classical opera escapes most Americans of both African and European heritage.

Those who believe beauty is culturally relative usually view it as temporally relative as well, reasoning that factors that constitute beauty may change over time even within a cultural group. One who believes specific elements of beauty are eternal and universal will probably prefer to pursue knowledge about universal aesthetics and universal theatre, rather than seeking enlightenment about aesthetics or the nature of theatre in cultural or temporal parameters. Those who believe characteristics of beauty vary according to time, place, and culture will probably regard the study of Afrocentric theatre as a legitimate pursuit.

Each individual's value system contains aesthetic and moral aspects that are not always easily reconcilable. Many creative developments in African American music have been denigrated because the music was background entertainment in places that offered alcohol, gambling, and prostitution as main attractions. Because the music and the musicians could be found in places Afrocentric and Eurocentric moral leaders proclaimed to be reprehensible, the music was frequently labeled "the devil's music," creating guilt by association.

When asking what constitutes grace or beauty of movement in a cultural group, analytical observation of group members when they are comfortable and at ease provides a valid and important source of information. If the observed persons appear to be imitating people the observer considers immoral, pimps for example, analyzing the movements free of interference from moral judgments becomes difficult. While moral judgments are important in every culture, some kinds of movement may be judged dirty or suggestive or lewd, and therefore aesthetically displeasing if moral judgments are permitted to override aesthetic evaluations. Especially if moral judgments are made across cultures, a movement that seems suggestive (a moral judgment) may also be deemed ugly (an aesthetic judgment). What a movement suggests in one culture's morality may be quite different from what it suggests in a different culture's morality.

An example of this complexity is illustrated in the film *Ethnic Dance: Roundtrip to Trinidad,* featuring Geoffrey Holder.[77] He does a dance called "the Yavalu" in which Dhambala, the god in the dance, inhabits the dancer's body, whose movements resemble those of a snake. The dance movements begin in the upper torso and spread to the arms, head, pelvis, and feet, and finally encompass the entire body. When Holder saw the dance performed in a nightclub in New York, he heard people around him whispering about how sexy the dance was. Holder says, "There is no sex in this dance." He explains the torso is the life center and everything rotates from it. The dancer's possession by the god Dhambala demands that the dancer release this energy. Holder suggests the Eurocentric New York audience was unable to appreciate the dance aesthetically because their moral indignation over the pelvic movements interfered.

Some people have discredited African American social dance on aesthetic grounds when their actual objections are to the movement of the torso that occurs in the dance. Their objections invariably involve preconceptions about the sexuality of the movements. Eurocentric moral objections to Afrocentric movement usually focus on the pelvis. Afrocentric aesthetic ideals differ with reference to movement of the spinal column up to and including the head and neck. Afrocentric ideals of graceful movement value flexibility of the spinal column while Eurocentric ideals of grace, which are in concert with Eurocentric moral standards, demand that the spinal column remain straight. Eurocentric ideals of grace are also characterized by pointed toes and rounded arms. Moreover, the hand follows the arm. But most important of all, the torso must remain rigid.

The concept of "keeping it real" is often viewed as an Afrocentric aesthetic goal when it is more of a social or political equity issue objecting to the practice of not actually seeing the person but seeing and responding to the person's stereotype instead. "Keeping it real" is a call for African agency, to participate in American society without abandoning one's cultural heritage. To not abandon one's cultural heritage requires one to embrace some fairly widespread aesthetic goals. Some of these goals are relatively concrete and straightforward: to talk, gesture, and dress in certain ways. Other such goals are more abstract and amorphous. The more abstract and amorphous goals manifest in the more traditional art forms that large numbers of African Americans patronize. Cultures generally develop subtle and complex systems of determining what is more or less beautiful while remaining sufficiently pliable to accommodate variations of time, place, and individual taste. Afrocentric culture is not an exception to this concept. African Americans who engage in some form of art with a modicum of effectiveness for an African American audience must conform to Afrocentric concepts of beauty. While Afrocentric concepts of beauty do not always conflict with Eurocentric concepts of beauty, when such a conflict occurs the artist cannot reasonably expect to please both.

Only after developing and articulating Afrocentric ideas about what culture is, what aesthetics does, and how aesthetics functions in a culture to control individual and group behavior, and those ideas are polished through interaction, can we expect to pursue a valid analysis of African American culture's artistic production. Inherent in this effort to describe an Afrocentric aesthetic is the assumption that Afrocentric art has some unique characteristics. Some African Americans insist a work of art ought to stand or fall on its own merit based on whether or not African American people accept or reject it. Under ideal conditions this idea would have validity. But African Americans do not exist under ideal conditions.

One of the most unfortunate circumstances Black Americans continue to face is the attempt, whether conscious or unconscious, to destroy African cultural heritage and discredit its evolution into African American culture. This effort has not been totally without results, especially among more highly educated African Americans. Therefore, a concerted effort to educate African Americans in their own cultural traditions is necessary. To assert some African Americans are more thoroughly educated in the traditions of Europhile American culture than they are in their own is not an exaggeration. Likewise some African Americans have been miseducated to believe the dominant culture is an innately superior one.

An artist cannot create a work of art that is not influenced by his or her own culture. Yet a few African American artists have made public claims that African American art does not exist. Instead, they proclaim they are artists who just happen to have a darker complexion or a birth certificate that says "Negro" and factors of racial identity are irrelevant to the art they create. These artists do not want their work to be regarded as African American art because they consider that a demeaning identifier. Only with supreme difficulty can one imagine a British playwright, an Italian sculptor, or a German composer proclaiming, "I am not a British or Italian or German artist! I am simply an artist!" Why, then do some African American artists find it necessary to renounce their cultural identity in their quest for a reasonable level of acceptability as an artist and as a person?

In fairness, some African American artists object to pronouncements that they are among the best Black directors or composers or actors because they are among the best at what they do when compared to all human beings on the planet. Some would liken their objection to these racial modifiers to a sports commentator saying Michael Jordan is one of the best Black basketball players of all time.

American miseducation requires young people to understand and appreciate European and Europhile American arts including theatre art, and instills the idea that these Eurocentric aspects of American culture are far superior to its non-White aspects. Standardized examinations reflecting this cultural myopia are required of all Americans who attend traditional schools or seek admission to traditional colleges and universities. Obtaining a job that enables a middle-class lifestyle is virtually impossible without satisfactorily completing a significant segment of this miseducation process. Students are rarely required to absorb such information about any of the other cultures that comprise American culture. This miseducation process has worked so well for so long that it now appears to be endowed with such admirable characteristics as logic, truth, objectivity, and universality.

One of the principal techniques used in this miseducation process is the implementation of Eurocentric American criteria to evaluate arts that are created within the framework of Afrocentric culture, as well as other non-White cultures. Suppose we decided to pass judgment on what makes a good orange by using apples as a standard for judgment. We would undoubtedly reach the conclusion that all of the oranges that we had observed were of an inferior color (too yellow on the outside, not white enough on the inside), too acid a taste, too juicy a texture; and we could go on and on with our list of deficiencies. This analogy is not as farfetched as many wish to believe. Just as we know how an orange is supposed to look and taste in order to determine whether or not any specific orange is a good orange or a bad one, a specific work of art for an African American audience cannot be judged with validity unless Afrocentric aesthetic standards are appreciated and applied by the individual doing the judging.

Commercial theatre is widely regarded as the pinnacle of American theatre, and money determines the hierarchy of American commercial theatre. To a large extent, the myopic nature of mainstream American theatre results from its commercial nature and impacts Black and White theatre artists in much the same manner. Commercial theatre is widely regarded as the pinnacle of American theatre and money determines the hierarchy of American commercial theatre. White people in the top 4 percent income bracket purchase the vast majority of commercial theatre tickets. The same group finances, and therefore controls, the values and aesthetic tastes of noncommercial theatre. The distinctions between professional and commercial theatre are not always obvious. The theatres across America that call themselves "regional theatres" are professional theatres that employ professional actors, directors, designers, etc. Regional theatres operate as not-for-profit corporations financed by tax-exempt charitable contributions from WEPPEOs who secure tax exemptions for themselves and the corporations they control by making charitable donations to not-for-profit organizations such as schools, hospitals, symphony orchestras, art museums, and theatres.

These WEPPEO-financed theatres maintain their tax-exempt status as charitable institutions by asserting they benefit the communities they serve. These theatres' mission statements assert the funding they receive from tax exemption and charitable contributions enables them to provide educational and cultural enrichment and similar altruistic goals. They say these financial rewards enable them to place a higher priority on their community's educational and cultural needs than would be possible if they were dependent on ticket sales as their primary source of revenue. Some not-for-profit theatres remain true to their mission statements. Others have slowly abandoned education and cultural enrichment goals while continuing to claim tax-exempt status as charitable institutions.

Despite its fickle and sometimes schizophrenic nature, the American theatre establishment occasionally proclaims a Black playwright worthy of praise. Most Black Americans who observe the vicissitudes of the mainstream theatre establishment have applauded this praise for the Black recipients and economic benefits it garners for them. But many of these recipients of praise have lived to see their pedestal unceremoniously removed to make room for a new Black dramatist *du jour*. The acute shortage of pedestals for Black dramatists means the few who enjoy acclaim today will quickly fade from mainstream theatre's attention once they "discover" the next August Wilson.

The mainstream theatre establishment has mostly measured August Wilson's success by the money his plays have attracted. The dominant source of ticket sales in American commercial theatre is White people in the top 2 or 3 percent income bracket. If August Wilson or the next August Wilson is to be evaluated from an Afrocentric location, that process cannot be based on how many well-to-do White people purchase tickets or by the prestigious awards or favorable reviews the plays garner from equally well-to-do White people.

An appropriate evaluation of Wilson's work begins by acknowledging the dozens of Black playwrights who came before him, and we have no doubt that Wilson would concur. The next step in an assessment of Wilson's work begins by questioning the assertion made by many White critics and theatre-goers that, "August Wilson is one of the greatest playwrights of our time." Decades before we knew August Wilson existed, we were regularly motivated to question some White critic's unequivocal dictums about a Black theatre artist either because the critic did not seem to take the artist's cultural location into consideration or the critic seemed unaware of some salient facts. Any assertion about Wilson's work that fails to fully consider his cultural location deserves to be questioned, whether the assertion praises or denounces his work. Citing such sources of praise for Wilson as successful Broadway and regional theatre productions, *New York Times* reviews, and Pulitzer Prizes would validate the notion that prestigious Eurocentric institutions are competent and appropriate evaluators of African American theatre art. An Afrocentric view contends an Afrocentric location provides the best place to observe, understand, appreciate, and evaluate the dramatic art of African Americans and further infers that while Eurocentric critical accolades represent laudable achievement, they hold little if any significance for Black artists who want, as Wilson himself put it, "to participate in society as African people with their culture intact."[78] For Wilson to entitle his landmark speech "The Ground on Which I Stand"[79] indicates he understood the significance of location in any appraisal of his work.

Afrocentric standards for what constitutes "good" exist independently and transcend any work of art or individual artist. While Afrocentric criteria are based in traditional values that some critics and academicians endeavor to diminish, Wilson would undoubtedly contend that the mere fact that these critics and academicians hold degrees from White universities demonstrates either a willing embrace of the dominant culture's values, or considerable proficiency at pretending to do so. Although critics such as Ben Brantley of the *New York Times* seem fascinated by Wilson's mastery of word power, they do not seem to realize this and other aspects of Afrocentric culture are not eradicated by a college education or a good job, or a less vernacular pattern of speaking as exhibited by the characters in Wilson's last play, *Radio Golf*. Brantley calls *Radio Golf* Wilson's "thinnest work"[80] whereas we consider it his most mature and complex work. People with different cultural locations may observe the same performance and see a different play. Brantley recognizes Wilson's warning about "the clear and present danger of assimilation" in *Radio Golf*, but has missed similar messages in his other plays.

While Wilson's success in a theatre world dominated by White people is undeniable, we were amazed to discover that many individuals who had produced his plays were surprised and aggravated by his 1996 speech entitled "The Ground on Which I Stand." In their view, he was ungrateful. America's theatre establishment had welcomed him and he had the effrontery to demand to function as a playwright with his Afrocentric culture intact. He had spoken eloquently about the issue of African agency in interviews that aired on television in the USA and England long before 1996.[81] Moreover, these theatre professionals apparently failed to notice both the frequency and fervency with which his characters seek to keep their African culture intact and the force that prevents some of his characters from achieving this goal.

PART TWO
PRESENTATION

> n. 4 an offering to be seen; exhibition; showing: the presentation of a play or a motion picture.

Afrocentric presentation fits within the parameters of Afrocentric culture, which in part grows out of the oral traditions of Africa. Wole Soyinka describes these traditions as "sophisticated in idiom." Our forms of the theatre are quite different from literary drama. We use spontaneous dialogue, folk music, simple stories, and relevant dances to express what we mean.[82]

Afrocentric culture and the presentations it generates is a more complex phenomenon than moving African people and their lifestyles to America. Afrocentric presentations derive from two main antecedents: West African culture and English culture, and in a broader sense from African and European culture. But Afrocentric presentations are a constantly evolving complex mixture that derives from a variety of cultural sources. Analysis of such an amorphous subject requires freezing phenomena at some point in time to achieve descriptive coherence, inevitably resulting in oversimplification.

This inquiry into the nature of Afrocentric theatre as presentation embraces the range of forms Afrocentric theatrical presentations use and focuses on what the creators of Afrocentric theatrical presentations seek to accomplish. We will also describe what actual and potential African American audiences and expert evaluators value and regard as proper, right, and beautiful in the presentations they witness.

Afrocentric theatre is a total event that may include narrative storytelling, storytelling in dialogue form, persuasive speeches, sermons, song, dance, or instrumental music in any number of conceivable combinations. Afrocentric theatre can be either an event that evolves orally or a specific set of words fixed forever on a page. Afrocentric theatre emerged from a societal context in which Africans were brought to America, some enslaved, some free, all oppressed. Both free and enslaved Africans were viewed more as commodities than as fellow human beings by the larger society. Out of this societal context, Black Americans often ridiculed their White oppressors or captors in a type of presentation that was later coopted into the Negro minstrel. This societal context also spawned styles of preaching, storytelling, dancing, and singing, and the standards by which such presentations are evaluated. These presentations function as art in the Eurocentric sense of the term; but they also reinforce values, sustain mental health, enhance self-worth, and suggest strategies for coping with shared problems and dilemmas. These presentations are the foundation of Afrocentric theatre.

During the 1960s and 1970s, the dominant strategy for achieving a more overt acceptance of Afrocentric aesthetic values by African Americans seemed to necessitate a thrust that some viewed as negative. But such a step was undoubtedly necessary for the next step in the process. The seemingly negative thrust empowered African Americans to reject the notion that White artistic standards are universally appropriate. Rejecting centuries of miseducation was and remains a necessary preamble to a thought process that embraces an appreciation of Afrocentric aesthetic standards. Carter G. Woodson pointed out almost a century ago that in a society that provides such effective and abundant miseducation, physical oppression is not necessary except to make examples of a few of us who get "uppity" from time to time.

PRESENTATION

Many White people condemned this refusal by African Americans to accept the imposition of Eurocentric artistic standards as "racism in reverse." But the "racism in reverse" epithet could only be legitimate if Black people were empowered to use established legal and social systems and an ideology of Black supremacy to forcibly prevent White people from full participation in the rights, privileges, and benefits of the society through systematic subordination and discrimination. Afrocentric theatre has never sought to influence the kind of theatre White people do for other White people or to impose Afrocentric aesthetic values on White people.

Ironically, each succeeding generation of White Americans and Europeans finds greater affinity with Afrocentric culture and adapts and assimilates more and more of it. On the other hand, many White people feel so threatened by confident expressions of Black cultural legitimacy that they interpret them as anti-White. Any reduction in Black subordination is viewed as a loss of White entitlement. Some White people are so accustomed to the privileges they enjoy that the liberation of Black people seems equivalent to Black people enslaving White people. To use the "level playing field" analogy, some White people are so accustomed to the privileges they enjoy in a system of ideological White supremacy that as the playing field becomes less tilted in their favor, those who have benefitted most from White male privilege sincerely believe it has tilted in the opposite direction.

WEPPEOs have indicated by their condemnation of theatre of, by, and for African Americans that their superior judgment allows them not only to know what's best for African American artists, but also to understand what African American artists are doing and why. With the aid and comfort of these assumptions, WEPPEOs paternalistically inform African American artists what they should perceive as beautiful and what they should not. This process is not altogether a function of racism, since this elite group of White Americans also tell other White Americans what they should and should not perceive as beautiful.

The concepts of beauty embraced by WEPPEO-endorsed critics have, in some instances, caused African American theatre to morph into Eurocentric theatre in natural blackface. These transitions are justified on the pretext that the only aesthetic standards worth considering are the WEPPEO's standards. When Black people say our work deserves to be evaluated by different standards, WEPPEO-endorsed critics conclude a call for different standards is actually an excuse for lower standards. Influential people who endorse the tenets of objectivity and universality seem unable to conceptualize a difference between things without imposing a hierarchical arrangement on the things.

An Afrocentric evaluation of theatre is made difficult by the imposition of Eurocentric concepts delineated by Eurocentric terminology. This difficulty is not confined to Afrocentric artists in the USA. Ghanaian dramatist Efua Sutherland adroitly verbalizes the misunderstandings that are created by imposing Eurocentric terminology on African dramatic expressions. Sutherland described this phenomenon as "a clash of concepts" in a lecture she presented at Spelman College in 1969. She argued this clash of concepts results from "insistence on using foreign terminology to describe African dramatic expressions . . . . Each African language has precise and indigenous terms for its dramatic concepts and conventions, for every variety of performance . . . . Outside of a small sprinkling of people, the words *drama, theatre, stage, audience*, etc., are foreign words and incomprehensible in Africa."[83] English language terms must be used with care in order to position the concepts inside the parameters of Afrocentric values.

Sutherland provides an example of this need for Africans who speak English to reposition English words in order to make the concepts fit inside the parameters of Afrocentric values. She explains how the word "concert" came to be used in Ghana to mean any presentation in a European physical arrangement. While under British colonial control, Ghanian schools often presented staged programs of songs by schoolchildren. The performers were on a platform in front of an audience that sat in chairs arranged in parallel rows. The European colonizers called these programs *concerts*. Eventually, the term "concert" evolved as Ghanaians associated the term "concert" with all performances given on a stage before which people sat in rows and listened. If Ghanaians present a play on a stage before an audience seated in rows of chairs, they too are giving a concert. The content of the material presented has no bearing on what is called a concert. The Eurocentric arrangement of the presentation's environment determines its classification as a concert. The term "concert" was appropriated by the Ghanaians and conceptualized in a way that has meaning for them.

We find ourselves confronted with a clash of concepts. Although our observations and evaluations are written with English words, we try to get the concepts symbolized by the words to fit within the parameters of Afrocentric values.

Chapter Six

Rituals

"You will observe with concern how long a useful truth may be known, and exist, before it is generally received and practiced on." —Benjamin Franklin

Rituals evolve out of the perceived needs of people who share a common set of values. Rituals evolve into formalized behaviors that validate a society's values, and inculcate those values in the society's members. Although the most frequently discussed rituals are solemn ceremonies, all rituals are not. Whether solemn or not, rituals share at least three characteristics: (1) behavior becomes formalized through an evolutionary process; (2) group consensus regards the behavior as having some specific and important functional effect; (3) the event validates the group's system of values. Afrocentric rituals provide a means to identify and describe traditions and ideals that cause the behaviors that make Black theatre different from White theatre. If one understands these traditions and ideals and acknowledges that they are as important to Black theatre as Dionysian religious rituals are to Greek theatre, one is less likely to discredit Black theatre for failing to accomplish things it never intended to accomplish.

Since they are obliged to fit inside the parameters of Afrocentric values, African American rituals, including theatre rituals, are expected to achieve at least three important functions: (1) a sense of community, (2) some useful purpose, and (3) spiritual involvement. Rituals evolve from people whose shared values warrant regarding them as a community. Malidoma Patrice Somé defines community as "any group of people meeting with the intention of connecting to the power within a community."[84] A community:

(1) values its rituals as useful, beneficial, and functional; (2) participates in and cherishes the behaviors it has formalized and accepted through an evolutionary process; (3) embraces a shared belief system and cultural memory. Afrocentric rituals affirm and celebrate a sense of togetherness, of community, of sharing common ideas, deals, and idioms. Conscious awareness of belonging together is often emphasized by such physical contact as joining hands. This sense is often verbally depicted by the term "family." Verbal responses of affirmation and encouragement enhance this sense of community. Spiritual togetherness is affirmed and heightened by these verbal and physical forms of togetherness.

Fellowship is both a way to affirm a sense of community and a force for validating a group's system of values. Afrocentric values expect to enable a spiritual force by honoring those who built the foundation on which their achievements rest. Afrocentric values acknowledge that the capacity to accomplish a ritual's intended goals derives from forces that cannot be seen, heard, or touched. While individuals bear personal responsibility to participate, coming together in fellowship empowers the ritual to accomplish its purpose.

While a sense of community is present in live theatre of all cultures, its relative importance varies. WEPPEOs may attend live performances because they are expected to be there or they expect others whom they deem important to be there. How people watch motion pictures and television demonstrates even greater contrast. Attendance at motion pictures almost always fails to foster the sense of community evident at live theatre performances. One can attend a motion picture with hundreds of others and still feel alone. Television viewing is an even more private activity. People often watch television while actually alone and become irritated when someone interrupts their television viewing. In contrast, people who went into rural communities in Africa bearing the gift of television were frequently told, "Instead of providing many small televisions so each family has its own, we would prefer one large television so we can watch together." Before they had television, gathering together to listen to stories was the most frequently practiced ritual in these small rural communities. They welcomed the technology that allowed them to learn stories from the outside world, but they did not understand why people who could create the marvel of television would use it to stifle the communal power of fellowship.

Rituals are communal practices that enable a group's members to better cope with events that profoundly impact their lives. These events include such natural phenomena as seasonal changes in climate. Rituals such as funerals, marriages, and various rites of passage directly address specific changes in relationships with loved ones. General and cumulative rituals such as regularly recurring religious worship ease the inevitable difficulties that life brings. Rituals promote harmony, balance, unity, collective memory, and continuation of the group in the face of all sorts of potentially disruptive occurrences.

In a contemporary society where religious rituals no longer hold dominion over the entire populace, other rituals emerge to satisfy individual and group needs to cope with occurrences over which people seem to have little or no control. In an environment where everything is a marketing plan, what seems to be a ritual can be a highly profitable business. American rituals now encompass a range that includes elitist Eurocentric art forms such as symphony concerts, grand opera, and Broadway theatre, as well as such nonelite events as baseball, football, basketball, hockey, and professional wrestling. Black Americans have coopted one such Eurocentric ritual and saturated it with Afrocentric values. Marching bands at historically Black colleges and universities have created football halftime shows that transform a previously Eurocentric ritual into a decidedly Afrocentric one.

Rituals do not emerge full blown overnight. During the Black arts movement of the 1960s the word "ritual" described performances in and for a cultural community that attempt to alter the values of that community. These presentations were developed and performed by several Black theatre groups during the 1960s. Although they were solemn ceremonies, presentations had not been formalized through an evolutionary process, nor did a broadly based Black community regard them as having a specific functional effect. Sometimes artists perform for people who are not of their community or in communion with them. Rituals require community. Without community there can be no ritual.

Some years ago, we were asked to write a paper focusing on the question: Does the Art Ensemble of Chicago integrate ritual drama in its performances? As we confronted this question, we recognized a larger question. Can artists create work that is simultaneously *avant garde* and ritual? By its nature, ritual is both vernacular and commonplace. Commonplace art is often demeaned as trite or clichéd by elitist critics. While the Art Ensemble of Chicago is certainly not trite or clichéd, its performances cannot possibly be rituals. The Art Ensemble of Chicago no doubt serves a valuable purpose by pushing the envelope. They are part of a significant movement in Afrocentric American music called "free jazz" by some and "avant-garde nationalism" by others. The movement solidified in the 1960s. "Three early cultivators of the style were Sun Ra . . . Charlie Mingus . . . and Cecil Taylor . . ."[85] But what the Art Ensemble of Chicago and similar musicians do never became a significant force among the masses of Black music lovers.

The conventions of the Eurocentric concert format are a significant part of the Eurocentric baggage carried by many Afrocentric musicians and many of their most appreciative audience members. The very idea of coming to a concert—a Eurocentric event—predisposes behaviors that are antithetical to the purposes of Afrocentric ritual. The definitive concert requires separation of the audience from performers and does not allow participation in the performance by the audience. Although, the Art Ensemble of Chicago's presentations include behaviors that have the surface appearance of ritual, they are not rituals unless their audience joins with them as a community.

However, the Art Ensemble of Chicago can be appreciated and evaluated as theatre art even if their presentations do not embody the ideals of ritual.

Just as wearing Eurocentric formal attire did not make the Modern Jazz Quartet's music Eurocentric, African paraphernalia in a context of the *avant garde* music of the Art Ensemble of Chicago does not necessarily make their music either Afrocentric or ritual. The Art Ensemble of Chicago's music may very well deserve to be regarded as Afrocentric, but their music and performance style is also *avant garde*. Ritual and *avant garde* are mutually exclusive and contradictory phenomena. Artists who succeed at being *avant garde* consciously choose to be out ahead of their community. Consciously choosing to be out ahead of one's community has created such honored Afrocentric musical innovations as bebop. While innovation is often a good thing, one cannot simultaneously be both *avant garde* and a part of and easily understood by one's community.

Many Black theatre groups in the 1960s and 1970s sought to adapt traditional African ritual concepts to contemporary African American life in order to achieve the responses that traditional African rituals achieve in their environments. Most of these efforts failed because the community they sought to serve did not see their efforts as beneficial or useful. Presentations called *rituals*, created by Black theatre groups in the 1960s and 1970s deliberately sought to change African Americans' values rather than validate or strengthen existing ones. These Black theatre groups sought to expose fallacies in the dominant culture's effective and abundant miseducation process and persuade masses of African Americans to abandon their Eurocentric cultural baggage. As with the Art Ensemble of Chicago, the presentations these Black theatre groups call rituals did not actually function as rituals in that they found no permanent place in the hearts and minds of a significant segment of the Black community.

Black theatre groups that created these events intended and expected their presentations to counteract the dominant culture's miseducation of African Americans. Many undoubtedly believed their rituals would become so ingrained in African American life that they would become rituals in the traditional sense of the term. But miseducation has led to double-consciousness, which in turn has created an ongoing dilemma. Like other Americans, Black Americans want the abundant comforts and conveniences America has to offer. Black Americans know their most reliable route to America's abundant lifestyle is a good education. But good education is a lot like good hair. Each is an unalterably, intensely Eurocentric idea. Is the cost of acquiring America's comforts and conveniences the abandonment of one's African cultural heritage? Can Afrocentric performing artists strengthen their community's desire to retain cultural heritage without forcing their community to abandon aspirations to acquire America's comforts and conveniences?

At least one set of practices established in the 1960s, the celebration of Kwanza, has survived; and its acceptance has evolved to the point that it deserves to be regarded as ritual.[86] When Maulana Karenga first proposed Kwanza, it was not a ritual. Decades later, Kwanza has evolved so that it is valued by a large and still growing community. Those who celebrate Kwanza believe it promotes and enhances their system of values. Its continued celebration implies Kwanza has recognizable beneficial outcomes. Kwanza has become a ritual. In addition to Kwanza, Asante and other Afrocentric humanists have established Afrocentric rites of passage for young African Americans in a variety of institutional settings.

Events that Black theatre groups call rituals are efforts to recapture lost or misplaced Afrocentric values that embody the spirit and spirituality of African predecessors. These performances do not seek to duplicate actual African rituals in some sort of archaeological revival. Instead, these rituals seek to adapt traditional African ritual concepts to contemporary African American cultural needs, and evoke the spiritual responses traditional African rituals evoke in their own environments. Accurately reproducing surface details of African rituals is not a goal of these Black theatre rituals. Consequently, it is inappropriate and invalid to find fault with these presentations for lack of authenticity or accuracy of detail. Valid standards for determining success are more likely to be found in responses from people for whom the rituals are intended. We find it interesting that while some have demeaned these newly created rituals on the grounds that they are newly created, the detractors do not protest any of the newly created American holidays that were invented by a well-known greeting card company for no purpose other than to sell more greeting cards.

Religious Rituals

Information about what African Americans value in their performing arts can be obtained by examining their highly regarded rituals. Since church services contain ritual elements that are held in high regard by African Americans, a determination of the most highly valued ritual elements in such church services provides important information about Afrocentric aesthetic values. Our descriptions of these elements of Afrocentric religious rituals are based on our accumulated observations of Afrocentric church services. But we must hasten to point out that we do not regard all church services that are carried on by African Americans as African American church services. Some are very nearly European American church services carried on by individuals who just happen to be Black.

At least three concepts distinguish Afrocentric religion from Eurocentric religion. (1) Afrocentric religion is behavior-based whereas Eurocentric religion is based in a specific set of beliefs, tenets, and ideology. (2) Afrocentric religion is community-based whereas Eurocentric religion is based in individual beliefs and responsibilities. (3) Eurocentric religious worship is conceptually apart and different from everyday life; whereas, Afrocentric religious worship is everyday life—a total way of life for everyone in the community—a continual activity that encompasses everyone at all times, at all places. These differences undoubtedly explain why Eurocentric scholars believe Kemites had "religious obsessions" in the conduct of their daily lives.[87]

John S. Mbiti is an African theologian and scholar whose work is not directly concerned with retention of African culture in America. However, his descriptive views of African religion provides a basis for identifying such retentions. He states, "Because traditional [African] religions permeate all the departments of life, there is no formal distinction between the sacred and the secular, between the religious and nonreligious, between the spiritual and the material areas of life."[88] The entirety of Mbiti's statement suggests the secular does not exist in a traditional African sense. Since all of life is religious, there can be nothing that is not religious. Persons who are born in a traditional African environment do not make individual choices to accept or reject the religious dogma of their community. Choice with respect to religion is nonexistent. Religion is the entirety of everything, so people are inevitably religious. Traditional African religion encompasses the total existence of a community and is for the community rather than for the individual. The ordinary and mundane artifacts and activities of every one of the community have as much religious significance as any special artifacts, activities, or individuals.

In Eurocentric thought the sacred is fundamentally different and distinct from the secular. Eurocentric religion is special. It is not ordinary. Eurocentric culture tends to regard the practice of religion, the church, and the clergy as a special thing, a special place, a special group of people. Eurocentric religion exists outside and exclusive of the normal day-to-day activities of the world. People who are considered worldly come in contact with the religious when they attend the special place called church on a special day and time. Diop attributes the Eurocentric separation of secular and sacred to the materialism of the Greeks who "were never to pass beyond material, visible man, the conqueror of hostile Nature." He says the "rugged life on the Eurasian plains apparently intensified the materialistic instincts of the people living there . . . it forged moral values diametrically opposite to Egyptian moral values."[89] Although many African Americans view the religious and the secular as separate, the Afrocentric view does not separate the religious from the secular. This seeming contradiction reflects the fact that African American culture is an amalgamation that retains some fundamental behavioral characteristics of African religion while embracing some ideological details of Eurocentric Christianity.

Rituals achieve a useful purpose by providing participants with inspiration, information, or insight that enables them to cope with change. Although change opens new and potentially exciting future possibilities, it also disrupts or destroys some element of the past. For example, a wedding is supposed to help make the change in relationships acceptable to those who previously felt a sense of belonging to one of the espoused. The often heard statement to the parents of the bride at a wedding, "You are not losing a daughter, you are gaining a son," characterizes one of the purposes of the ritual. Rites of passage make the person completing the ritual feel that a level of competence and independence has been achieved, but the rites also allow parents and surrogate parents to cope with their feelings of abandonment as the child becomes more independent.

Eurocentric culture makes a fundamental distinction between ritual and theatre that is fine art, whereas the Afrocentric view does not recognize such a distinction. The salient factor in this distinction is usefulness. An Afrocentric view may regard a ritual that accomplishes some useful function to simultaneously function as art. Eurocentric notions of art for art's sake and fine art exclude rituals from the category of fine art. Rituals aim to serve a useful purpose and Eurocentric fine art excludes usefulness as a criterion for aesthetic worth. Persons who believe in art for art's sake cannot reasonably condone the notion that factors that contribute to the value of a ritual can exist in a work of theatre art.

Traditional Eurocentric ideology regards the cognitive and the emotional as fundamentally different, and in a sense, opposing things. Cognitive knowledge is highly valued in both Eurocentric and Afrocentric cultures, but Afrocentric thought regards knowing and feeling as inseparable aspects of a whole process by which human beings receive stimuli from outside themselves and learn from them. Since Afrocentric culture values feeling more highly than Eurocentric culture, a Eurocentric perspective views the emotional stimuli of traditional Afrocentric church services as uncultivated, uncivilized, possibly even primitive or barbaric.

The pervasive influence of Eurocentric religious concepts on African Americans might lead one to assume that some significant, basic, and essential differences between religious rituals and secular ones exist in African American culture. While such an assumption may seem accurate on the surface, its rigid application could confuse the issue. For African Americans who regard religion as all encompassing, the difference between the religious and the secular is largely a matter of style and convenience in the arrangement of the presentation. Our observations about ritual characteristics of Afrocentric church services are therefore applicable to secular presentation as well. An exemplary expression of the nonexistence of a religious and secular dichotomy in Afrocentric culture was voiced in the early 1970s by Wendell P. Whalum, then chairman of the Department of Music at Morehouse College. While discussing the evolution of African American music, he has said there are two, two-syllable words, "Jesus" and "Baby," that enable the same song to be used in both religious and secular contexts. With that principal simple alteration in wording, a song changes from gospel to blues. In such a transformation, numerous subtle changes are likely to take place as well.

Word Power

The dichotomy between the religious and the secular or the lack thereof is not the only fundamental difference in Afrocentric and Eurocentric points of view about ritual and theatre. Afrocentric ritual theatre's aesthetic priorities do not conform to Eurocentric tenets for evaluating drama.

Eurocentric aesthetics traditionally employs a hierarchical arrangement of six components. Aristotle lists these components in the *Poetics*, in descending order of importance, as plot, character, theme, dialogue, music (often translated as mood and rhythm), and spectacle. In a relatively recent enhancement of this model, professors George and Portia Kernodle link Aristotle's three most important components (plot, character, and theme) that they describe as "structure," and the lesser three components (dialogue, music, and spectacle) comprise the "texture." The Kernodles explain, "The texture is what is directly experienced by the spectator, what comes to him through his senses, what the ear hears (the dialogue), what the eye sees (the spectacle), and what is felt as mood through the entire visual and aural experience."[90]

No matter how far some modern and post-modern theatre movements have ventured away from the middle of the Eurocentric theatre stream, they remain in the stream circumscribed by Aristotelian rules. Some of these movements challenge the system's boundaries, but they remain in the stream, and the stream remains intact. Each Eurocentric theatre movement rebels against conventional Eurocentric drama by violating limitations imposed by conventional Eurocentric thought. Absurdist playwrights challenge conventional notions of objectivity and assert that reality cannot be reduced to a model of linear logic by portraying an irrational universe. But their surface reality is not significantly different from the Eurocentric models they claim to be rebelling against. Ibsen and Ionesco are remarkably similar when contrasted with the classical operatic forms of Beijing or Yoruba culture.

Afrocentric theatre is neither a rebellion against nor a violation of Eurocentric aesthetic standards. Afrocentric theatre perceives and expresses reality in fundamentally different ways and functions with fundamentally different aesthetic standards from Eurocentric aesthetic standards. Afrocentric theatre places significantly more emphasis on dialogue, music, and spectacle, than on plot, character, and theme. An aesthetic that grows out of an oral tradition and regards rhythm as the central factor in presentation must necessarily place a higher aesthetic value on texture and a lower value on structure.

Confusion often results when using the Eurocentric literary process of analyzing theatre from a script rather than from a presentation. Because this literary process uses the term "dialogue" to describe both vocal utterances and words written in a script, what the ear hears in presentation gets confused with literary values and cognitive meanings of written words. Readers of written words control the chronological sequence and time allotted to ponder them. Viewer-listeners see and hear in the space and time allotted by the presenter. There is a vast difference between how words written in a play's script impact a reader and how vocal quality, mood, rhythm, and visual perceptions impact a viewer-listener when these stimuli converge as a single message.

Dialogue in an Afrocentric context is similar to the Eurocentric concept that considers dialogue "what the ear hears." But the relative value of how dialogue is presented and how its meaning is conveyed differs. The differences are subtle, but there are differences. An appreciation of the term "nommo," generally translated into English as "word power," may serve to illuminate the differences. Since the English translation does not convey the term's cultural context, we have summarized Molefi Asante's discussion of nommo in *The Afrocentric Idea*. Asante says nommo is productive, imperative, calling forth, and commanding. African society seeks harmony and nommo creates harmony from spoken materials. An African view of communication is affected by a strong collective mentality where the group is more important than the individual. Since African art is always functional, public discourse as an art form is complete only when it is productive, hence functional. Theatre is "public discourse as an art form," which is a creative manifestation of what is "called to be." Theatre is created by artists to satisfy a societal need, and it is functional because it has meaning in the speaker's and audience's worldview. Meaning is derived from social, political, and religious moments in the society's history. Theatre is essential to society and inseparable from its worldview because nommo is the generative power of the community. Hence, there is little distinction between audience and speaker.[91]

Our view of nommo has been enhanced by observation of ways that some African societies seek harmony by placing higher value on harmony than on assigning guilt and punishment. Traditional West African processes for arbitrating disputes seek not so much to punish guilt as to restore harmony. Similarly, traditional African religious leaders often assign tasks to individuals who have strayed from the path of righteousness. But neither penitence nor punishment is the goal of the tasks. Rather, the tasks aim to restore harmony. The purpose of the "bride price" is even more widely misunderstood. It too aims to restore harmony. The "bride price" is not a purchase price but a token of recognition that the bride's departure leaves a void in the bride's parents' home. While no token of appreciation will fully fill the void, the "bride price" expresses recognition that a daughter's departure constitutes a significant loss to her parents.

Several decades ago an African American singer, we do not recollect the name of the song or the singer, sang "It ain't what you do, it's the way that you do it." We have often explained this facet of nommo by relating an old story about a good church-going sister who was asked by a friend, who was unable to attend church that day, "Did Rev. Jones preach a good sermon this morning?" "Oh yes," the sister answered zealously. "What was the sermon about?" her friend asked. The sister replied, "I don't rightly know what it was about, but it sure was a good sermon." The good church-going sister understood the texture of the sermon was of far greater value than its structure.

Vocality

African Americans use vocal effects or vocality to enhance the emotional intensity of their music or speech. The following summary of several terms used to describe African vocality is derived from Earl L. Stewart's *African American Music: An Introduction*. We have modified Professor Stewart's description to focus on spoken-word uses of vocality. Descriptions of these devices are not optimally conveyed through the written word. If live presentations are not readily accessible, we recommend listening to recorded music and speech. While there are far too many excellent examples to list here, two classic exemplars of many of these vocal devices can be found in the recorded music of James Brown and in sermons recorded by Rev. C. L. Franklin, Aretha Franklin's father.

When these devices are used by preachers, storytellers, and other spoken word artists, there is very little noticeable difference between guttural effects and related utterances, interpolated vocality, and vocal rhythmization. Another way to view these terms is that there are several different ways to describe a single phenomenon. Guttural effects include screams, shouts, moans, and groans. Skilled presenters rarely use guttural effects haphazardly or indiscriminately. Rather, they are used at moments when their presence adds emotional emphasis or heightens the emotional drama. Two types of shouts are commonly used. The intoned shout sounds more like singing than speech. The nonintoned shout sounds more like speech than singing. Both types add to the rhythmic complexity of performances and offer speakers a nonverbal option to generate emphasis. Interpolated vocality adds vocal sounds or words and also has two basic forms. One is substantially rhythmic, consists of inarticulate sounds, and is generally spoken. The second uses words, often to restate or extend a theme, and is also called "interpolated verbalism." Vocal rhythmization uses vocal sounds mainly for rhythmic purposes. Whether sung (as in scatting) or spoken (as in rapping), the emphasis is on rhythm rather than melody.[92]

Further insight into the relative values of structure and texture may be gained by examining the African tradition from which Afrocentric theatre continues. Lewis Nkosi explains that because, there is very little pretense toward naturalistic representation . . . an actor can often pause to introduce extraneous matter or explanations to the action or comment on the appearance of members of the audience, drawing extra laughs, without minimising the dramatic impact of the action. The result of all this is to make it very difficult for an African to think of drama merely as literature because the force and integrity of the drama is realisable only in its performance.[93]

The most important characteristic of dialogue is the manner in which words are presented. Traditional Afrocentric church services provide examples that are well known and accepted by a broad array of African Americans. A sermon on the twenty-third psalm probably contains ideas and cognitive information that is very well known to anyone and everyone in a typical congregation.[94] Whether the presentation is religious or not, the key factor is how well the presentation is made, how effectively the presenter generates empathetic responses. The presenter need not enact a story with a beginning, middle, and conclusion as Eurocentric realistic drama does. Eurocentric drama uses language to deliver cognitive information that conveys character exposition and conflict, resulting in a climax, followed by a resolution.

Afrocentric ritual theatre can be based on a dramatic premise as simple and straight forward as the twenty-third psalm. First, the premise is established. A premise can be a simple declarative sentence such as, "The Lord is my shepherd." The arrangement of actions uses the premise to build emotional intensity. Plot complications that create conflict or suspense are acceptable, but not necessary. Many such presentations contain no discernable conflict. In the context of Afrocentric ritual, suspense is of little consequence since the congregation already knows the story.

Eurocentric plot is often described as a line moving through time. The line rises to a climax and descends to a denouement or plot resolution. This linear cognitive content delivery presents all in the audience with the triggering climactic data at the same instant. In contrast, an Afrocentric preacher or storyteller who presents a story such as the twenty-third psalm is expected to build the congregation's emotional intensity to a climax. When generated through ascending emotional intensity, the climax does not occur at the same moment for every member of the congregation. Similarly, the peak of emotional intensity is followed by a reduction that is neither linear nor simultaneous for all members of the congregation; nor is it a denouement since it need not resolve conflict, eliminate suspense, or resolve the story's loose ends. The rise and fall in emotional intensity is not an attribute of the sermon alone; it occurs over the entire service. Pre-sermon activities take as long as needed to achieve an appropriate level of emotional involvement before the sermon begins. These pre-sermon activities are important steps in the process of achieving a dramatic climax. Typically, a respected elder determines when the proper level of involvement has arrived and so indicates through a pre-arranged action. The presentation of secular poems and stories accomplishes this preliminary function by having the congregated encourage the presenter to perform until a sense of communal readiness has been achieved. The presenter must sense when it is time to begin and do so at that time.

Ordering actions to elicit empathetic responses is more important in Afrocentric theatre than in Eurocentric theatre where the emphasis is on the use of language to provide an ordered sequence of cognitive information—a story. Afrocentric ritual drama has story content, but this ordered sequence of cognitive information is less valuable, less necessary to the event's success than ordering the sequence of actions to achieve appropriate emotional responses. Afrocentric ritual theatre does not require conflict or plot complications. Plot complications that emerge from conflict are not necessary; neither is a denouement to resolve conflicts and plot complications. In Afrocentric ritual theatre a script structured as a linear story with a beginning, a middle, and a conclusion is often not necessary and sometimes not desirable.

We find striking similarities between some of the hieratic Kemetic ritual texts (in translation) and Afrocentric ritual theatre presentations. Many Kemetic rituals are based, not on stories, but on dramatic premises, as are Afrocentric sermons. Both use such devices as call-responses, chants, hymns, repetitions, and musical instruments to affect emotional intensity.

Rhythm and Movement

The element of rhythm is a dominant force in Afrocentric ritual theatre. Afrocentric religious ritual is almost totally dependent on tempo and rhythm to order presentations into a beginning, a middle, and an end. Tempo builds in rate and intensity, and volume usually builds to a climax and then recedes. Asymmetry is an Afrocentric ideal, both rhythmically and visually whereas Eurocentric aesthetic choices tend more toward symmetry and regularity in color, pattern, and rhythm. In Afrocentric theatre, rhythmic asymmetry is often an overriding factor in dialogue as well as music choices. Syllables may be added or deleted from words and words or phrases may be repeated to create more intense rhythmic responses.

In Afrocentric performance, rhythm dominates the communicative modes of speech, music, and movement. Black preachers generally regard the rhythmic elements of music, movement, and speech as valid and useful tools for heightening emotional the intensity of religious rituals. All three of these elements, music, movement, and speech, function together to establish empathy with the congregation. The preacher's movement, music, and speech grows in intensity, causing the congregation's response to grow in intensity.

A preacher may make a simple straightforward statement like, "The Lord is my shepherd." If the preacher receives a vocal acclamation of low to medium intensity—a few amens, a few my-Lords—the preacher may say "The Lord is my shepherd" three or four times using rhythm and vocal inflection to generate affirmations of greater volume and intensity. What matters here is not the cognitive content of what is said but the way it is said. If the preacher says, "The Lord is my shepherd" six or seven times, each new and different repetition is aimed at garnering more unanimous and more enthusiastic affirmation.

A syllable or a whole word may be omitted from a phrase if it interferes with the rhythm. This concern for rhythm is the origin of many idioms of "Negro dialect." When Black poets alter a word's pronunciation to make it conform to a desired rhythm pattern, they are accused of not speaking "good English." When White poets make similar alterations, the process is called "poetic license."

Afrocentric ritual involves body movements that are communicative and aesthetically pleasing that could be considered dance. Most Black preachers and their congregations would never use the term "dance" to describe their body movements during a service. Many Christian denominations call dance "sinful." Christian morality appears to be at odds with traditional African dance in that one of the most salient features of traditional African dance is its emphasis on movement of the torso, more specifically the pelvis. Traditional African ideals of grace place a high value on movement of the torso, reasoning the torso is the center and source of human life. This point of view permits some freedom and flexibility for expression through movement of the arms and legs, such providing rhythmic emphasis via movement and sound by clapping hands and patting feet. In contrast, the Eurocentric ideal of grace places high aesthetic value on very specific arm and leg movement, while requiring the torso to remain rigid. The best example of this ideal is classical ballet, where any movement of the torso, especially of the pelvis, is considered aesthetically displeasing and is absolutely forbidden by the rules. This prohibition of pelvic movement is also a significant factor in the Eurocentric classification of ballet as a fine art.

Scripted Afrocentric theatre retains the focus on community found in Afrocentric rituals. Eurocentric masterpieces, from *Oedipus Rex* to *Hamlet* to *The Glass Menagerie* to *Who's Afraid of Virginia Woolf*, to *Glengarry Glenn Ross*, to *I Am My Own Wife* emphasize individuality and focus on an individual's differentness. Afrocentric theatre has as a fundamental goal bringing a group of people together to celebrate being together. Although the stated purpose of Afrocentric rituals is usually to observe some specific event such as birth, puberty, marriage, or death, at the foundation of each purpose is the more basic goal of affirming a sense of community. Going to church satisfies a nontheological need, fellowship, which is a way to affirm a sense of community and is an impetus to validate the group's values.

Afrocentric rituals benefit from a community's conviction that close proximity and harmony with others enhances outcomes individuals might have achieved to a lesser extent by working separately. The belief that being in harmony and close proximity enables the whole to be greater (or stronger) than the sum of its parts is a fundamental principle for many Afrocentric societies (which is not to say that other societies might not adhere to this principle as well). The belief that strength can be derived from context also affects Afrocentric language usage. English is often bent to fit Afrocentric context by assigning meanings words that differ from their objective Eurocentric definitions. The word "bad," depending on the context, may mean bad or it may mean especially good. The view that context can change the essence of a thing is in direct contradiction to Platonic philosophy and fails to meet Eurocentric standards of objectivity.

Traditional rituals are expected to have some future effect outside the ritual event itself. A funeral ritual is supposed to have a useful future effect on the soul of the deceased as well as on those who grieve for the deceased. From a Eurocentric location, cause-and-effect relationships that cannot be scientifically explained are primitive superstitions. Afrocentric poets and playwrights whose goal is to be useful by teaching, persuading, or motivating often generate responses from Eurocentric locations that label such efforts as propaganda and claim their work not art and not theatre.[95]

Ironically, these Eurocentric theories of fine art seem to have little, if any, impact on the realities of Eurocentric theatre. The pre-nineteenth-century Eurocentric notion that the purpose of drama is to teach and to please has not been driven out of the Eurocentric mind by contemporary Eurocentric values that are more materialistic and scientific. Most Eurocentric textbooks that describe the nature of theatre recognize that propaganda or rhetoric can be an integral part of Eurocentric theatre art. At the very least, these theories of fine arts generally acknowledge and approve of a theatre art that has such incidental aftereffects as changes in opinion that result from insights.

A dilemma seems to exist. Eurocentric values appear to regard theatre art and rhetoric as two separate phenomena that cannot be mixed. But Eurocentric values also appear to welcome persuasive messages in theatre. The dilemma is resolved by recognizing that Eurocentric values welcome persuasive messages in theatre so long as the messages are consistent with Eurocentric values. Eurocentric critics really do not object to theatre that expresses controversial ideas or combines drama with rhetoric. What Eurocentric critics object to is advocating ideas that do not conform to the values of the people who comprise the leadership or controlling class, the WEPPEOs.

To further complicate matters, WEPPEOs often seem willing to permit certain specific forms of dissidence. The fact that some dissidence is tolerated in the USA is often misconstrued. Advocacy of an idea that is as antithetical to American capitalists as Marxism is tolerated if the advocate adheres to a Eurocentric theoretical framework and avoids pragmatic action. Marxism is as Eurocentric in its view of history and economics as capitalism is. The fact that WEPPEOs occasionally tolerate radical Eurocentric ideas does not mean they will condone advocacy for Afrocentric behavior, even if the behavior does not pose a significant threat to WEPPEOs. Many White people who derive no actual benefit from maintaining the status quo are convinced they have a vested interest simply because they are White. Occasional attacks by WEPPEOs on some Afrocentric position enhances the view among White people who have no power that simply being White gives them a vested interest in the controlling establishment.

Spirituality

A third function of Afrocentric ritual theatre is to create spiritual involvement, sometimes called emotional involvement. Afrocentric values do not make the Eurocentric presumption that human behavior is either rationally motivated, resulting in fine behavior, or emotionally motivated, resulting in coarse behavior. Afrocentric values do not presume human behavior can be classified in an arbitrary manner as one of these or the other. Further, Black people have used the term "soul" for decades, to respect and venerate behaviors that contain emotionally and spiritually motivated elements. Such behaviors are highly valued among African Americans, whether they are called *soul* or something else. In recent decades, aspects and styles of soul have been called *funk*, *jive*, *hip*, *hip-hop*, *be-bop*, and the list goes on.

Scripted African American theatre such as James Baldwin's *The Amen Corner* exhibits many manifestations of soul. The play's action flows to the rhythms of the language and music of the Black church. The play's dominant force is its rhythm. The audience becomes swept up in this rhythm and is thereby compelled to participate. *The Amen Corner* affects its audience in a manner similar to the empathetic responses elicited by Black church rituals. The play's use of rhythm elicits empathetic responses from those who are gathered together (the audience) and reinforces their sense of togetherness. *The Amen Corner* is also similar to Black church ritual with respect to its content. The play is about love, about the enduring strength that love gives, about love among the people who comprise a particular Black family and among the extended family that is the congregation portrayed on stage, and further to the congregation that comprises the theatre audience. This love transcends the petty bickering, jealousies, and family fights that comes alive in the theatre enabled by many of the presentation techniques that Black churches use.

Ironically, *The Amen Corner* is weakest as a play when it is strongest as literature. There are several scenes between Alexander family members that exhibit Baldwin's strength as a novelist while depending too much on words to reveal character and move the plot forward. What is told needs to be told, but some of it would be told more effectively through deeds rather than words. Playwrights need to let the actors act. In these scenes, words overwhelm deeds, the tempo slows, and the rhythms become less pronounced. Word power has more to do with how words are spoken (deeds) than the intrinsic or literary meaning of the words. This ebb in the action is especially pronounced in scenes involving the father. Because he is confined to a sickbed, visual interest through movement is difficult to achieve. While ideas are repeated, the repetition is not used here to create rhythmic involvement from the audience through the use of empathy. Although some aspects of *The Amen Corner* exemplify Afrocentric aesthetic priorities, other aspects exemplify Eurocentric priorities that regard the word, in a literary sense, as the principal element of drama. This emphasis on words is apparent in the practice of publishing and reading scripts rather than producing and attending plays. Such an emphasis on words results in playwrights being thought of as "writers" rather than as "wrights." Scripts are more highly valued for their literary worth than for their impact in presentation. Those trained in Eurocentric traditions of literary analysis seem to have difficulty accepting the idea that a dramatic presentation cannot be captured on printed pages. This literary point of view fosters, among other things, the idea that improvisational theatre, music, and dance are inherently inferior to forms of these arts that commit words, notes, or movements to a page to be executed by interpretative artists exactly as written.

While Eurocentric theatre values the ability to create an illusion of spontaneity, actual spontaneity is an essential and valued component of Afrocentric arts including ritual theatre. In order to be deemed good by Afrocentric standards, spontaneous creation of art requires at least two attributes: mastery of the art form and spiritual involvement in the performance. The jazz idiom in music provides ample evidence of the artistic validity of spontaneity that grows out of both mastery of the art and spiritual involvement in the performance. Highly regarded African American performers often develop the capability of becoming one with the event, the other performers, and the audience. While artists are generally aware of this transformative experience, they may call it something other than spiritual involvement. Whatever this transformative experience is called, a mastery of craft is an indispensable prerequisite for it. Highly competent performers are able to excel because they practice often, well, and with sufficient discipline to master their craft. Disciplined mastery of craft enables artists to create spontaneously because when they perform they can concentrate on the event, the other performers, and the audience rather than on their craft. Eurocentric evaluators often attribute the ability to create spontaneously to "gift" or "natural" ability. Black folks are not "natural" actors or instrumentalists or singers or dancers or basketball players. The allegation of natural ability to explain Black people who excel at theatre, music, dance, or basketball offers a seemingly rational explanation that supports the ideology of White supremacy.

Chapter Seven

Space and Time

Western rationalism views both space and time as "universal" phenomena. Ironically, Western rationalism also lionizes Albert Einstein for his theory of relativity while continuing to think of time as an unalterable irreversible impenetrable linear progression.

In traditional Afrocentric ritual, the dramatic event is not obliged to create an illusion of time and place other than its own. The traditional performance techniques of African American preachers and narrative storytellers provide evidence to support this assertion. The widespread acceptance of these performance techniques suggests that the creation of an illusion of some realistically formulated time and place other than the theatrical event's actual time and place is not an especially highly valued quality among African Americans. Eurocentric theatre tradition aims to create illusions of reality of time, place, and character other than the actual ones. This Eurocentric aim, along with an architectural separation of actors from audience and comfortable seats attached to the floor in parallel rows, encourages passive observation that is rarely interrupted except for occasional applause for approval after the fact or politeness or just because other people are applauding.

In the Afrocentric ideal, everyone participates in the theatre event, but not all in the same manner or to the same extent. The Afrocentric ideal that maintains a sense of real and present time and place frees the theatre audience to participate spontaneously in the event in response to the spiritual involvement the presentation evokes. Optimally, there is no such thing as an audience in Afrocentric theatre, only variations in the level of participation. Afrocentric theatre's most immediate concern is to stimulate overt emotionally motivated spontaneous participation that is fundamentally different from such Eurocentric responses as applause, which is a response to rational judgment. Nor should this overt emotionally motivated spontaneous participation be confused with traditional Eurocentric liturgical unison responses that are meticulously planned, usually coordinated through written instructions, as to what to say and when to stand, sit, etc.

The Afrocentric ideal of evoking audience participation is exemplified by Afrocentric musicians and preachers. Although musicians and preachers strive to motivate everyone to participate fully, each participant is expected to "testify" according to the degree of her or his own personal involvement and commitment. Afrocentric playwrights, designers, performers, and theatre critics must not and do not expect their audiences to sit still and listen passively to the theatrical event. These expectations influence Afrocentric presentations in many ways. The techniques actors use to concentrate will vary, based on whether or not the actor needs to listen to verbal responses from the audience and make impromptu verbal responses in reply. The manner in which playwrights construct dialogue is affected by the knowledge that the audience can be depended upon to make certain kinds of verbal or behavioral responses to the dialogue and action.

Afrocentric Space

The Afrocentric ideal of evoking audience participation manifests as a physical design concept that seeks spatial unity. Since all who are present are considered participants, there should be no figurative or literal barriers between those who primarily present and those who observe the presentation and respond to it. All visually observable elements: scenery, lighting, costumes, makeup, architecture, even how performers' bodies look and move, either contribute to or distract from motivating the congregation to participate.

AFROCENTRIC THEATRE

The Afrocentric ideal of spatial unity is at odds with the ideal of aesthetic distance that permeates Eurocentric design concepts that separate actors from audience. Although Eurocentric theatre produces empathetic responses between actor and audience, the goal is for the empathy to be detached and nonparticipatory. Architecture that separates actors from audience fosters restraint and detachment, creates aesthetic distance, and enhances the highly valued Eurocentric quality of objectivity. Most Eurocentric theatres include several feet of actual space between the first row of seats and the stage. Augmenting the actual physical distance with structural barriers makes the audience's observation place seem more distant. Many Eurocentric theatres have an orchestra pit which adds an additional barrier between actor and audience. Raising the stage several feet above the first row of seats creates an additional barrier on the other side of the orchestra pit. Eurocentric theatre spaces usually have a proscenium arch. This large opening in the wall that separates the stage space from the auditorium can be closed with a curtain that blocks the audience's view of the stage whenever the tenets of Eurocentric realism determine the audience's view should be blocked. Recent advances in lighting technology have virtually eliminated the need to close the curtain for scene changes as most now take place by fading the lights to achieve a blackout. Nevertheless, many theatres still open the curtain to signal the play's beginning and close it for intermissions between acts.

Although some Eurocentric theatres value audience participation and involvement, the ones we have observed encourage participation by overtly violating Eurocentric aesthetic distance to confront the audience. These confrontations are not necessarily belligerent, but they enhance the concept that actors and audience are different entities. The spatial arrangement of most Eurocentric theatres reflects and enhances this relationship by first providing Eurocentric distances and barriers and then crossing over them. Even when the physical separation between audience and actor is crossed or violated, the psychic or emotional separation seems to remain. To cross or violate a real barrier is not the same as insisting there is no barrier.

SPACE AND TIME

Afrocentric ideals with respect to relationships between performers and audience are in conflict with most of the theatre spaces that exist in America because they were designed and built to house Eurocentric theatre. Establishing relationships between performers and audience that is consistent with Afrocentric values is fraught with dilemmas when the performers are framed by a proscenium arch; the performance space is separated from and raised above the audience space; and the audience sits in parallel rows of seats that are attached to the floor.

Many theatre critics and historians theorize about the invention of the proscenium arch. Some say it has crippled the theatre; others say it is the best thing that ever happened to the art of the theatre. Most who have criticized the proscenium arch have offered alternative ways of dealing with a fixed architectural entity. Although the proscenium arch is probably the most difficult of the available arrangements for Afrocentric theatre, the Eurocentric architectural alternatives, theatre-in-the-round, thrust, and open staging, do not provide spatial relationships that enhance the goals of Afrocentric theatre. Most renditions of these Eurocentric alternatives contain fixed architectural elements that separate the actor's space from the audience's space. Often a substantial neutral zone increases the distance between actors and audience. The Afrocentric ideal of spatial unity precludes any such fixed architectural separation or barrier.

Afrocentric audiences are free to spontaneously comment on and participate in presentations when moved to do so. Such participatory involvement is enhanced when architectural spaces expedite interaction between performers and audience by eliminating any impression of barriers or impediments. While the audience is not often invited into the performance space, the architecture should not appear to prohibit the possibility. While the need for actual audience accessibility to the performance space is rare, the audience's perception of accessibility to the performers increases the potential for overt empathetic response. While Afrocentric values hold such overt responses in high esteem, Eurocentric values seem to regard such responses as annoying and unwelcome intrusions and possibly even as uncivilized, since overly emotional behavior is viewed as insufficiently objective.

Many of the most popular and widely accepted Afrocentric rituals take place in churches, theatres, or motion-picture houses that were designed and built to house Eurocentric presentations. The seats for the audience are usually attached to the floor in parallel rows facing in one direction. Often a space six feet wide or more separates the performance space from the audience space, and an architectural barrier such as a bannister rail or a rise in floor level of several feet prohibits the spatial unity of performers and audience. Eurocentric architects include these elements because Eurocentric church and theatre architecture has evolved to successfully accommodate Eurocentric church or theatre functions. When Afrocentric events take place in these facilities, they must overcome Eurocentric architectural elements that work against the success of Afrocentric events.

The space between the front row of audience seats and the raised performance area must be used in a manner that destroys the Eurocentric goal that caused such a chasm to be regarded as necessary. Eurocentric notions about actor-audience relationships require such a void in order to physically establish aesthetic distance. In some African American congregations, this space is occupied by the most active respondents to the presentation. These respondents are thereby able to accompany their spontaneous verbal responses with body movements that are not constrained by the people occupying the fixed rows of seats behind them. Although Afrocentric presentations occur in these Eurocentric spaces, an ideal Afrocentric solution to reconfiguring such spaces has not evolved.

The reconfiguration for the New Lafayette theatre in Harlem provides an architectural design example that adapts a Eurocentric space for Afrocentric dramatic events. The architectural firm for the New Lafayette Theatre Project, Hardy Holtzman Pfeiffer Associates, understood what the theatre's artistic leadership wanted: a space without impediments or barriers that physically or spiritually separate audience from actors. The architectural firm explained:

> The New Lafayette will require an environment of exploration and participation. In order to unite artist and audience into the theatrical event as one total community, an architectural cohesion between the event of the production and the life of the audience must be found. This cannot be accomplished within traditional terms; they are too well known, too constricting, too redolent of things past.[96]

The theatre was located at 200 West 135th Street in Harlem, New York, but it was destroyed by fire. Robert Macbeth, the founder and director of The New Lafayette, describes the fire from his point of view in Woodie King, *Black Theatre: the Making of a Movement*.[97]

The "Celebration of Blackness" commemorating the opening of the Institute of the Black World in Atlanta, Georgia, January 17, 1970, provides an example of effective adaptation of space to an Afrocentric presentation's needs. Although the "multipurpose room" in the Morris Brown College student union building was not designed for such a presentation, the structure contained no architectural barriers to prevent physical and spiritual unity between performers and those who were present to participate as observers. As Black artists from throughout Africa and the Americas performed, some people sat in chairs around the perimeter of the room, others sat on the floor in front of the chairs, and others stood behind the chairs. The chairs could be moved and were moved at various times throughout the celebration. Food and soft drinks were available immediately adjacent to the room, and people felt free to exit the room, purchase refreshments, and return at will. An atmosphere of relaxation, fellowship, and community encouraged moving about, talking to those who were performing, and talking to others who were witnessing the performance. A vaguely defined area in the middle of the room was used for presentations, but not all presentations took take place in that area, and the size and shape of the performance area changed as performance needs changed. The Katherine Dunham Dance Company required a large unobstructed area, so adequate space was cleared. At the other extreme in space requirements, Ms. Val Gray Ward began her presentation in the midst of a crowd of observers and throughout her performance she moved around the room without ever separating herself from the observers.

The Ira Aldridge theatre at Howard University was designed by Hillyard Robinson,[98] an African American architect, and constructed in 1961. The theatre has a traditional Eurocentric stage with a fly loft, but the design excludes the most prominent Eurocentric impediments to actor-audience interaction. Instead of the barrier created by a stage that is several feet higher than the first row of seats, three steps traverse the entire width of the stage, making the performance space and the auditorium floor easily accessible to each other. While the theatre has a proscenium and front curtain, the opening is the full width of the auditorium with no visible arch on the sides or above, so the building's structure does not create the perception of performances taking place inside a picture frame. Although the theatre is adaptable to Eurocentric productions, the perception from inside the space is architectural unity, making the theatre among the Afrocentric-friendliest ever constructed.

The most Afrocentric theatre space we have ever worked in is the theatre originally constructed under Efua Sutherland's supervision for Abibigromma near the center of Accra, Ghana. Some years later, when a much larger performing arts center was constructed on the theatre's original site, the building was removed and reassembled on the University of Ghana's campus in Legon. The building is actually an eight-sided structure, but when inside the octagonal space, one feels as if one is inside a circular structure. One side of the octagon is entirely devoted to a proscenium arch that can function as such for traditional Eurocentric plays. But the stage is not high enough to create a formidable barrier between performers and audience. None of the theatre's chairs are attached to the floor. The floor inside the octagon is flat and is not covered by a roof. The space is easily reconfigured and is frequently used with the audience surrounding the play's action and with the play's action surrounding the audience.

Acting in Afrocentric Space

Eurocentric assumptions about what an actor is supposed to do and how she or he is supposed to do it are difficult to reconcile with Afrocentric concepts of performance. Eurocentric culture assumes theatre involves mimesis. The actor acts with the intent of getting the audience to accept a character portrayal as real and plausible. Eurocentric audiences willingly suspend disbelief in order to accept the actor as a real character, as someone other than who, where, and when she or he is. In doing so, the actor is supposed to concentrate so deeply and completely on being this other that the audience's presence is at least partially shut out from the actor's consciousness. Black actors who master this modern, realistic technique in Eurocentric acting classes find it disconcerting when their concentration is broken by the Afrocentrically proper, overt involvement of an Afrocentric audience.

In Afrocentric theatre, behavior, but not necessarily the words, occurs in a specific and expected manner and arrangement. If the manner and arrangement of performance is not accomplished, the aftereffect the ritual is supposed to cause may not occur. Further, performers' behavior often elicits overt interaction between audience and performers that indicates when the spiritual involvement needed to invoke the desired aftereffect has probably been reached. Both the performers' behavior and the audience's response are more important than creating an illusion of surface reality through the use of realistic mimetic technique that performers are actually characters other than themselves in some other time and place. Afrocentric ritual drama does not seek to achieve the realistic/naturalistic ideal of Eurocentric theatre. Eurocentric realistic mimesis and Afrocentric specifically arranged behavior are not opposite ends of a continuum. They are not mutually exclusive characteristics. Rather, they have different orders of priority in

Afrocentric ritual theatre on the one hand, and Eurocentric realistic theatre on the other.

To function effectively in Afrocentric theatre actors must move beyond the linear goal of creating a realistic plausible character. Functioning in concert with Afrocentric actor-audience relationships requires an approach to actor training that prepares actors to perform as themselves and portray other characters. Although this approach does not reject the idea of realistic mimesis, Afrocentric actors must perceive and respond to audience behavior that occurs in response to the performance. The tactic of blocking the audience out of one's conscious awareness does not serve the Afrocentric performance skills that allow the actor to perform as herself or himself and portray more than one character in a single performance event.

Audience members may verbally express evaluative opinions about Afrocentric presentations during the presentation and in face-to-face communication with the performers following the presentation. Although the Eurocentric theatre conventions of applause and curtain calls seem redundant in Afrocentric presentations, they are, nevertheless, established conventions in Black theatre. The fact that African Americans believe applause and curtain calls are appropriate appendages to presentations is indicative of double consciousness since these conventions seem to contradict Afrocentric assumptions about what presentations are for and what relationships ought to exist among performers and between performers and audience. Applause and curtain calls function as marketing tools to sell a production and its stars. Curtain calls elicit applause, thereby fostering positive opinions about productions and stars. Eurocentric theatre is a commodity and curtain calls help sell that commodity.

In the late 1960s and early 1970s we experimented with eliminating curtain calls in our productions, but we soon reinstated the practice. African American audiences "demanded" curtain calls in the belief that applause and curtain calls are important and necessary conventions of *the* theatre.

Carter Woodson's ideas about miseducation and DuBois' concept of double consciousness have led us to postulate that if Eurocentric opinion-makers claim something is one of the "finer things in life," many African Americans will insist on having their share of it. The question of whether or not a particular "finer thing" actually benefits African Americans seldom arises in this context. Actors deservedly want the praise curtain calls provide. On the other hand, playwrights, directors, designers, stage managers, and other production workers deserve praise for their work as well. These other contributors to a production's success seldom, if ever, get curtain calls. The miseducation process has created a dilemma. Afrocentric theatre ought to manifest Afrocentric values regarding the use of space and time, but Eurocentric concepts of space and time imposed on Afrocentric theatre create conflicts. Double consciousness and miseducation about how people of all cultures ought to behave at *the* theatre has impeded acceptance of Afrocentric concepts of performer-audience relationships in space and time among many African Americans.

Afrocentric Time

Orthodox Afrocentric values evidence points of view about time that differ from orthodox Eurocentric views of time. The Celebration of Blackness exemplifies an Afrocentric view of time as it manifests in presentation. Pre-event advertising announced a starting time for the Celebration of Blackness, but the event started when it was time to start, a somewhat later time than the advertised starting time. The event concluded when a communal sense was reached that the activity had completely run its course. Hence, the Celebration of Blackness continued for several hours past the preannounced time for the event to end. A communal sense that it is time for an event to begin and end determines an event's actual beginning and ending times. This concept of time is seen in Afrocentric preaching and some Afrocentric musical forms such as jazz and gospel.

How African Americans conceptualize time can be extrapolated by examining the traditional African view of time. John S. Mbiti explains, "Time has to be experienced in order to make sense or to become real." Therefore, the assignment of numbers to designate a date or an hour of the day several months or years in the future has no real meaning in traditional African thought. Mbiti categorizes in English as "no-time" things that have not taken place or have no likelihood of taking place soon. Most of what is called "the future" in English does not exist, cannot be conceptualized. "What is certain to occur, or what falls within the rhythm of natural phenomena, is the category of inevitable or *potential time*." The reckoning of either actual (experiential) time or potential time is traditionally done on the basis of phenomena rather than on a numerical basis.[99]

Afrocentric time is not a linear continuum from the past into the future, but an experiential surround that contains us. We exist in time. Events must begin and conclude in time rather than on time. Mbiti describes the Swahili word "Zamani" as "the ocean of time in which everything becomes absorbed into a reality that is neither after nor before." This African concept of time is often alleged to be primitive on the grounds that it does not enable precise calculation of scientifically predictable events. Yet there are numerous examples of extremely precise calculations in such disciplines as astronomy and architecture in Africa dating back four to five thousand years.

Eurocentric values infer Afrocentric time is primitive and Eurocentric time is more advanced, objective, and universal. But often, Eurocentric stereotypes imply something worse than primitiveness. Eurocentric people, regardless of ethnicity or skin color, often conclude a person who manifests Afrocentric time indicates she or he is lazy, indolent, and disinclined to work or exertion. Both in contemporary urban Africa and among African Americans, the impact of Eurocentric time is pervasive and inevitable. The resulting conflict over these differing concepts penetrates every conscious aspect of African American life and creates a distressing instance of double consciousness.

Modern Eurocentric values hold punctuality in very high esteem. For those in economic power, punctuality is indispensable. For factory owners and people who hold high-level management positions in the military-industrial complex, punctuality is absolutely essential for the maintenance of power and profits. WEPPEOs have infused punctuality with an aura of responsibility, respectability, morality, patriotism, and other idealistic qualities. Punctuality is clearly a valid ideal for the culture that invented it. A mass production economy cannot survive if punctuality is not a highly valued behavioral attribute. Assembly-line mass production fundamentally altered the Eurocentric economic system by enabling significant increases in productivity, which in turn significantly increased profits for factory owners. These owners and their upper echelon managers understandably place a very high priority on keeping the production line on schedule. In the mass-production environment, life revolves around the time clock. Tardiness is a punishable offence. Owners reward upper echelon managers who convince workers that punctuality is as lofty an attribute as morality, responsibility, respectability, or patriotism. But the practices that increase profits for owners and upper echelon managers also tend to increase monotony and devalue skill among lower echelon workers.

African and African American culture, as well as some other cultures, conceive of time in a way that is antithetical to the profit motives of mass production by valuing the excellence of workmanship, beauty, and usefulness of a product over producing larger quantities of identical products in a shorter period of time. These cultures' values allow people who are directly involved in productive activities to exercise some judgment about when their work commences and ends rather than acquiesce to an absentee owner's mechanical device that measures time with numbers to generate greater profits.

Presenters who seek to accommodate Afrocentric concepts of time to a Eurocentric theatre environment must address such issues as should performances begin promptly at the announced time even if audiences do not arrive promptly? Should audience members who have adapted to Eurocentric time object if an Afrocentric performance does not begin promptly at the announced time? Should theatres do what African American churches do and set aside time for interim activities that reinforce feelings of community while the audience assembles? Frustration and disappointment among African American audiences and presenters grow out of a lack of uniformity and consistency in resolving these conflicting concepts of time.

The prevailing concept of time in any given society seems to be influenced by a variety of factors. Some variation with regard to concepts of time also exists within a society among its individual members. Our generalizations about Eurocentric concepts of time should not be construed to imply that all Eurocentric people are always prompt. Nor do we suggest all Eurocentric people strive to maintain a predetermined schedule. Rather, those who dominate Eurocentric culture insist on punctuality and punish tardiness. Punishments are sometimes formal, such as monetary fines for union theatrical workers who are late. Other punishments are informal, such as inflicting implicit feelings of guilt. Such factors as economic class, ethnic identity, climate, and degree of industrialization and urbanization seem to share responsibility for variations in commitment to this Eurocentric concept of time and related behavioral ideals.

People who control industrial production and its profit stand to gain much more from punctuality than their workers do. Even workers who are punctual generally seem significantly less passionate about the ideal of punctuality than those who reap the profits of industrial production. Rural agrarian Eurocentric societies are generally less committed to the use of numerical means of recognizing time, such as calendars and clocks, than urban industrial Eurocentric societies.

In the Mediterranean region, genetic distinctions between Caucasians, Asians, and Africans have been rather amorphous for centuries. People of the Mediterranean coast of Europe seem far less committed to Eurocentric ideals of time than people in other parts of Europe. This variation raises the possibility that differences in race or ethnicity among Europeans may impact the behavioral ideal of punctuality. Attitudes about punctuality among Germans and southern Italians exemplify such differences. Although explanations of such differences often focus on such items as Germany's colder climate and southern Italy's warmer climate, racial or ethnic differences between Germans and southern Italians are as discernible as climate differences. Those parts of Europe that are closest to Africa and where European racial characteristics are not as "pure" also have a warmer climate than their neighbors to the north. Whether such measurable factors as climate or such amorphous factors as race have greater impact on concepts of time remains an open question.

Visual and Rhythmic Asymmetry

The goal of symmetry is to achieve a sense of balance by creating equal patterns in space or time on each side of the center. Visual symmetry may achieve balance by making one side of the center a mirror image of the other side. Rhythmic symmetry may achieve balance by making things equal or regular in time such as a pattern of consistent strong beats in consecutive measures of music. Asymmetry achieves balance while making things unequal or irregular either rhythmically in time or visually on each side of the center in a contained space. Asymmetry occasionally occurs in Eurocentric cultural artifacts despite a marked preference for symmetrical balance. Afrocentric cultural artifacts exhibit a marked preference for asymmetrical balance but Afrocentric cultural artifacts inevitably use some symmetry as a foundation for contrast with the asymmetrical event.

These cultural tendencies manifest in something as simple as how people walk. Rhythmically, the standard Eurocentric assumption about walking is symmetry. Rhythmic symmetry is achieved when walking by spending exactly the same amount of time on each foot. Visual symmetry is achieved when each side of the body is, as nearly as possible, a mirror image of the other side. These aesthetic standards of symmetrical balance are evidenced, for example, in the music of John Philip Sousa and in the way band members are expected to march while playing a Sousa march. In contrast to the drum cadences and manner of marching of most Eurocentric university bands, most marching bands at historically Black colleges and universities exhibit rhythmic and visual asymmetry. Evidence of these differences is readily accessible since both types of marching bands regularly appear on television during football season.

Similarly, some African American males exhibit a behavioral style of walking, talking, and dressing called "pimping" in the vernacular. Men who affect this style do so to enhance their esteem among peers and to amplify self-worth. Among the most noticeable characteristics of pimping is the walk, an asymmetrical stroll with both visual and rhythmic implications. Visually, asymmetrical balance is achieved by leaning the torso to one side and positioning the arms and legs in such a way that the body is balanced without allowing one side of the body to become a mirror image of the other side. Visual asymmetry contributes to rhythmic asymmetry by encouraging the amount of time spent on one foot to differ from the duration on the other foot. The foot that receives the longer duration is on the side toward which the torso leans. The rhythmic result is uneven beats.

While the example of pimping is significant because of its widespread vernacular use, the aesthetic goal of asymmetrical balance is seen in many other more organized and institutionalized settings. Even the manufacture of automobiles has been impacted by decades of customizing by non-White cultural groups as some recent models with asymmetrical design elements have advertising campaigns with music and visual symbols aimed at appealing to non-White cultural groups and the younger White consumers who voluntarily identify with them. All manner of products now use African American musical idioms ranging from rhythm and blues to hip-hop to reach mainstream audiences in television commercials.

African American dance, music, theatre, and the visual arts, in both religious and secular settings, are influenced by the same cultural factors that created the behavioral style called pimping. While most Black men do not consider pimping an acceptable mode of behavior for themselves, several highly regarded Afrocentric aesthetic principles can be derived by observing the style. One such principle may also be observed in the behavioral styles of America's most popular athletes and musicians. Afrocentric aesthetic goals in many different activities involve not only exhibiting superiority in performing the requisite skills, but while doing so, creating the impression that the skills are accomplished easily, effortlessly, and naturally. But the skills do not come naturally. Instead, the appearance of casual ease is actually a learned and practiced part of the performance.

The musical characteristic called syncopation is by far the most salient, significant, and widely accepted manifestation of asymmetry. In *African American Music: An Introduction*, Earl L. Stewart explains:

> The essential rhythmic characteristic of virtually all African American vernacular styles is *syncopation* . . . syncopated rhythms give a feeling of temporarily contradicting the strong beats of the prevailing meter. Syncopation is the principal means by which African American melodies, or melodic phrases, obtain their distinctiveness. The feeling or suggestion of syncopation sometimes results from the placement of a stressed word or syllable on an unstressed pitch, which is followed by a stressed pitch that contains an unstressed word/syllable . . . .[100]

In the spiritual "Go Down Moses" . . . syncopation appears first when the word "down" and the second syllable of "Mo-ses" occur on the weak second beat rather than the strong third beat of the measure. Its next occurrence is on the word "land" . . . halfway between beats three and four. In the following measure, the word "ole" begins halfway between beats one and two. Two measures later, the second syllable of "peo-ple" begins halfway between beats three and four.[101]

Since African American music has become American music, the use of syncopation has become fundamental to some of the newer and less respected forms of Eurocentric music. These less respected forms of Eurocentric music tend to enjoy their greatest popularity among White people who are younger, have less power and privilege, and are less motivated to conform to Eurocentric traditions. On the other hand, such respected Eurocentric composers as George Gershwin, Claude Debussy, Igor Stravinsky, Maurice Ravel, and Leonard Bernstein have occasionally incorporated Afrocentric musical idioms into their work. When both the music and the environment in which it is performed are "sanitized," even patrons of elite Eurocentric music (opera, symphony, etc.) may regard the presence of an occasional Afrocentric musical idiom as acceptable.

Asymmetry (or syncopation) is often emphasized by contrasting it with a symmetrical (nonsyncopated) event by placing the two events in close proximity.

> Nonsyncopated motives and phrases also occur in African American music, but seldom for extended periods, unless the underlying accompanying musical events are syncopated. . . . Syncopation in African American melodies usually occurs on several rhythmic levels at the same time. . . . Syncopic stratification is one of the principal stylistic attributes that distinguish African-derived styles from most nonblack styles. . . . African American music often features several highly rhythmic parts played simultaneously. One common effect is to have a highly syncopated melody performed with a nonsyncopated accompaniment.[102]

Stewart gives an example of:
> The tension that arises when the melody is syncopated and the bass is not, and . . . the feeling of release or resolution when both parts arrive on a strong beat together . . . . When several melodies (or musical events) occur at the same time they form . . . a rhythmic plexus: an interconnected network of musical events . . . . When this happens the listener does not hear the individual events, but instead hears the cumulative effect, or union, of all of them. This effect is called rhythmic concrescence . . . . a type of rhythmic harmony . . . . the effect that is implied when terms like rag, swing, funk, feel and soul are used to describe the rhythmic affect, or emotional character, of certain styles. In other words, when Duke Ellington suggests that "It Don't Mean a Thing If It Ain't Got That Swing," or James Brown commands an audience to "Make It Funky," they are both alluding to the importance of rhythmic concrescence as a precondition for the enjoyment of the other dramatic offerings of the music.[103]

We recall the fun Duke Ellington seemed to derive from asking his Eurocentricly sophisticated audiences at such elegant venues as the Newport Jazz Festival and the Rainbow Room at 30 Rockefeller Plaza in Manhattan to please "pop your fingers after the beat."

Chapter Eight

Heroes

He who is priest of the living . . . performs right actions without seeking reward for them.[104] —Kagemni, officer of Pharoah Snefru

---

Molefi Asante describes Kagemni's discourse on the subject of devotion:
> Those who minister to the living must have the character to do right without looking for any type of reward; one should do right because it is right. This is the full meaning of devotion. When we think of a full measure of devotion we immediately think of one who is willing to give his or her life for what they think is right.[105]

A hero performs right actions with neither expectation of reward nor fear of consequences, even if death is a possible consequence.

Some years ago, we attended a Vodoun religious service in Ghana with a group of American college students. After the service, we went to a nearby establishment that sold food and beverages to interact with some of the principals who had allowed us to participate in their religious service. When we departed, one of the students, a White male, left his bag containing a video camera under the table. A youth, approximately twelve years of age, noticed the bag, grabbed it, and ran after us to return it to its rightful owner. The embarrassed but grateful American offered the young Ghanaian money as a token of his appreciation. The boy refused. The American became more insistent. The boy continued to refuse as the boy's father and I approached. The boy's father quickly decided the young American did not get the point, so he turned to the older American with the white beard and asked me to "Please explain to him, I do not want my son to expect to get a reward for doing the right thing." And so, teachings from at least as early as the reign of Sneferu, which began in 2613 BC, are handed down from father to son in Ghana today.

Heroic Values

Heroes and standards of heroism provide a structure for informing a society of behavioral expectations and aspirations. A major function of heroism is identity bonding, an inclination to empathize with heroes to the extent of emulating their values and behaviors. Identity bonding encourages others to regard a hero's values and behaviors as achievable goals and emulate them. Americans who exhibit attributes that others emulate are often called role models. While not all role models exhibit laudable values and behaviors, society benefits when the values and behaviors role models exhibit are heroic.

America's market economy uses the predilection to emulate highly admired people by hiring star athletes and other celebrities to develop or endorse consumer products. Many Americans view heroes as role models and role models as heroes. While we will focus on heroes who transcend the marketing of shirts and shoes, we recognize and respect the aesthetic standards that lead young Black men to view high-profile athletes as heroes. Black basketball players, for example, have altered an athletic contest to conform to Black aesthetic priorities. Just putting the ball through the hoop is no longer enough. The game now demands putting the ball through the hoop while exhibiting creative improvisation and athleticism.

Heroes of great depth and truth can inspire identity bonding among more cosmopolitan people of other cultures. This phenomenon should not be confused with extolling the universality of Eurocentric heroes disguised as members of other ethnic groups. Shakespeare's Othello is an exemplar of this phenomenon. Shakespeare describes Othello as Black but Othello is not Black. Othello is a Eurocentric hero in blackface. Eurocentric characters who seem to be Black are actually Eurocentric heroes. This phenomenon is not some sinister conspiracy. Rather, it is a case of creative artists functioning within their own cultural framework, seeing the world from their own cultural location. Eurocentric heroes in blackface function as models of how White opinion makers expect Black people behave. If Black people believe these characters are legitimate Black heroes, the tendency for Black people to behave in ways that benefit White people is increased. Moreover, behavioral ideals of attractive Black characters who are marketed as heroes on television and in motion pictures often make some significant sacrifice that benefits one or more White folks, often to some Black person's detriment, thereby propagating the idea that Black people achieve heroism by acting to benefit White people, even if their own best interests are sacrificed in the process.

Eurocentric heroes must have the genetic potential to be heroic. The idea that nature equips aristocrats to behave heroically was invented to justify transferring wealth and power from aristocrats to their children. Aristocracy as a political and economic system is founded on the belief that such heroic qualities as honor, dignity, and the capacity to lead are genetically transferred. This ideology is the source of the "highborn" and "lowborn" assumptions that abound in Eurocentric mythology and are effectively propagated in Shakespeare's plays. When a "lowborn" person performs heroically, the Europhile presumes, as Shakespeare's plays instruct, the hero is an aristocrat whose credentials have been lost. The idea of someone who is not an aristocrat by birth behaving heroically is inconceivable in this frame of reference.

Even though aristocratic assumptions are supposedly in disrepute in the United States, the debate over the presence of heroism in such works as *Death of a Salesman* continues. *Death of a Salesman* is generally regarded as one of the finer examples of modern Eurocentric drama. Yet many Eurocentric experts emphatically proclaim the play is not a tragedy. The crux of the explanation as to why *Death of a Salesman* is not a tragedy is based on presuppositions about aristocratic breeding and the genetic transfer of heroism. Ultimately, the assertion that the play is not a tragedy hinges on the fact that Willy Loman is, as his name implies, a *low* man, therefore he cannot be a hero, therefore the play cannot be a tragedy.

The hypothesis that innate superiority results from aristocratic birth and male gender is the basis for conflicting views about definitive traits of a hero. The assumption that a hero must have magnitude is both legitimate and cross-cultural. While a hero must have magnitude, the presumption that magnitude can be genetically transferred from father (White, of course) to son provokes disagreement. Eurocentric tragic heroes must have the capacity to suffer greatly and their suffering must transcend their personal discomfort. An Afrocentric hero's actions and their outcomes must transcend the hero's individual needs as well. Afrocentric heroes must do what is right despite potentially dire consequences, but their actions do not inevitably lead to suffering. Afrocentric American heroes are prototypical manifestations of the group's hopes, aspirations, and values, whose actions are independent and external to the White establishment's desires and expectations.

The faith-based belief that only aristocratic White males are plausible as heroes perpetuates notions of racial and gender superiority. In the Eurocentric tradition, women, even the daughters of aristocrats, practically never achieve heroism. There are exceptions, such as Antigone, Joan of Arc, and Othello, but the rarity of these exceptions strengthens the rule's credibility. Notions about gender and racial inferiority are perpetuated by a mythic structure that also propagates negative stereotypes about White males who possess neither wealth nor aristocratic lineage. On the other hand, some contemporary WEPPEOs seem willing to consider an exception for a lack of aristocratic breeding in instances of unquestioned excellence in military skills or similarly combative athletic contests.

Afrocentric culture places a high value on nonaggressive athletic skill, bravery, courage, and wit to resolve crises or achieve victory over one's adversary. Two of the most frequently observed forms of wit use (1) strategy in lieu of brute force in a serious context, and (2) comic irony in a context of diplomatic rhetoric.

Although many comic Afrocentric heroes prevail through the use of wit, additional character traits must accompany wit to achieve heroism. For a character who prevails through the use of verbal diplomacy to be truly heroic, verbal diplomacy must be accompanied by comic irony. Talking one's way out of danger with wit and comic irony is a manifestation of heroic behavior. Irony enables a character's plight to be seen in a larger context, which in turn enables the audience to view the character's survival strategies as an effort to cause the survival of something far larger than one individual's comfort and convenience.

Traditional Afrocentric Heroes

Verbal diplomacy that is regarded in Afrocentric culture as heroic can be exemplified by the Signifying Monkey, a mythological hero, who is the main character in a poem of the same title. There are numerous versions of *The Signifying Monkey*.[106] While not a play in a Eurocentric sense, *The Signifying Monkey* is a theatrical event in an Afrocentric sense. Performing a poem such as *The Signifying Monkey* involves a ritual form. The congregation cajoles the reluctant storyteller into performing. This initial part of the ritual is essential. The storyteller does not begin until provoked by demonstrative request to do so. The storyteller must be coaxed into performing, not because of a reluctance to perform or to bolster the storyteller's ego, but because that is what is supposed to happen, and for assurance of the congregation's enthusiastic participation.

Overt participation by the congregation is as important in Afrocentric secular ritual as it is in religious ritual. The need for preliminary cajoling is a similar phenomenon to pre-sermon events of Afrocentric religious ritual. Each initiates the congregation's participation. Each offers a preview of the congregation's willingness for overt verbal participation in the presentation. Elements of Afrocentric religious presentations, such as asymmetry of rhythm and movement and the use of repetition and empathetic response to emphasize the importance of rhythm, are present to a comparable degree in such secular ritual presentations as well.

The Signifying Monkey's structure (plot, character, and theme) is simple. The complexities and subtleties grow out of the texture—how the presentation's nommo enhances the congregation's immediate experience. The scene opens with the Signifying Monkey high in a tree as the "King of Beasts" passes by. For no particular reason except to alleviate boredom, the monkey decides to "start some shit." Monkey calls out to Lion and tells him a fallacious, malicious story about how the Elephant has recently degraded Lion.

Although mentioning Lion's cowardice and lack of skill as a fighter is mandatory, the storyteller is free to *ad lib* in order to exhibit virtuosity as a player of the dozens. The congregation's response will determine the extent of the negative things the storyteller says in the form of the dozens, but they should focus on things Monkey claims Elephant said about Lion, Lion's mother and grandmother, and the uncertain identity of Lion's father. Throughout, the storyteller may expand or abridge the story depending on the congregation's level of overt participation.

The story continues with Lion going off in a rage after Elephant. When Lion meets Elephant face to face, Lion confidently tells Elephant how badly he is going to beat him. Lion attacks Elephant, but Elephant wins the fight easily, beating Lion unmercifully for some time and with considerable flamboyance. Lion, beaten and humiliated, drags his battered, bloody carcass back through the jungle, whereupon Lion is greeted by the Signifying Monkey from high atop a tree where he can safely signify.

Monkey describes the terrible beating Lion received from Elephant and jokingly describes Lion's injuries in painful detail. Monkey proclaims for all to hear that Lion is not as big and bad as he claims, and finishes by telling Lion that given his present sorry condition he had better give him some respect or Monkey will come down out of the tree and give Lion another ass whipping. Monkey has so much fun enumerating the ways he will give Lion another whipping that he starts to laugh uncontrollably at the defeated and demoralized Lion. Monkey slips and falls to the ground. In a flash, Lion has his paw placed menacingly on the neck of our hero.

Here begins Monkey's apology. Monkey explains that he did not really mean any harm by the things he said. It was all in fun. Monkey apologetically proclaims he has the utmost respect and esteem for Lion. Lion is not impressed. So Monkey tries a new tactic. Monkey musters an attitude of bombastic belligerence and yells at Lion:
> Get your foot off my neck, let my head out the sand,
> and I'll kick your ass like a natural man.
> You damned well better be holding me down,
> 'cause if you turn me loose, I'll stomp you
> six feet under the ground.

Monkey continues to yell threats until Lion is so angry:
> The Lion jumped back, he was ready to fight,
> but the Signifying Monkey was already out of sight.

Monkey scrambles into the tree and continues to signify, this time concentrating on Lion's stupidity.

Certain key attributes make the Signifying Monkey a heroic character. (1) As an allegorical representative of those who are small, weak, and oppressed, he has heroic magnitude. (2) Because he lacks size, strength, and respect, he must depend on cleverness, innovativeness, persistence, and tenacity for survival. (3) He survives with panache. He uses his verbal virtuosity to parry

HEROES

Lion's aggressiveness and hostility in a manner that seems almost effortless. His unabashed exhibition of wit overcomes Lion's physical strength and hostility. A character such as the Signifying Monkey must exhibit all three of these characteristics to some degree in order to be considered a hero.

Shine, in *The Titanic* [aka *Shine*], is a similar hero.[107] According to Black urban mythology, Shine is the only Black man aboard a ship as legendary for its exclusion of Black passengers as for failing to live up to its hype as the quintessence of White technological superiority. Touted as unsinkable, the *Titanic* sank on its maiden voyage. On the night of April 14-15, 1912, the ship struck an iceberg and sank some 1,600 miles from its New York City destination. Only 705 persons survived, in part because there were not enough lifeboats aboard the ship. Most of the survivors were women and children. Different investigations fix the number who died at 1,490, 1,503, and 1,517.

The facts about the ship's sinking are not as crucial to appreciating Shine's heroic qualities as Black America's readiness to find comic irony in this Eurocentric pathos. The Afrocentric perception of the situation was: (1) the ideology of White supremacy led to a policy of racial discrimination in booking passage aboard the ship; (2) White folks thought their technology had created an unsinkable ship; (3) when news of the ship's sinking spread over the USA, Black folks knew none of the people who died were Black; and (4) they knew White folks' technology is not always as miraculous as it is reputed to be. As Leadbelly often sang:
   Jack Johnson tried to get on board,
   The cap'n said we ain't haulin' no coal
   Fare thee well, Titanic, fare thee well.
Shine, the mythological only Black person aboard the Titanic, was deep in the ship's bowels shoveling coal when it struck that iceberg. The only plausible explanation for a Black man aboard that ship was a job shoveling coal. But Shine represents something greater than a shoveler of coal, even greater than a trans-Atlantic swimmer. Despite the presumption of Shine's inferiority, he survived where many wealthy, powerful White men did not.

Still, mere survival was not enough to make Shine a hero. Shine is a hero because: (1) he is an allegorical representative of those who are undervalued and oppressed; (2) he survives because his persistence and tenacity enable him to swim 1,600 miles across the North Atlantic, and his mental discipline to not be diverted from acting in his own best interest, even when the temptations include promise of great wealth and offers of sex by and with the White captain's blonde, voluptuous daughter; and (3) he survives with panache by exhibiting cleverness, innovativeness, and verbal virtuosity as he dismisses diverse temptations with comic irony and swims 1,600 miles almost effortlessly.

Rhetorical skill is an attribute of great value in Afrocentric culture. At the very least, rhetorical ability is a survival mechanism for avoiding hostile aggression from self-appointed enforcers of White supremacy. In addition to its pragmatic value, the ability to use the language imaginatively and effectively may also create an art form when synthesized with other elements requisite to the creation of a work of art. The ability to perform certain word games is characteristic of heroes in Afrocentric ritual drama. "The dozens," a juvenile African American word game, is probably the best known, most frequently played, and most easily identified. The game consists of a series of verbal challenges, usually alternating between two persons. The apparent object of the game is to subdue the opponent by extemporaneously denouncing, in rhyme, the opponent's parents.

Frequently, the structure of the dozens is no more than repeating the assertion "I have had sex with your mother and so have a wide variety of others under some rather bizarre circumstances." But the important consideration is not the structure; it is the texture, how successfully such assertions are directly experienced by the audience. One of the most highly valued abilities in playing the dozens is the ability to create visual images with words. When White people display this ability in other contexts it is usually called poetry.

People who analyze poetry generally ignore the dozens or proclaim it is trash. In either case, they consider the dozens unworthy of their attention. A great deal of the dozens' content is sexually explicit and filled with words most Americans consider vulgar, making the dozens unacceptable by both Eurocentric and Afrocentric moral standards. But the dozens have a useful societal purpose. When considered apart from moral issues, the dozens is a game. One wins the game by making one's opponent angry enough to exhibit distress and loss of self-control. Players of the dozens use the most inflammatory statements they can devise to get an opponent to lose self-control. The game's social function is to encourage and strengthen the capacity to retain self-control in the face of insult and abuse. African Americans' survival has demanded the ability to remain outwardly pleasant and inwardly vigilant when confronted by insult and abuse. Playing the dozens teaches African Americans to survive. In this context, one might find a plausible connection between the current increase in young African American men in prison and a decrease in the lessons learned by playing the dozens. We do not want to blame the victims here. Unfair and unjust incarceration is wrong. But since it is a reality, strategies to avoid unfair and unjust incarceration seem appropriate.

Some word games are less controversial than *The Signifying Monkey*, *The Titanic*, or the dozens. Overpraise is a game that can be directed at oneself or at one's opponent. Mohammed Ali's self-overpraise is well documented. Of course, nobody would consider Mohammed Ali a hero if his self-overpraise was not a reasonably accurate prediction of his actual performance. Instead of claiming "I am the greatest," the reverse of self-overpraise uses exaggerated humility to disarm one's adversary. This form of overpraise may seem on the surface to be sincere humility, but the presence of comic irony indicates the exaggerated humility is not sincere. The overpraise game's unstated irony is "I hold your ability as an adversary and your intelligence in such disdain that I am certain you are stupid enough to think I am sincere when I say you are better than me." Sometimes heroes need to be self-effacing to achieve a goal. Overpraise may be the most viable path to survival against overwhelming odds, and outwitting an adversary while exhibiting irony and panache may enable one's dignity to survive as well. An African chief named Kwame Ansa exemplified panache when he wrote the ranking Portuguese emissary in 1482 as Portugal sought to establish a permanent presence in the Gold Coast. Chief Ansa demonstrates a sense of irony and wit in his use of overpraise as he writes:

> I am not insensible to the high honour which your great master the Chief of Portugal has this day conferred upon me. His friendship I have always endeavoured to merit by the strictness of my dealings with the Portuguese, and by my constant exertions to procure an immediate lading for the vessels. But never until this day did I observe such a difference in the appearance of his subjects: they have hereto been only meanly attired, were easily contented with the commodities they received; and so far from wishing to continue in this country, were never happy until they could complete their lading, and return. Now I remark a strange difference. A great number richly dressed are anxious to be allowed to build houses, and to continue among us. Men of such eminence, conducted by a commander who from his own account seems to have descended from the God who made day and night, can never bring themselves to endure the hardships of this climate; nor would they here be able to procure any of the luxuries that abound in their own country. The passions that are common to us all men will therefore inevitably bring on disputes; and it is far preferable that both our nations should continue on the same footing they have hitherto done, allowing your ships to come and go as usual; the desires of seeing each other occasionally will preserve peace between us.[108]

Chief Ansa's eloquence and skill with words enabled him to forestall the immediate invasion of the Portuguese as they sought another tactic to accomplish their end.

Scripted Heroes

Being Black and living in the USA is an experience saturated with ironies that heroes in Afrocentric theatre are often able to clarify and intensify for audience members who share an experiential frame of reference that results from being Black and living in the USA. These nuances are readily observed by Black theatregoers and frequently missed by individuals who do not share their experiential frame of reference. The nuances are missed, not because of less perceptual acuity or intelligence, but because values and experiences differ across cultures. These cultural differences lead to describable differences between Black heroes and White heroes.

The release of Melvin Van Peebles' motion picture *Sweet Sweetback's Badass Song* was a pivotal event in the genre that came to be called "Black exploitation" or "Blaxsploitation" films. Many opinion makers, Black and White, expressed enthusiastically negative views about *Sweet Sweetback's Badass Song*. Van Peebles has attributed much of the negative reaction to a failure of the film's detractors to perceive the difference between a Black exploitation film and a film about Black exploitation. An appreciation of Afrocentric heroes frequently depends on the audience's ability to perceive such differences as those required to distinguish between a film that exploits Black people and a film that shows how Black people are exploited.

A respected White drama critic who attended the opening of a Black play entitled *Dr. B. S. Black* perceived that, "It uses all the broad earthy clichés that banished such performers as Stepin Fetchit and Rochester from a [White] liberal's respectability list." The critic further observed that "this play actually is a throwback to the playlets of Bert Williams and the days when sly, shiftless blacks and their womenfolk were figures of fun." The title character in *Dr. B.S. Black* is a man of less than modest means who rises above his circumstances. He does not simply survive, he controls his fate by using his imagination and verbal skills and prevails with panache. When a Black comic hero controls his destiny while exhibiting wit and comic irony, Black audiences seem willing to accept some accompanying racial clichés. When evaluating Black characters, one crucial question must be: Who is in control?

This deservedly respected critic of Eurocentric drama was undoubtedly well-versed in both Eurocentric dramaturgy and the history of Black people who have performed before White American theatre audiences. Yet the critic was puzzled by the fact that the nearly all-Black "first night audience seemed to find humor in the characters."[109] The critic was especially puzzled by the audience's demonstrative acceptance of the production because Black cultural nationalism dominated behavior on Howard University's campus in 1970, the time and place of this opening night. The audience laughed unreservedly because they could differentiate between a play that makes fun of Black stereotypes and a play that uses Black comic stereotypes to expose an issue of concern to Black people. Black audiences in the 1970s in Washington, D.C., Memphis, Houston, and Atlanta readily recognized that the play uses stereotypes to make fun of Black people who disrespect other Black people on the basis of skin color and social status and these audiences were comfortable laughing at those stereotypes.

The Stepin Fetchit and Rochester characters to which this respected critic refers are scripted in a manner that Black audiences generally find demeaning. Black audiences that find the Stepin Fetchit character unacceptable do so primarily because he is inevitably manipulated by a White character, often to his own obvious disadvantage. Black audiences see Stepin Fetchit's character's dominant trait as an inability or unwillingness to address the question of what is in his own best interest. Since he never addresses this question, he is a perpetual victim. Stepin Fetchit could exhibit all of his usual stereotypical mannerisms and remain acceptable to Black audiences if he showed a glimmer of recognition that he is being manipulated or that he acts the way he acts, not because is actually that slow and dense and subject to manipulation, but because he knows he must play the role of a coon in order to survive.

Rochester, the character Eddie Anderson played on radio, television, and motion pictures, was more acceptable (or less unacceptable) to many Black people. Rochester often created the illusion of outsmarting his boss, played by Jack Benny. Eddie Anderson's role in the various Jack Benny sagas was actually quite progressive for its time, largely because the Rochester role was played in concert with Jack Benny's role which made fun of Jewish stereotyping. Jack Benny's character was the stingiest man on earth for comic effect. So the Rochester role was a stereotype on a show that made fun of stereotypes. Despite Rochester's ability to outwit "Mr. Jack," the audience is never allowed to forget Benny is the stereotypical stingy boss and Rochester is the stereotypical cheeky servant. Rochester is part of a long Eurocentric tradition of brash servant characters who generate laughter by seeming to outwit their masters. But the cheeky servant can be cheeky without disturbing the ideology of aristocracy because the boss—in this instance, Benny—is genetically destined to be the dominant figure and the servant—in this instance, Rochester—is genetically destined to be the servant. Benny's cultural sensibilities and Anderson's acting skill permitted Anderson to shrewdly communicate a difference between what his character did for a living and who he was as a human being.

Many Black plays have comic heroes, and some of them exhibit traits that seem stereotypical. Among the most memorable of such characters are Joe Smothers, in *Strivers Row* by Abram Hill; Jesse B. Semple, in *Simply Heavenly* by Langston Hughes; Mrs. Grace Love, in *Contribution* and Charlene, in *Idabel's Fortune* both by Ted Shine; Rev. Purlie Victorious Judson, in *Purlie Victorious* by Ossie Davis; Tommy in *Wine in the Wilderness* by Alice Childress. Tommy is an African American woman, as are Grace Love and Charlene. Many heroes in plays by Black playwrights are women. This female presence is true of plays that grow out of a sense of comic irony as well as serious plays. In recent years, African Americans have loved and hated the Madea character created and portrayed by Tyler Perry. Eurocentric critics who used to disregard and disrespect Tyler Perry have mostly stopped. Their desire to uphold the tenets of Eurocentric culture pales in comparison to their respect for money and those who make a lot of it. On the other hand, Black people who object to Perry's work do so out of sincere belief that his work has negative consequences for Black Americans. While we suspect this opinion has validity we do not share it because, in our view, it blames the victim.

Tyler Perry, like other Black Americans, is a victim of racism. The argument that dominates negative valuation of Perry's work by Black people is that his images, especially the Madea character, fuel the fires of race and gender stereotypes. Perry cannot be blamed for the fact that negative Black stereotypes exist. Although Perry's characters remind people these stereotypes exist, his plays and motion pictures do not put the negative spin on the character types that have become so familiar that they seem to be present even when they are not. Instead, Perry concocts much of his characters' comic potential from an open awareness that the characters are outrageously exaggerated caricatures. Perry does not deserve to be rebuked for creating exaggerated, shallow comedic characters. Such caricatures abound in both Eurocentric and Afrocentric culture. Jerry Lewis has been proclaimed a comic genius for creating outrageously exaggerated, incredibly shallow caricatures. The difference is Lewis' characters do not provoke people to say "That's the way White folks act."

When playwrights like Shakespeare and Moliere and Neill Simon generate laughter that grows out of character, the people who possess the character trait the audience laughs at are probably uncomfortable, possibly even angry. Most of the best comedy makes somebody uncomfortable. Perry's comedy is presented in an unpretentious style that openly admits it is a presentation and not a peek at reality. Further, Perry uses comedy as a corrective force that seeks to be useful to Black people. Some Black people are discomforted by Perry's work, not so much because of what his work says or how he says it, but because of what White folks might think of Black folks as a result of seeing it.

HEROES

Some Black folks are embarrassed when Black folks laugh in public, possibly out of concern that White folks won't take us seriously if they see us laughing at things most White folks do not find funny. These Black folks do not seem to understand that White folks who demean us will find an excuse to demean us no matter how circumspect we are, so we might as well laugh when we want to. Moreover, laughing at the ironies of being Black in America helps keep Black people sane. Perry does not whine about the sometimes sad circumstances in which his characters find themselves. Instead, he says, "This is our world. We live in it. Let's laugh at its ironies, do our best to fix its problems, and have a good life to the best of our abilities." Tyler Perry's plays and motion pictures are funny. They make Black people laugh, especially when no White people are watching.

When Eddie Murphy lampooned the Buckwheat character of *The Little Rascals* and *Our Gang* series of motion pictures from the black and white movie era, the same Black people who complain about Tyler Perry complained about Eddie Murphy. In both instances, some people do not perceive a difference between lampooning racist stereotypes and racist stereotyping. As with Perry's portrayal of Madea, Murphy's Buckwheat character on the *Saturday Night Live* television program generated a great deal of its comic potential from the audience's awareness that the character is an outrageously negative stereotype. This awareness allows one to see beneath the surface of the stereotype and recognize Murphy is not recreating the stereotypical Buckwheat character but lampooning the fact that this outrageously stereotypical character ever existed. Again, the Black people who objected to Murphy's portrayal did not seem to object to the presentation but to their fears about the presentation's effect on White people.

A person who has not been exposed to a diverse assortment of real Black people but who has been exposed to the stereotypical images of Black people regularly presented on television, motion pictures, and live theatre will probably not appreciate the comic irony of Murphy's portrayal of

Buckwheat. In order to appreciate this comic irony, one must know the images Murphy lampoons only exist in the minds of the White people who controlled the *Our Gang* series of motion pictures and the audiences who believe those images are reflective of real human beings. This knowledge of what Murphy is lampooning allows one to recognize that Murphy is not making fun of a Black child or of Black children in general. This recognition enables one to find humor in Murphy's lampoon of the momentous prejudice of the folks who created and perpetuated the aberration named Buckwheat, as well as the other numerous pickaninny characters and the White audiences who love them and believe they are true representations of Black children.

The comic and the serious in Black drama are not always distinctly different. Comic plays may provoke tears, and serious plays sometimes provoke laughter. Although comedy is often equated with frivolity, Afrocentric comedy frequently projects heroic ideals that aim to influence Black people's behavior. Such ideals are vividly presented in a comedy called *Strivers Row* that premiered in 1940 in Harlem. Since then, *Strivers Row* has continued to provide laughter, life lessons, and an iconic character named Joe Smothers, better known as Joe the Jiver. As Joe exits a taxi and enters the Van Striven home where a debutante ball is in progress, he says:

> [To the taxi driver] Scram Joe meter, you an' that gas eater can't beat me for no change, I'm no Sam from Alabam. [To the young Black man who has answered the door] Twist that slammer, Gatemouth. That cat may be from the deep south. That nickel-snatching taxi driver. [To the Van Strivens and their guests] What's happening folks, I'm Joe, the Jiver!

When Mrs. Dolly Van Striven objects to his presence at her daughter's debutante ball, Joe responds with:

Don't play me cheap, I ain't no Bo Peep. Let me get you straight, 'fore it is too late. I'm here to stay, so on your way. [To the audience] That chick comes on like an Eskimo.[110]

Joe exhibits characteristics that are indicative of Afrocentric comic heroism. As an allegorical representative of ordinary hard-working Black people who have the kind of job that elite White liberals have labeled menial, Joe has heroic magnitude. He has verbal skills and uses them with a flair for irony to express monumental contempt for the Eurocentric values and status symbols of the Black inhabitants of Strivers Row who mechanically mimic wealthy White role models. Verbal skill alone does not make a comic hero, but Joe's verbal skill encourages Black people to eschew artificial barriers that divide the few Black people with symbols of social status from the many Black people who have slightly less economic equilibrium. Joe makes choices in such areas as clothing style and speech pattern that bourgeois Negroes consider in poor taste, but his initiative, cleverness, persistence, and tenacity, as well as his advocacy for Afrocentric values, generate identity bonding. Further, Joe exhibits sufficient imperfection to avoid an audience's reluctance to identity bond with a character who seems too good to be true. The conclusive determination of Joe's status as a hero is his ability to control his situation for his own, and the group he represents' best interest. Joe lacks social and economic status, but he is in a situation where such status is not just important, it is necessary for survival. Joe's situation is structured to ensure his inferiority, yet he establishes his personal worth and accomplishes his goals on his own terms, and does so with panache.

Strivers Row exhibits another trait that illuminates the idea of control as it relates to Afrocentric heroes. The play has no White characters to provide a White frame of reference or point of view. The issues that are addressed in the play are viewed by the playwright as issues Black people must address for themselves and resolve for themselves. An African American character cannot be a hero if his behavior never rises above the level of reacting to White people. As is the case with *Strivers Row*, many Black plays, have no

White characters. Although some Black plays have White characters, the heroic characters act on their own initiative in order to control their own destinies.

The character Purlie Victorious Judson, in *Purlie Victorious* by Ossie Davis, is a hero that is similar to Joe the Jiver in many ways. Although his verbal skills are more characteristic of a Black preacher than of a secular hero, he uses those skills to manipulate circumstances that are designed to victimize him and nearly succeed in causing his demise. Judson succeeds in accomplishing his goals on his own terms in an environment that is designed to oppress him, and he does so with wit and panache.

Langston Hughes published several books and many columns in the *Chicago Defender* that featured the character Jesse B. Semple (Simple) prior to creating the play with music entitled *Simply Heavenly*. The play is reminiscent of Langston Hughes' newspaper column and subsequent books in the same serialistic style with an episodic story line held together by the Semple character and David Martin's music, which grows spontaneously from the play's action and locale. *Simply Heavenly* was first produced as a play in 1957. The story line is derived from a book by Langston Hughes published in 1953 entitled *Simple Takes a Wife*.

Jesse B. Semple is the prototypical Harlemite. His most extraordinary quality is his ordinariness. Relationships with women, the cost of living, landladies, taxes, alcoholic beverages, and the U.S. Army are Semple's catastrophes and the subjects of his frequent barroom oratory. But the thing about Semple that strengthens his identity bonding to heroic proportions is that he can trace the ultimate cause of all his problems to the fact that he is Black. As Semple explains it, "something's always happening to a colored man!"[111] Semple is not a gangster or a sports or show-business personality, or a successful professional man. He does not drive a Cadillac or wear flashy clothes, but neither is he a pathetic victim of circumstances. Semple is concerned with the ordinary things of life.

He is disturbed by the fact that Black people never get mentioned in the newspapers in connection with nonsensational, positive, or beneficial activities. Semple asks, "Unless we commit murder, robbery or rape, or are being chased by a mob, do we get on the front page, or hardly the back?" Semple points out that he has read about Karl Krubelowski and Giovanni Battini and Heinrich Armpriester seeing flying saucers, but never about Roosevelt Johnson or Henry Washington, or anyone that even "sounds like a Negro," seeing one.[112]

Much of *Simply Heavenly*'s humor comes from satire about the predicament of Black people in a society dominated by White people. This humor is often missed by White audience members. In the song "Let Me Take You for a Ride," Zarita invites Semple to go for a ride in a friend's convertible. She sings, "Let me take you for a ride!" And Semple responds, "Let the breeze blow through my hair!"[113] Semple laughs at things that make Black people different from White people to eliminate or reduce the hurt and embarrassment that often results when White people ridicule those differences and infer the differences are indicative of Black inferiority. Semple sees irony in the fact that unlike the White people in the advertisement for everything from convertible automobiles to hair dye, his hair does not blow in the breeze. He uses comic irony to deflect the potential pain of racially based ridicule. On another occasion, Semple says, "I been caught in some kind of a riffle ever since I been Black."[114] Black audiences see the irony that Semple's difficulties are not of his making. Despite the inevitable difficulties that arise from being Black in America, Semple manages to control his own destiny.

In the context of social issues of the 1950s, Semple expresses pride in his Blackness and confidence in himself with comic effectiveness. He asserts that in the recently integrated army, he would "rise right to the top today and be a general." Further, he insists he wants to command a White regiment from Mississippi. He goes on to explain that he would "do like all the other generals do, and stand way back on a hill somewhere and look through my spy-glasses and say, 'Charge on! Mens, charge on!'" After his imaginary White troops succeed in battle under his leadership, he forgives them for their past racial transgressions and presents them with medals for bravery. He concludes by asking his White troops to stop fighting him and join him in a drink to celebrate their victory.[115] As with all Afrocentric comic heroes, Semple provides an illustration of how Black people come to terms with hostile environments, control their circumstances, and achieve their goals. Comic heroes recognize the incongruities and ironies of their environment and are able to laugh at them. A true comic hero causes the audience to recognize not only the foibles of others but their own foibles as well.

Some Black women characters accomplish their goals on their own terms in an environment designed to victimize them. Three such heroines are Ted Shine's characters Charlene in *Idabel's Fortune* and Mrs. Grace Love in *Contribution*, and Tommy in Alice Childress' *Wine in the Wilderness*. These female characters differ from most male heroes with regard to the style in which their wit and panache are exhibited. The exhibition of wit and panache by these heroines is more subtle. This is in sharp contrast to Tyler Perry's Madea character, who is far less subtle than the most outrageous of the male comic characters we have mentioned. In the case of Tommy, her wit is disarmingly natural. Charlene and Mrs. Love carefully contrive their wit to disarm people. Charlene is a maid and Mrs. Love is a cook. Each deliberately creates the impression for the White people who observe them that they have certain attributes of the "mammy" stereotype. Dramatic irony is created as the audience is slowly made aware that these women are not exactly what they seem to be. Their subterfuge enables each of these women to accomplish their goals in an extremely hostile environment.

Tommy, Charlene, and Mrs. Love display attributes similar to those Black people regarded as stereotypical and unacceptable in such characters as Beulah of the radio program *Beulah*, Sapphire on radio and television's *Amos 'n' Andy*, and Mammy and Prissy in the film *Gone with the Wind*. These characters are not racial stereotypes because they possess key factors that we have described earlier as attributes of heroism: (1) they are allegorical representatives of women who are undervalued and oppressed; (2) they survive because their persistence, tenacity, and discipline enable them to absorb abuse and disrespect with grace and dignity in order to not be diverted from acting in their own best interest; and (3) they survive with style by exhibiting cleverness, innovativeness, and verbal virtuosity. Despite circumstances that make them vulnerable to the control of others, these women survive with panache.

Sometimes a character struggles to overcome hostile circumstances that require the endurance of pain and suffering. Such characters are often considered tragic heroes. These characters seek to achieve a goal that leads to inevitable confrontation with forces opposed to their goals. The essential differences between comic and tragic heroes have to do with how they deal with forces that oppose the accomplishment of their goals. Tragic heroes confront opposing forces, whereas comic heroes try to navigate a route to their goals that avoids confrontation and the pain and suffering that often follows.

A recurring phenomenon has generated a type of Black hero in theatre and other art forms who has faced American racism throughout life. Suddenly, and often without apparent provocation, the hero gets tired of coping with the overwhelming burdens of racism. This hero makes a decision, takes a stand, and makes a commitment with full awareness that their stand may result in death or some barbaric punishment such as castration for males or rape for females. But this hero says "I don't mind dying" and means it. In real life, such a hero may or may not actually die as a result of taking such a stand. Mrs. Rosa Parks must have expected, if not to die, at least to be thrown in jail and subjected to physical abuse when she refused to give up her seat to a White passenger on a bus in Montgomery, Alabama in 1955, thereby initiating a series of events that precipitated the Montgomery Bus Boycott and Rev. Martin Luther King, Jr.'s rise to prominence.

Most Black Americans have been forced on some occasion to say to themselves "I don't mind dying" and actually mean it in order to retain some sanity and self-respect. But taking action in the face of obvious risk of harm or possibly even death is not enough to make a tragic hero. Such a decision does not, in and of itself, indicate the type of dignity that results from esteem and respect. Nor does such dignity automatically result from pain and suffering, even when the pain and suffering is totally unjustified. Exhibiting dignity while experiencing comfort and convenience is not especially worthy of esteem or respect, but exhibiting dignity while enduring unjustified pain and suffering may be regarded as heroic when accompanied by other attributes that heroes must exhibit.

Racism inevitably imposes considerable pain and suffering. Racism's recipients often find it more difficult to tolerate the pain and suffering of others than to endure it themselves. A desire to relieve others' pain and suffering is often a Black hero's motivation to action. The hero acts without regard for her or his own personal safety. The action is not taken to achieve martyrdom or suffer for a cause. The heroes' strongest impulse is to survive, but survival includes access to human dignity, not self-centered individual dignity, but community dignity. This struggle can override the impulse for individual survival.

The hero who overrides the impulse for individual survival knows the societal structure is programmed to inflict pain, suffering, and possibly violent death to any Black person who overtly objects to subhuman status. In this context, suffering is not inflicted by the gods or as a result of some internal character flaw, but by agents of White racist oppressors. Most of those agents are White but some of the agents are Black. In a society that is structured to overwhelm Black people with denials of human dignity, a Black hero is often required to choose to either assert human dignity or to acquiesce. The mere assertion of self-worth in the face of oppression is insufficient to generate heroic status. A Black heroic character in a play must also exhibit actions that reflect Afrocentric values and priorities.

Audiences identify with a hero according to the dictates of their values and to the extent they consider themselves connected to the hero. A hero decides to overcome an obstacle in an effort to control destiny and ensure the survival of a community while exhibiting characteristics of sufficient magnitude for his or her actions to rise above the personal.

A few Black heroes in serious plays by Black playwrights are known to a broader American public, the Younger family in *A Raisin in the Sun* for example. A Black play that has achieved some success before White audiences may still be a significant and worthwhile play by Afrocentric standards. The mere fact that White audiences find a play with Black characters acceptable does not guarantee the play is or should be unacceptable to Black audiences. White audiences often find Black characters exotic or endearing or "true to life" when Black audiences see none of these attributes. As a result, some Black people are suspicious of any play with Black characters that acquires ardent support from White audiences. By delving deeper into this apparent contradiction, we discover that while attending the same performance, White audiences' cultural baggage causes them to see a different play from the one Black people's cultural baggage causes them to see.

In the case of *A Raisin in the Sun*, Black audiences generally see a positive image of an African American family dealing with issues that are important to Black people. The central issue is the continuation of the family as a unit in an environment structured to oppress and exploit them. This central issue raises several specific questions. The playwright Lorraine Hansberry raises the question of abortion as it relates to Afrocentric values. Other questions addressed are: Who should handle the family finances? Who owns the insurance money? Who is head of the household? It is important to recognize that each of these is a different question with potentially a different answer. The quest for higher education is another important issue for Black audiences who often find validation of their own decisions in the Younger family's decision to sacrifice so Beneatha can become a medical doctor. Implicit in the play is the idea that the Younger family's adults regard higher education as an important mechanism, not only for the financial rewards to the recipient of the education, but especially for the intrinsic value to the Black community of desperately needed services of health professionals. The family's generations differ about the details of what constitutes security for the family, but all the family's members work to achieve it. The broader theme that brings the issues together into a coherent whole is concern for the progress of the race. Strategies differ from one member of the Younger household to the next, but they all desire to see the race progress.

Walter Lee Younger grapples with the issues facing his family, and in doing so he emerges as a hero. Walter is the only character in the play who changes his behavior as a result of self-realization. Walter's character does not change; his values do not change; only his behavior changes. This change in behavior actually reveals his character in a way Walter has sought to conceal. The man he claims to be and tries to be early on is not the man Walter Lee Younger, Sr. taught him to be. Lena forces Walter to confront his deeply rooted values by insisting that his son Travis is in the room when Walter "negotiates" with Lender for what amounts to a bribe for not moving into Clybourne Park. The presence of his son forces Walter to have the key moment of self-realization in the play and his speech turning down the Clybourne Park bribe delineates him as a hero.

In the late 1950s when the play was first presented, White audiences and critics did not consider Walter a hero. He seemed to evoke an image many White liberals found threatening. The refusal to see him as anything but an angry Black man, a kind of mid-twentieth-century buck stereotype, seemed to revolve around Walter's aspiration to own a business and his critique of his White employer. Lena is not a mammy stereotype by any means, but she is a grandmother and a domestic worker. Liberal White audiences and critics seemed to derive comfort from envisioning her as a mammy figure and gain solace from sympathizing with the long-suffering Black female domestic worker who finally gets a decent place to live. After all, she is not moving into a neighborhood inhabited by the kind of White people who regularly purchase Broadway theatre tickets.

In the 1950s, White Americans' access to Black females in theatre, motion pictures, television, or especially in real life was highly limited. The only Black female characters carved into the consciousness of White Americans when *A Raisin in the Sun* premiered on Broadway are exemplified by two "beloved" characters first played on radio by White actors and later by Black women on television. Sapphire was a continuing character on *Amos 'n' Andy*. Beulah was the title character on *Beulah*, although the show was really about the White family that employed Beulah as a maid. *Amos 'n' Andy* was on CBS television from June 1951 to June 1953, and *Beulah* was on ABC television from October 1950 to September 1953.

For those not yet born in the 1950s, the concept of such limited awareness of Black female characters may be difficult to imagine. There were seldom more than two or three Black women appearing on national television in the same year. Except for the *Amos 'n' Andy* show's Sapphire, Kingfish's stereotypical scolding, nagging, bad-tempered wife, every other Black female character on national television in the 1950s appeared only in her work environment, where she was a maid and the show's central characters were members of the White family for whom she worked.

When *A Raisin in the Sun* premiered on Broadway, social science data was fostering the idea that African American culture preferred a matriarchal family structure. Some years after the play's premiere, Daniel Patrick Moynihan's 1965 *Report* from the U.S. Department of Labor changed the idea's status from sociology theory to national policy. White theatregoers and critics seemed comfortable concluding Lena Younger was a matriarch despite exposition in the play that contradicts that idea.

In contrast to Lena, Walter is a young Black man who is both angry and virile. White liberal guilt was a popular recreational activity in the late 1950s and early 1960s. Liberal White audiences and critics seemed to assuage their guilt by diminishing or ignoring Walter's anger. By viewing Lena as a bossy old matriarch, they are comforted from the disquieting prospect of recognizing Walter as a force with which to be reckoned. This avoidance of Walter as a representative of angry and virile Black males has been legitimized by focusing the conclusion of White sociologists that Black families, especially poor ones, are ruled by matriarchal figures. The tradition of matrilineal succession and the respect and power women enjoy as a result is definitely a part of Black America's African heritage. But to see this play from the White sociologists' point of view of the matriarchal family is to miss the play's essence. Although the play is undisputedly about the entire Younger family, the play's central character and the head of the Younger household is Walter Lee Younger, Jr.

Two factors in *A Raisin in the Sun* seem to go unnoticed by those who believe the play is about Lena. Walter's father and Lena's husband, the head of the Younger household for more than thirty-five years, has recently died. Most families require a period of adjustment following such a trauma. Second, Walter respects his mother both as mother and as the elder of the family. Walter's behavior is comparable to an African chief who must listen to the elders before important decisions are made. The chief does not have to follow the elders' advice, but he must listen to it and respect it. Lena states, at the end of Act II, Scene 2, "I'm telling you to be the head of this family from now on like you supposed to be." Some White people misconstrue the respect Lena receives from Walter and Ruth and requires of Beneatha to be matriarchal rule. The concept that Lena's rule prevails in the Younger household has little to do with the content of the play and a great deal to do with prior assumptions, sometimes known as prejudices.

When a Black female character is strong of body, mind, and opinion, the prevailing White view sees her as the head of the household who has emasculated any and all males in said household. Any suggestion of respect by an adult male family member is assumed to be indicative of subservience. Just as White males seem to consider a Black male's assertion of strength or independence an implicit assertion of White male weakness, any woman's assertion of strength or independence seems to be regarded by White males as a similar implicit threat.

The economic and social forces of White male oppression have caused a large percentage of Black households with no regularly employed adult male in residence. The absence of a male breadwinner in many African American homes has resulted in the inaccurate assumption that African American values generate households dominated by women. This lack of male presence is a horrific social problem rooted in the economic exploitation of Black males that has very little to do with the content of *A Raisin in the Sun*. Walter Younger, Jr. is an employed adult male in residence. Further, Walter Younger, Sr. was a wage earner who was present in the home from the day he married Lena until the day he died. Any connection between *A Raisin in the Sun* and the phenomenon of African American households without a male wage-earner is fabricated by the observer's prejudice.

Joseph Walker's dedication statement for his play *The River Niger* says, "The play is dedicated to my mother and father and to highly underrated black daddies everywhere."[116] *The River Niger* has a Black hero who communicates positive values for Black people and provides identity bonding for "underrated black daddies everywhere." The play's hero, Johnny Williams, sacrifices himself to save his son. Survival of the family and progress of the race represent higher priorities for Black heroes than the "save your own skin no matter what" concept of survival. The ideal of freedom expressed by African artists suggests a man is not free to let his brother go without food and shelter when he has enough of both to share. Johnny Williams does not consider himself free to place a higher value on his own life than he places on his family's legacy.

A Medal for Willie by William Branch exemplifies a Black woman who embodies the characteristics of heroism. The play was written in 1951 and centers around the posthumous awarding of the Distinguished Service Cross to CPL Willie D. Jackson. The act of bravery that earned Willie the medal also cost him his life. The ceremony to award the medal to Willie's mother takes place at the Booker T. Washington High School Auditorium. Mrs. Jackson is a quiet, hard-working woman who raised a son and a daughter in a small southern town. Her son Willie went to Korea because he could not get a job in his hometown. A general, accompanied by the mayor and the superintendent of schools come to the Black high school to present Mrs. Jackson with her deceased son's medal. Mrs. Jackson's environment is structured to place her in a subservient role. The White male authority figures expect her to behave exactly as they have told her to behave. She has been given an acceptance speech to read, but as she begins to read it, she chokes on the hypocrisy of the words. Instead, she eloquently expresses contempt for the local and national authorities responsible for the injustices her son suffered. To conclude, she gives the general back the medal and tells him to take it back to Washington, and "give it to the ones who send boys like my Willie all over the world to die for some kinda freedom and democracy they always gets the leavin's of!"[117]

Mrs. Jackson exemplifies many heroic characteristics found in Afrocentric mythology. Her acceptance speech shows the process of soul searching that serious heroes undergo. Her actions exhibit values and ideals that Black people regard as heroic. Mrs. Jackson, like other Black heroes, maintains a sense of self-worth in the midst of a hostile environment. Playwrights who create Afrocentric heroes, both comic and serious, create characters whose awareness enables them to perceive irony in other people's circumstances, as well as their own.

At least one heroic character in each of August Wilson's ten-play cycle expresses the idea that Eurocentric images of God function to the disadvantage, possibly even the destruction of African people. These characters fight temptations to accept the dominant society's social contract. In order to reap the rewards of the American dream, African people must reject their heritage, even their concept of God. Each of Wilson's heroic figures vehemently rejects Eurocentric images of God and Wilson validates their heroism with their vigorous and earnest pursuit of an African image of God. In reality, many people who are committed to African cultural authenticity are also adept at assuring White folks they accept Eurocentric values so they can reap the dominant society's benefits. This complexity is exemplified in the last play he wrote before his death and the play that chronicles the last decade of the twentieth century, *Radio Golf*. Harmond Wilks could be rich, famous, and mayor of Pittsburgh if he would only renounce his cultural heritage. But he refuses to do that.

Chapter Nine

Characterization

"There is no one black spokesperson, no one point of view, no one form or style of expression. Black writers are as diverse as their experience is complex. They differ as much as they share in common." —Douglas Turner Ward[118]

Afrocentric theatre does not always seek Eurocentric modern realism's ideals of characterization. Modern realistic ideals of characterization did not begin to emerge in Europe until the late 1800s. Just as American advertising seeks to convince people every new consumer product is, by virtue of its newness, better than any similar product that preceded it, Eurocentric critics generally interpret the relative newness of realistic characterization as evidence of its superiority over any style of characterization that existed before the advent of realism. This point of view could be described as aesthetic Darwinism since it presumes such evolutionary movement invariably constitutes progress. As with proponents of social Darwinism, the "survival of the fittest" assertion fails to address the question, "Fit for what?"

Hip-Hop Characterization

In recent years, an Afrocentric form that is a direct descendant of both traditional African storytelling and vernacular poetry such as *The Signifying Monkey* and *The Titanic* [aka *Shine*] has attracted attention in mainstream theatre circles. The hip-hop aesthetic has garnered cross-cultural popularity and generated significant entertainment industry revenue. Generally considered an aspect of the music industry, hip-hop culture has a spoken

CHARACTERIZATION

component that had its infancy as poetry slams in small venues that do not generate much revenue. As with its antecedents, hip-hop performers need not pretend they are someone other than themselves in some time and place other than at the performance.

As hip-hop culture morphed from a Black American thing into an international, multicultural, multibillion-dollar industry, those early opportunities for exposure in small venues led to such Broadway successes as *Russell Simmons Def Poetry Jam* and a musical by a man named Stew, entitled *Passing Strange*. While *Russell Simmons Def Poetry Jam* and *Passing Strange* garnered favorable reviews, these productions did not succeed as a result of massive support from traditional Broadway theatregoers. Only the more adventurous among traditional Broadway theatregoers, along with a younger demographic and a culturally diverse (Hispanic, Asian, and Black) older demographic enabled Broadway success as defined by both financial profitability and plaudits from journalists who evaluate theatre for media outlets.

Conceived by Stan Lathan and Russell Simmons and directed by Stan Lathan, *Russell Simmons Def Poetry Jam* opened at the Longacre Theatre on November 14, 2002, and closed on May 4, 2003, a run of nearly six months. A review by Philip Hopkins states:

> One of the best things about *Russell Simmons Def Poetry Jam* is how hard it is to describe. Part theater, part performance art, part poetry and revival meeting, the only way to sum up the show is to say that it must be experienced, not just because it's unique, but because it's also moving, hilarious, powerful, and thought provoking. This is not your parents' theater, and its certainly not their poetry. But if you or they want a memorable encounter with the combustible cultural mixture that is America today, there is nowhere else to go on Broadway.[119]

Stew's *Passing Strange* premiered in New York as an off-Broadway production at the Public Theatre, running from May 14, 2007, through June 3, 2007. It began previews at the Belasco Theatre on Broadway on

February 8, 2008, officially opened on February 28, 2008, and closed on July 20, 2008. Stew wrote the book and lyrics and coauthored the music. He also played the leading role, both the main character in the story and the storyteller or griot. *Passing Strange* won the 2008 Tony Award for best book of a musical. Ironically, *Passing Strange* bears little resemblance to a typical Broadway musical. Its form more closely resembles traditional Afrocentric storytelling.

The mainstream critics predictably categorized *Passing Strange* as an autobiographical coming of age play, and failed to focus on the clearly stated theme that is echoed in the title. The theme is clear but cleverly concealed in the allure of the play's rock concert environment. The central character in *Passing Strange* "finds himself" when he comes to the realization that he is passing for Black. When he comes to this realization, he has left the comfort and predictability of his Black middle-class upbringing in Los Angeles. He is in Europe, surrounded by Europeans, and he is passing for Black. He discovers the allure of a more cosmopolitan life by Eurocentric criteria has subverted his self-interest and his identity. The idea of a Black American passing for Black in Europe raises related questions: Are certain individuals presented to Black people as role models- as examples of success- who gained their success by passing for Black? Should we take pride in and emulate Black Americans who voluntarily self-exile and bask in their European success? Does America still offer enticements to pass for Black? How does Stew's notion of passing for Black relate to Molefi Asante's view of African agency?

Just as hip-hop is an evolutionary continuation of a genre exemplified in the 1930s and 1940s by such musical artists as Cab Calloway and Louis Jordan, hip-hop as theatre art is a continuation of traditional African storytelling and African American vernacular poetry. Every two years in late July or early August, theatre artists gather in the friendly confines of Winston Salem, North Carolina at the National Black Theatre Festival. There, one can observe this cross-generational continuation. Theatre artists whose work predates and informs the hip-hop era, such as Idris Ackamoor and Rhodessa Jones, Ricardo Pitts-Wiley, and Ntozake Shange share the festival with theatre artists of the hip-hop era such as Malcolm Jamal Warner (the son on "The Cosby Show"), Daniel Beaty, and Will Power. Generational and stylistic differences seem insignificant at the National Black Theatre Festival and other venues where audiences are more receptive than Broadway to Black aesthetic values.

Values and Character Motivation

Afrocentric theatre, like most other theatrical genres, is intended for a relatively homogeneous audience. Black people tend to presume plays by Black playwrights with a mostly Black cast are intended for Black audiences. Comparably, White people are likely to presume a play presented in a venue that traditionally presents Eurocentric plays for predominantly White audiences is intended for them even if the play is by a Black playwright with a mostly Black cast. Sometimes Black people and White people attend a play presuming it will address their cultural identity, and each cultural identity is satisfied the play addressed their cultural identity. At other times, cognitive disharmony results for one cultural identity or the other or both.

Plays that resonate best with Afrocentric audiences presuppose shared experience and common cultural identity. When Black audiences do not perceive such a sense of community, that resonance is diminished or destroyed. A Black audience is likely to conclude a play is not intended for their cultural enrichment or enjoyment if the character exposition seems overstated or redundant. Conversely, overstated or redundant character exposition may be indispensable if White audience members are expected to derive cultural enrichment or enjoyment from the play. Absence of such character exposition may very well cause audience members who do not share experiences and cultural identity with the play's intended audience to conclude the characters are insufficiently explained, inadequately motivated, or two-dimensional.

Following an opening night performance of *Strivers Row* in Atlanta, a deservedly respected White critic who sincerely sought to encourage Black theatre in that city posed a question about the delineation and motivation of one of the play's principal characters, Joe Smothers. He asked if Joe Smothers was a pimp, a thief, or an honest wage earner. He also questioned the depth and sincerity of Joe's possible romantic relationships with several of the play's female characters.[120] *Strivers Row* was first produced in Harlem, New York over seventy years ago with later productions in several other cities, and to the best of our knowledge, questions such as these have never been raised by African Americans who have seen the play. African Americans who are motivated to comment about Joe Smothers's character usually affirm their familiarity with someone just like Joe Smothers. Because a character known as Joe the Jiver always dresses in the very latest fashion, his costume must change for each time and place the play is presented. We sought permission from Abram Hill, the playwright, to present a revival of the play in Atlanta in the early 1970s with Carlton directing and Barbara designing costumes. Since the script sets the play in 1940, Abram Hill asked if we intended to stage it as a "period piece" with 1940s costumes. We enthusiastically responded in the negative, insisting that Joe Smothers was (and still is) alive and well and living in every urban Black community in America. The Black audiences who saw Samuel L. Jackson as Joe Smothers decked out in the latest 1970s fashions found the character enjoyable, recognizable, and clearly delineated. Other Black audiences have experienced similar recognition enjoyment and clarity from the first performance of *Strivers Row* more than seventy years ago to the present day.

Eurocentric modern realism presumes a need to inform audiences about a character's past, often revealing or at least implying details of events or relationships that occurred many years earlier than that of the action of the play. These details provide Eurocentric audiences with insight into a character's present behavior through the use of oversimplified Freudian psychoanalysis that assumes awareness of certain past events or relationships reveal why a person behaves the way he does today. Often this alleged insight is dependent on some revelation about the character's sexual behavior. If a man's dominant traits are negative, we discover that his mother mistreated him as a child. Modern Eurocentric dramatists often seem fervently committed to the tenets of Freudian psychoanalysis as a means of explaining human behavior.

In Afrocentric drama, plot does not have to grow out of character. Plot can be incited by environmental and experiential forces or delineated through narrative, or characters may simply be presented without historical explanation based on Freudian assumptions. Character insights through oversimplified Freudian psychoanalysis seem a necessary part of modern realistic Eurocentric theatre and make these plays much longer than they would be if Freudian inferences were removed. In contrast, many early Black arts movement plays are described as short rather than full-length. The terms "short" and "full-length" do not simply describe the time it takes to perform a play, they also impose a specific point of view about what audiences should be told about a play's characters. Eurocentric critics have been known to express value judgments, asserting lack of competency and maturity in playwrights who only write short plays and presuming a lesser status is deserved by playwrights who do not exhibit an ability, in their view, to explicate multifaceted characters in a full-length play.

Imposition of Eurocentric values to explain characters' behavior can stifle a Black play's thematic intentions. Eurocentric audiences at Douglas Turner Ward's *Happy Ending* often find the play's characters morally reprehensible. Eurocentric concepts of morality lead to the conclusion they are all thieves. Eurocentric values presume the audience should be able to discern what motivates such apparently wrongful behavior and what negative consequences will befall the perpetrators. Eurocentric values assume stealing ought to result in some sort of negative effect; if not punishment, at least some sense of guilt that implies punishment within the framework of Freudian psychology. But the characters in *Happy Ending* suffer no such negative outcome. On the contrary, when they learn they will probably be able to continue their activities, they celebrate the news as a happy ending; hence, the title of the play.

Characters in *Happy Ending* are well conceived and described, when examined from a context of Afrocentric values. The only clarification needed to explain the fact that these characters engage in a practice that some White people regard as stealing is they only take things that would otherwise be wasted by their extremely wealthy White employers. Most Black Americans call this practice "totin' privileges." The only character exposition needed for a Black audience is that the characters' White employers are so wealthy they have no sense of what they own or what it is worth. The characters in *Happy Ending* communicate several facts that expose their moral standards. They never take more than they need, so they are not greedy. They work hard, so they are not lazy. They exhibit willingness to help other members of their family, so they are not selfish. No Freudian explanation is necessary and no punishment is deserved.

Whether they have objected to the concept of "totin' privileges" or not, many White critics have surreptitiously discredited these plays, and other thematically similar plays, by labeling them "social protest" plays. Douglas Turner Ward's *Day of Absence*, a longer companion piece to *Happy Ending*, has also been labeled "social protest" in an apparent attempt to imply its usefulness in the perpetuation of Afrocentric values somehow reduces its aesthetic worth. Inherent in the message of *Day of Absence* is the premise that, in the time and place of the play, Black people know a great deal more about White people than White people know about Black people. This phenomenon results from accumulated knowledge over several generations of invisible Black people who cook and serve the food, take care of the children, clean the filth, and haul away the garbage of their WEPPEO [wealthy, elite, powerful persons of European origin] employers.

White people seldom have similar intimate awareness of Black people since WEPPEOs have generally had about the same amount of empathy for their Black domestic servants as they have for a piece of their furniture. WEPPEOs have expanded the way they regard their Black servants to include Black people in general and encouraged other White people to consider Black people to be a threat to their wellbeing. We see evidence of this disregard in the way WEPPEOs discuss their most intimate private affairs before Black people with a total absence of concern. On the other hand, Black domestic servants have traditionally told their White employers only what their White employers wanted to hear. Black people seldom allow their honest feelings and opinions to intrude on this tradition. *Day of Absence* dramatizes a basic truth that Black audiences recognize. This truth is probably most impressively articulated by Ralph Ellison in his seminal novel *Invisible Man*. In the prologue, the protagonist says, "I am invisible, understand, simply because people refuse to see me."[121]

To concisely explain the full implications of Black people as invisible is difficult. Sensibilities may be heightened through exposure to some of the major works of art that focus on this theme. *Invisible Man* is an excellent introduction to the concept. *Day of Absence* focuses on the idea that White people simply refuse to see Black people from a comic point of view. The play's farcical premise is that all the Black people in a small southern town disappear without a trace. This transformation from figurative to literal invisibility results in all the essential human needs of the town's White population going unmet. Three of the town's leading citizens complain to the mayor:

> INDUSTRIALIST: Half of the day is gone already, Henry. On behalf of the factory owners of this town, you've got to bail us out! Seventy-five percent of all production is paralyzed. With the Nigra absent, men are waiting for machines to be cleaned, floors to be swept, crates lifted, equipment delivered and bathrooms to be deodorized. Why, rest rooms and toilets are so filthy until they not only cannot

be sat in, but it's virtually impossible to get within hailing distance because of the stench!

BUSINESSMAN: Business is even in worse condition, Henry. The volume of goods moving 'cross counters has slowed down to a trickle, almost negligible. Customers are not only not purchasing, but the absence of handymen, porters, sweepers, stockmovers, deliverers and miscellaneous dirty-work doers is disrupting the smooth harmony of marketing.

CLUB WOMAN: Food poisoning, severe indigestitis, chronic diarrhea, advanced diaper chafings and a plethora of unsanitary household disasters dangerous to life, limb, and property! As a representative of the Federation of Ladies' Clubs, I must sadly report that unless the trend is reversed, a complete breakdown in family unity is imminent . . . . Just as homosexuality and debauchery signaled the fall of Greece and Rome, the downgrading of Southern Bellesdom might very well prophesy the collapse of our indigenous institutions . . . . Remember, it has always been pure, delicate, lilywhite images of Dixie femininity which provided backbone, inspiration and ideology for our male warriors in their defense against the on-rushing black horde. If our gallant men are drained of this worship and idolatry, God knows! The cause won't be worth a Confederate nickel!

The characters in *Day of Absence* are deliberately two dimensional and farcical. Most characters are not even given names, but are simply referred to by occupation, such as Supervisor, Mayor, Industrialist, Businessman, and Clubwoman. The play is intended to be performed as a minstrel show in reverse—a Black cast performing in whiteface—with two exceptions: a northern White television newsman played by a White actor in straight makeup, and Rastus, played by a Black actor as a farcical character in straight makeup.

CHARACTERIZATION

Livin' Fat by Judi Ann Mason explores the idea of "totin' privileges" in a slightly different context. David Lee, the play's central character, has a college degree but is unable to find employment except as a janitor in a bank. When the bank is robbed, he finds over $50,000 in an envelope that the robbers dropped in their hasty departure. When David Lee attempts to call attention to the money immediately after the robbery, he is unable to get the attention of the bank authorities or the police. He is another one of those invisible men Ralph Ellison wrote about decades earlier. David Lee takes the money home and decides the money is payment to his mother, father, and grandmother for the hard times they have suffered. No explanation is necessary for a Black American audience to understand that David Lee would go to jail if he tried to be "honest" and returned the money. Black Americans know David's explanation would not be believed by White law enforcement officers in a small Southern town.

The only sagacious decision is to keep the money. The characters have no subsequent feelings of guilt since their standards of morality and justice conclude no wrong has been done. An important item to note is that David's parents are God-fearing, church-going folks. Prior to arriving at the decision to permit David to keep the money, David's father insists on "praying over" the moral issues that are presented by David's acquisition. Why do some people find it difficult to accept the notion that an ideal of ethical behavior is presented in *Livin' Fat* and in *Happy Ending* while continuing to idolize Robin Hood?

Other plays have used African American actors with whiteface makeup for reasons other than to convey the idea of a minstrel show-in-reverse. Carlton and Barbara Molette's *Rosalee Pritchett* is a serious play that uses African American actors in whiteface makeup to portray all of the White characters. The playwrights' notes to the director state that:

> We are opposed to the idea of having the Guards played by whites. They should be played by Black men in white-face makeup. It's not that we have anything against white actors in the Goodoleusofa, but

they just ain't capable of the kind of objectivity that is necessary in the portrayal of these roles.[122]

The assertion that White actors are incapable of objectivity is made satirically, a sort of antiequal-opportunity argument in reverse. However, the request that Black actors portray the White roles is a sincere one based on sincere doubt that most White actors can and will accurately portray these Black playwrights' perceptions about the behaviors and motivations of the White characters in this play.

Frequently a character's desired meaning is not exposed through European rules of character exposition but through experiences held in common among the African American audience members. These shared experiences lead to shared attitudes and values that do not need to be explained to African American audiences. White people are often oblivious to these attitudes and values and have difficulty accepting the truth of Afrocentric culture. One such truth that underlies African American character behavior is that Whites, in general, are frequently held in contempt by African Americans. Contempt and hatred are not synonymous, however; most Black people who hold White people in contempt do not hate White people. Consequently, Afrocentric heroes frequently have contempt for White people in larger-than-life or heroic proportions.

Shine in *The Titanic* is an African American mythological hero whose heroism is closely connected to his contempt for White people. Even though it is presented from a comic perspective, Shine's monumental contempt is, in large part, why the Shine character conveys a sense of truth to African American audiences. Leadbelly's recording *Fare Thee Well, Titanic* expresses similar contempt. While each of these African American cultural artifacts expresses contempt for White people, neither expresses hatred. Yet many White people are reluctant to recognize this exhibited contempt as a truthful expression of Black feelings. Nobody wants to think of himself or herself as worthy of contempt.

Eurocentric critics expect Black theatre to exhibit authenticity in characterization. This means Black characters who fit preconceived notions of who and what Black people are. Characters they consider authentically Black lend themselves to stereotypical exaggeration and simplification. So they consider pimps, prostitutes, drug addicts, and petty thieves authentic. Characters who do not fit their preconceived notions of authentic Blackness, such as doctors, lawyers, professors, bankers, and businessmen seem more difficult to stereotype, exaggerate, and simplify. The standard Eurocentric critics use to determine authenticity in a Black character seems to be twofold. The characters must (1) rise above their Blackness and (2) be motivated by the same stimuli in the same way that White characters are motivated.

No Place to be Somebody by Charles Gordone contains characters that most White critics regard as well-conceived and well-drawn. As the first Black play to win the Pulitzer Prize, *No Place to be Somebody* garnered more critical acclaim than any other play by a Black playwright in the two decades between *A Raisin in the Sun* and *A Soldier's Play*. Ironically, *No Place to be Somebody* is an extremely effective argument in favor of the myth of White racial superiority. The play attempts to make heroes of Black people who compulsively seek not just to enter White society but to establish their most intimate relationship with a White person. The play is dangerously deceptive because Charles Gordone is effectively colorful in his use of Black vernacular language and in his portrayal of some of the most negative characters to inhabit the Black experience while subtly, possibly unconsciously, presenting a message of White supremacy.

The play is so well constructed and the characters are so authentic in their external detail that Black audiences are often beguiled by those attributes into ignoring the play's dominant thematic elements. The characters who are presented in a negative light seek self-actualization within a Black cultural framework, but they not only fail to achieve it, they also fail to survive. The characters who achieve success relentlessly seek vicarious self-actualization through intimate association with some White character whom society permits to be somebody. The flaw in Gordone's theme is that human beings do not self-actualize vicariously.

No Place to be Somebody is reminiscent of Harriet Beecher Stowe's *Uncle Tom's Cabin* in that both works encourage Black people to bond their identity to a White person's goals and aspirations. Every Black character in *No Place to be Somebody* who has an opportunity to "be somebody" owes that opportunity to an intimate relationship with a White person. Each of those Black characters will "be somebody" only to the extent that their goals and aspirations connect to those of their particular White person.

Many White people find the character of Uncle Tom, as delineated in Harriet Beecher Stowe's novel and in numerous theatrical adaptations of her novel both dignified and lovable. *Uncle Tom's Cabin* was an important piece of abolitionist rhetoric when first written. Uncle Tom was a remarkably successful symbol supporting the nineteenth-century Eurocentric effort to abolish slavery in America. Mrs. Stowe crafted a lovable (to White people) character who effectively epitomized the inequities, cruelty, and un-Christian nature of slavery. But the White people who found Uncle Tom lovable loved him not as a fellow human being, but as they would love an obedient old pet dog. Mrs. Stowe crafted a character who could be embraced, not only by the relatively few nineteenth-century White Americans who endorsed the idea that Black people deserved full equality under the law, but also by the preponderance of nineteenth-century abolitionists who felt slavery was an un-Christian abomination while also holding the view that Black people were inherently inferior to White people. On the other hand, the overwhelming majority of Black people find the character pathetic or disgusting or worse. Black people generally see Uncle Tom as a man who willingly and complacently devalues himself. He relinquishes his destiny to

CHARACTERIZATION

the White family that claims he is their property. As a result, Black people use the term "Uncle Tom" to symbolize willing and complacent acceptance of inferior status.

The source of Uncle Tom's subservience is his recently acquired Christianity. White Christians have taught Tom that God made Black people inferior to White people, and Tom accepts this notion as a tenet of Christianity. Uncle Tom is the quintessence of all that is implied by the statement, "The God of the slave owner does not emancipate slaves."[123] When Tom's Black compatriots tell him to run away because he is going to be sold, he refuses. He is loyal to his master and has faith in "de Lawd." He wants to be free, but since he has accepted the White man's religion, Tom sings spirituals and waits for "de Lawd" to free him. He has been so completely emasculated by the system he calls Christianity that he allows Eva, a little girl no more than eight or ten years of age, to order him about and use him as a plaything. When Eva stamps her foot, Tom jumps.

Tom not only fails to control his own destiny, but he also opposes the idea of controlling his own destiny. He does not even speculate about what is in his own best interest. He is not selfless in the normal sense. He literally has no sense of self. He is entirely sincere in his belief that what is best for "his White folks" is best for him. Even in the self-realization that comes with his impending death, Tom fails to "be somebody" as he passively permits Simon Legree, the brutal White overseer, to beat him to death. Uncle Tom's behavior would not be so degrading if his willingness to subjugate his own best interests to better serve the needs, even the whims, of "his White folks" was not accompanied by such piousness. An Afrocentric hero in Uncle Tom's position would make a larger-than-life effort to save all the slaves on the plantation. Such an effort might require Uncle Tom to sacrifice his own efficacy to achieve the greatest good for the greatest number. In a comic context, he might develop an elaborate confidence scheme. In a serious context, he still might die in the end, but his demise would result from a valiant effort to save others.

Uncle Tom's Cabin was written by a White woman. White men taught nineteenth-century White women to believe they could only "be somebody" through obedience and subservience to a White male. Ms. Stowe's position is not surprising as she sincerely regarded Uncle Tom's behavior as exemplary. In a "stage Negro" tradition that has lasted to the present time, only the Black woman (Cassy) has the strength to take overt action against Simon Legree. The only other characters who have positive arcs are George and Eliza Harris, who aspire to "be somebody" and work to control their own destinies. But even the Harrises evoke negative concerns in twentieth-century and later African Americans. The Harrises believe their human aspirations and stronger wills result from their partial European ancestry, which is recognizable in their skin color and hair texture. The Harrises imply that to be "almost White" is to almost "be somebody."

A character who bears some resemblance to Uncle Tom appears in *The Escape: or a Leap for Freedom* by William Wells Brown. The character Cato appears in this nineteenth-century play by an African American playwright, but Cato only seems on the surface to be an Uncle Tom. Cato is regarded as a true and acceptable character by Black audiences over one hundred years after the play was written because Cato pretends to be an Uncle Tom in an effort to control his own destiny. Even though Cato has more stereotypical attributes than Ms. Stowe's Uncle Tom, Cato strives to control his own destiny and eventually succeeds. As a consequence, contemporary Black audiences find Cato an acceptable humorous character.[124]

The phenomenon of the Uncle Tom stereotype obviously did not end with Emancipation. *Purlie Victorious* by Ossie Davis is a play of the 1960s. Gitlow Judson, Rev. Purlie Victorious Judson's brother, appears to be a throwback to the negative stereotypes of an earlier era, but he is not. Gitlow and Purlie Victorious use different tactics, but they have similar goals. Purlie Victorious believes confrontation and protest is the best way to deal with Ol' Cap'n Cotchipee. His brother Gitlow is a tactical Uncle Tom. Gitlow believes he can get much more from Ol' Cap'n for far less work by seeming to be an Uncle Tom. Ol' Cap'n calls on Gitlow to testify about how Negroes really feel about integration.

> OL' CAP'N: Gitlow Judson, as God is your Judge and maker, do you believe in your heart that God intended white folks and Negra children to go to school together?
>
> GITLOW: Nawsuh, I do not!
>
> OL' CAP'N: Do you, so help you God, think that white folks and black should mix and 'sociate in street cars, buses, and railroad stations, in any way, shape, form or fashion?
>
> GITLOW: Absolutely not!
>
> OL' CAP'N: And is it not your considered opinion, God strike you dead if you lie, that all my Negras are happy with things in the southland just the way they are?
>
> GITLOW: Indeed I do!
>
> OL' CAP'N: Do you think ary single darky on my place would ever think of changing a single thing about the South, and to hell with the Supreme Court as God is your judge and maker?
>
> GITLOW: As God is my judge and maker and you are my boss, I do not![125]

Later, Gitlow makes a concise statement about standing up to fight like a man. He says running "emancipated more people than Abe Lincoln ever did." Although some see Gitlow as a throwback to the negative racial stereotypes of an earlier era, and Gitlow readily admits he is an Uncle Tom, he is quite different from the namesake character of *Uncle Tom's Cabin*.

Because Gitlow's Uncle Tomming is a tactic to manipulate situations in order to achieve his goals in an environment designed to victimize and oppress him, Black audiences find Gitlow funny, acceptable, and true despite his broad earthy clichés.

How Character Shapes Theme

Some Black characters have been reduced to inconsequential status by the introduction of a White character. The Black character would be regarded as heroic if the pivotal action were internally motivated and initiated, but the pivotal action seems to be initiated by the White character. By inference, the specific Black character and Black people in general seem incapable of initiating crucial actions on their own behalf. Two of the most widely seen and readily accessible examples of causing the drama's inciting action seem to be conceived, initiated, or articulated by White people are the television miniseries *King*, starring Paul Winfield, and the made-for-television motion picture *The Autobiography of Miss Jane Pittman*, starring Cicely Tyson. In both instances, a White character's presence is necessary to initiate an action that is required for the character to consummate a key act of confrontation. Some people who were present during events portrayed in the television miniseries *King* do not recall a lack of initiative or leadership by Martin Luther King, Jr. that is implied by the television screen presence of the White liberal labor leader from New York.

In the novel by African American writer Ernest J. Gaines, Ms. Jane Pittman tells her own story.[126] In the screenplay by Tracy Keenan Wynn, the story appears to be told, not by Ms. Pittman, but by a nice northern White male reporter named Quentin Lerner. Ms. Pittman's story seems to emerge onto the screen as a result of Lerner's desire to tell it. Making the reporter seem so obligatory to the telling of the story diminishes Ms. Pittman's status. Even the climactic moment when Ms. Pittman drinks from the "White" water fountain at the county courthouse is shared with Lerner. The scene is edited so the focus of attention and the suspense is divided between two

CHARACTERIZATION

different plot elements. The dominant focus is on whether or not Lerner will salvage his job by getting to Cape Canaveral in time to cover a space shot that his editor told him to cover and still complete his story about Ms. Pittman. Lerner wants to provide his story about Ms. Pittman with an exciting climax. Ms. Pittman has been asked to provide a symbolic impetus to the local civil rights movement by drinking from the "White" water fountain at the county courthouse. Whether or not Ms. Pittman drinks from the "White" fountain is diminished in importance because the focus shifts to Lerner's concerns.

Even when a Black character's behavior is fundamentally heroic, the character's stature can be significantly reduced by inserting a White male who becomes the focus of an important action, or initiates it, or tells the story from his point of view. Then the Black character seems to act only because action is required or desired by the White male and only seems to "be somebody" through this White man's identity.

An English-language theatre convention for interracial marriage was established, no doubt inadvertently, by William Shakespeare's *Othello*. The difficulties Othello faces in his tragic attempt to assimilate into White society established a tone that has continued to permeate the work of subsequent White playwrights who treat interracial marriage or persons with mixed-race parentage as subject matter. Out of this tradition has emerged a character type appearing in serious plays by both Black and White playwrights that has come to be labeled the "tragic mulatto." Tragic mulatto characters differ from other African Americans of light complexion in that they have an overwhelming urge to join the White world. This urge usually focuses on a desire to identify with the White parent or make a relationship with a White lover more permanent and public. Inevitably, White society rejects the mulatto character, and pain and suffering follow.

Black playwrights who have written about mulattoes have focused on the negative impact the mulatto character has on other Black people. In

Afrocentric plays, what happens to these mulatto characters is not a genetic accident. Further, the mulatto character who wants to be accepted by White society is not a hero. Rather, the hero is the Black mother, brother, or sister who recognizes his or her African American identity and survives by refusing to identify too strongly with the White parent or lover. The mulatto characters in *Mulatto* by Langston Hughes and *Ti Yette* by John Matheus are human beings with problems, and their problems include other people's reactions to their color and their mixed parentage; and they deal with their problems as best they can from the context of their values.

Plays with mulatto characters by White authors tend to imply "mixed blood" generates a sort of genetic dissonance that controls the lives of tragic mulattoes. White playwrights seem to say two different natures in conflict with each other live inside one human body: the primitive nature of the mulatto's African ancestry and the civilized nature of the mulatto's White ancestry. The tragedy of these mulatto characters grows out of their inability to overcome their primitive side. Or in some more sophisticated treatments, their tragedy grows out of White society's negative assumptions about their African blood coupled with their unswerving desire to assimilate into White society. White plays about mulattoes fail to recognize that Black Americans have never systematically, culturally ostracized African American people of mixed parentage. Further, when non-Black Americans have sought to assimilate into African American society, the African American societal response has generally been guarded acceptance. Afrocentric values dictate that the fact of mixed parentage is, in and of itself, neither tragic nor heroic. Since Black Americans who have sought to assimilate into White society have often confronted violent rejection, most Black Americans regard those who feel compelled to enter White society as individuals to be pitied, or as victims of the myth of White racial superiority, but certainly not as heroes.

Black theatre has created another type of mulatto character: the comic mulatto. Douglas Turner Ward's *Day of Absence*[127] exposes a comically

CHARACTERIZATION

ironic view of the phenomenon of "passing for White." As we have already discussed *Day of Absence*, we will focus here on the play's treatment of the comic mulatto idea. The play creates a situation in which all the Negroes in a small southern town are suddenly and inexplicably absent. As the impact of the Negroes' absence continues to farcically deteriorate, the town's leaders discover several citizens previously thought to be one-hundred percent pure White are missing as well. The Mayor's brother-in-law, two members of city council, chairman of the Junior Chamber of Commerce, the City College All-Southern half-back [this was before such an athletic team would have been integrated], chairlady of the Daughters of the Confederate Rebellion, Ms. Cotton-Sack Festival, and numerous miscellaneous nobodies are missing. The wife of one of the absent persons carries a placard that reads "Why Didn't You Tell Us, Your Defiled Wife and Two Absent Mongrels."

A Black hero who achieves his goals usually makes a useful statement to Black audiences. But an Afrocentric play may also make a useful statement to Black audiences by portraying Black characters who fail. *Ceremonies in Dark Old Men* by Lonne Elder is a sensitively detailed character study of a Black family. But none of the play's characters can be regarded as heroic. Even though they have the requisite skills to control their destinies, the characters succumb to the oppressiveness of their environment. They own a barbershop, they are all reasonably intelligent, and they all exhibit some capacity for survival; they could have succeeded. Despite these glimmers of potential, they manage to fail beyond any hope of redemption. But *Ceremonies in Dark Old Men* achieves a positive goal by exposing a negative set of circumstances and provoking the question, "Why did these people fail?" To the extent the audience gains insights into the forces that generate the Parker family's downfall, the play is successful. Some plays portray negative examples of Black characters to stimulate insight needed to avoid similar negative circumstances.

For some people, plays with heroes are unrealistic. Many actual situations are not populated with heroes, but are nevertheless worthy of presentation.

Some plays without heroes seem to say the human spirit seldom, if ever, rises above the level of the mundane situation being dramatized. Other plays without heroes present a negative situation that could be made more positive and try to provoke audience members to supply a link to the positive. In real life, all situations do not work themselves out so everyone lives happily ever after, and people are at least as likely to learn from negative experiences as from positive ones. In order to determine the difference between positive and negative presentations from an Afrocentric point of view, one must address issues that are far more complex than whether or not the Black protagonist prevails or causes laughter.

Black people in America exist in an environment of institutional racism. Those who are not compelled to suffer the consequences of racism on a continual basis generally fail to recognize the severity of its impact. When a character decides to risk pain and suffering or death for what White critics regard as no apparent reason, the White critics may have insufficient awareness of Black American existence. Eurocentric critics may conclude a character is not properly motivated because they fail to appreciate that being Black and living in the USA might provide motivation enough.

James Baldwin's *Blues for Mr. Charlie* provides an example of an African American character who disregards the harm that is likely to befall him and confronts the forces that seek to take away his human dignity. Richard Henry may not possess the requisite characteristics for status as a hero, but he provides an example of how institutional racism can collide with actual occurrence. Both the actual character Emmitt Till and the fictional character Richard Henry would seem to lack the awareness of the larger picture that motivated many civil rights demonstrators who made conscious decisions to ignore obvious danger and confront institutional racism. James Baldwin says *Blues for Mr. Charlie* "is based, very distantly indeed, on the case of Emmitt Till, the Negro youth who was murdered in Mississippi in 1955."[128] After the man indicted for Till's murder was acquitted, he claimed, as best we can recall, Till's behavior was so "uppity" that his death was necessary to maintain the honor of White folks. He insisted he did not want to kill Till, but Till left him no choice. Emmitt Till was murdered because he challenged institutional racism in his own very small and personal way. But his personal confrontation with oppression and Baldwin's exploration of the phenomenon may shed light on larger issues.

Baldwin explores a larger picture than the individual Black youth who challenged the racist traditions of a specific time and place. Baldwin explores the picture of institutional racism from a variety of points of view. He examines the incident not only from several Black points of view and a White liberal point of view, but also from the point of view of the White bigot who murders Richard Henry. Baldwin has sought to illuminate the concept that White people who commit demonic deeds within the context of institutional racism do not view themselves as demonic individuals. Baldwin averred "no man is a villain in his own eyes."[129] White bigots who commit violent acts against Black people do not do so because they choose to do wrong. No matter how misguided their actions may be, they are doing what they think is right. Their behavior reflects their values. The evil, Baldwin suggests, is the system that instills racist values, not the individual who responds to a perceived need to perpetuate and defend them.

Audiences are better able to perceive a play's thematic elements when characters express values that are in concert with the audience's values. While the dramatist's values and the audience's values may achieve a degree of harmony, the play and the play's intended audience may not be in harmony with other aspects of this culturally diverse society. Since such cultural differences inevitably exist, Americans will either continue to argue in favor of the superiority of one cultural location over another or learn to regard a diversity of cultural locations as valid, legitimate, and appropriate for their own situations.

Chapter Ten

Images in Theatre and Media

"All propaganda has to be popular and has to adapt its spiritual level to the perception of the least intelligent of those towards whom it intends to direct itself." —Adolf Hitler, *Mein Kampf,* 1933

Visual images communicate messages in theatrical presentations. Most Eurocentric analysis of theatre has focused on the script's words. This focus comes about as a result of classifying theatre as a subcategory of literature. Persons trained to evaluate literature have been regarded as the appropriate specialists to evaluate theatre. Literature specialists are usually astute enough to focus on the elements of theatre they are best prepared to evaluate. They ignore the elements of theatre, the visual ones, in which they have less interest or are less well equipped to evaluate, or both. But theatre art is at least as visual as it is verbal. Audiences see facial expressions, gestures, and bodily movement, as well as the clothing, jewelry, and makeup that adorn performers and the scenery and other objects that comprise the performance environment.

How the people of any cultural group use their visual perceptions to ascertain a sense of truth or plausibility is an essential factor in how they respond to theatre. Visual elements are as important in creating theatre as spoken words. The adage "seeing is believing" is as true as it is trite. As powerfully persuasive as words may be, widespread use of the term "eye witness" rather than "ear witness" illustrates the importance of visual perception in establishing proof of an occurrence. Since visual images of motion pictures and television are more easily accessible, we will focus on them. In America, how theatre audiences interpret and respond to visual images is not fundamentally different from how motion picture and television audiences interpret and respond to visual images.

Visual Cues

What we see is at least as dependent on psychological factors as on physical ones. One such psychological factor is that individuals acquire a set of visual cues that allow them to categorize what they see quickly and easily. Individuals retain information about things they have seen before, and use the information to interpret new visual experiences. One example of this phenomenon is how individuals interpret the illusion of three dimensions, whether in reality or in a two-dimensional painting or photograph or stage setting. The laws of physics that control perspective describe the basic visual cues that people employ to determine relative distance in the third dimension. Experience with these visual cues teaches that parallel lines appear to converge at a point on the horizon. One need not be cognizant of the science that explains optical perception to know when one looks down a highway, the road does not actually get narrower and the telegraph poles do not actually get shorter as the distance increases. Experience enables one to interpret the optical illusion of diminishing size to mean increasing distance. Without the relevant visual experience, one might assume the road actually narrowed and the telegraph poles actually got shorter. These and other visual cues are learned through experience. One who lacks experience with interpreting the impact of distance and weather conditions on color perception would no doubt assume the apparently purple mountains in the distance are actually purple.

Another issue related to how experience enhances the interpretation of visual cues can be summed up by the idea that all Black people look alike. Black people do not think all Black people look alike. On the other hand, some Black people think all Caucasians look alike. This phenomenon has a logical explanation that is only peripherally related to racism. Racism contributes to the likelihood that Americans will not have sufficient personal interaction with people whose phenotype differs from their own to accumulate the experience needed to enhance their visual awareness of other phenotypes. White people who rarely interact with Black people, or who only interact with Black people in the manner described earlier by referring to Ralph Ellison's *Invisible Man*, will probably not accumulate the visual cues needed to recognize differences between Black people who are similar in appearance. Experience develops perceptual familiarity that enables one to focus on factors that make a person different from others of similar appearance. Despite paying special attention to persons with unfamiliar phenotypes, subtle differences between such persons are more difficult to perceive and describe. When White people use the word "dark" to describe a person's complexion, they usually mean dark for a White person. "Olive" and "swarthy" describe the same complexion. Black people typically describe that same complexion as "light" or "bright" or "high yellow." Although one group calls this particular complexion "light" and the other calls it "dark," each group describes the complexion accurately in terms of its own normative experience.

In the 1960s, identification cards contained verbally descriptive data about height, weight, and complexion that seem less necessary since photographs became commonplace on identification cards. At least one liberal midwestern university inserted the word "light" in the space labeled "complexion" on the identification cards of students then called Negroes. This rather bizarre practice probably resulted from a scenario in which Negro students of light complexion by Afrocentric standards were labeled "dark" by some White staff member empowered to enter information on students' identification cards. Since the term "dark" was an uncomplimentary description in the early 1960s, some Negro students undoubtedly complained. After reading the label "light" on a brown-skinned student's identification card, we speculated that the university decided to avoid potential protests by calling all Negro students "light" regardless of their skin color. This anecdote suggests the relevant staff persons either could not or would not perceive differences in skin color among their Negro students or use descriptive terminology their Negro students found acceptable.

An individual whose visual experience is limited to persons whose skin is lighter than most Black Americans' will probably have difficulty perceiving and describing Black people's complexions. Many people with insufficient experience to see subtle skin color and hair texture variations among Black people also exhibit little, if any, interest in improving their visual awareness. People who work in theatre, motion picture, and television do not want to lose potential audience simply because their limited visual experience prevents them from easily recognizing differences among Black characters in a production. Various techniques to attract and sustain this audience have emerged over time. These techniques focus on enhancing visual differences between Black actors by exaggerating the controllable aspects of each actor's visual image. The most problematic factors to exaggerate are facial features. Since the late 1950s, any alteration of facial features that suggests a return to blackface makeup is likely to generate a negative response. Clothing and personal adornments such as jewelry are less problematic and easier to exaggerate. Manners, or visually observed behavior, may be exaggerated even more easily than clothes and personal adornments. Exaggerating Black characters' behavior, clothing, and personal adornments has evolved as standard practice in mainstream American theatre and media drama.

Normally, a theatre production's visual details are collaboratively planned by the director and various designers, with the stated goal of carrying out the intent of the playwright. When the visual details of a production are "right," knowledgeable observers derive a sense of truth from the visual messages they receive. Moreover, visual messages that convey a sense of truth enhance the observer's understanding of the structure, the characters, their behavior, and the resultant thematic ideas. Visual messages that are not in harmony with other elements of the production have a negative impact on the audience's understanding and appreciation of the whole.

When such elements of the play as plot, character, theme, mood, and rhythm and language are accompanied by visual messages that seem inappropriate to those who already possess accurate information about the surface details of the play's subject matter, cognitive dissonance is created. Cognitive harmony is uncommonly difficult to create in mainstream theatre and media presentations with Black characters when people in decision-making positions believe dissonant elements are actually in harmony. These individuals probably intend no harm. Their experience has provided few, if any, authentic images of the Black characters they bring to the stage or screen. Instead, their experience consists of a constant repetition of exaggerated stereotypical Black images over an extended period of time. They know nothing else about African American life, so they assume the exaggerated, stereotypical images they see on stage and in the media are authentic, so they present them to the public without remorse.

To blame an African American actor for creating a negative image is to blame the victim for the crime. Stereotypical characters should not be confused with the actors who portray them. Some people and organizations that advocate for African Americans' civil rights have, on occasion, expressed contempt for a Black actor who portrayed a character that in their view generated negative or stereotypical notions about Black people. Actors are not always in a position to determine what images will be presented ultimately to the audience, or how those images interrelate with the whole production, or how those images will be interpreted by various facets of society. For example, Cecily Tyson undoubtedly did not know the film *The Autobiography of Miss Jane Pittman* (discussed in chapter 9) would be edited so her character would seem to some viewers to be a pawn in the chess game between the White newspaper reporter and his editor.

Eunuchs are Safe

A Gallup poll conducted to determine the winners of the *Tenth Annual People's Choice Awards*, a CBS-TV Special presented on March 15, 1984, indicates Michael Jackson, Emmanuel Lewis, and Mr. T. were mainstream America's favorite African American characters at that time. This was the last such poll not influenced by *The Cosby Show* phenomenon, which premiered the following September. The poll further indicates America's favorite television programs included several with major continuing characters who are Black. In addition to *Webster* with Emmanuel Lewis and *The A-Team* with Mr. T., the other top three program in the "Favorite Overall New Television Program" category was *Hotel*, with a continuing Black character who plays the hotel's security officer. This character is remarkably similar to the Black continuing characters on *Hill Street Blues*. Among the "Favorite Comedy" and "Favorite Dramatic" categories, the only one with Black continuing characters is *Hill Street Blues*. One African American was included on the top three "Favorite All Around Male Entertainer" list: Michael Jackson. All three "Favorite Music Video" titles were by Michael Jackson.[130] The results of this poll suggest the aberrant Black character White people most want to see and is most often seen on primetime television is a male who appears to be asexual or dominated by a White person, or both. Not surprisingly, no Black females made the top three list in any "Favorite" category. Mammy and maid stereotypes are not submissive in the manner that Black male stereotypes are expected to be.

Organized objections to old stereotypical images, along with the growing sophistication of White audiences, demanded the emergence of a new Uncle Tom character in the 1980s. This new Uncle Tom was new only with respect to a few surface features. His patterns of behavior and motivation did not change. New visual features were added to circumvent objections to the old Uncle Tom stereotype. The new visual image is not that of an elderly man, but a male child. This Black male child, as a result of some bizarre set of circumstances, lives in a White man's house. The Black child has virtually no personal contact with other Black people.

Since Uncle Tom stereotypes are both submissive and asexual, some evidence must be present in the plot to dispel any thoughts that the White male is a pedophile. This relationship is sharply portrayed as that of father and son: White father, Black son. This classic "big me, little you" relationship permits a degree of White domination to which the Uncle Tom stereotypes of earlier eras seldom descended. The potential for visual enhancement of the "big me, little you" relationship was exploited by positioning cameras and actors to emphasize size differences on the television screen. Optical illusions were created by selecting a longer focal length for the camera lens, thereby causing a character standing in the foreground to appear larger in comparison to a character standing farther away from the lens. In addition, smaller than average Black children were presented with larger than average White males. This visual contrast, with such other characteristics as the relatively high soft voice that is usually present in diminutive male children, created a formula that was exceedingly popular among the masses of White Americans. Although *The Cosby Show*'s dominance was evident in Gallup poll preceding the March 1986 People's Choice Awards television program, Emmanuel Lewis remained a solid favorite in the "Favorite Young Television Performer" category. The cute and talented child actors on *Webster* and *Diff'rent Strokes* also played characters who were fundamentally subservient to a White male.

Other variations of this 1980s Uncle Tom stereotype were evident. One such variation, the jive genie of the short-lived *Just Our Luck* television series, was not diminutive in size, age, or vocal quality. Like other such mythological creatures, this Black genie exists for the sole purpose of fulfilling his master's fantasies. Total domination is visually reinforced by the genie's behavior as he bows, scrapes, and scurries about carrying out his master's wishes. Since genies are spirits, they are sexually safe. The kind of stable relationship that leads to marriage, child rearing, and the perpetuation of values is unthinkable in a genie. The jive genie also exposes another facet of the Uncle Tom stereotype reconfigured to span from the 1980s into the new millennium, the Black eunuch. A eunuch is a male with the physical attributes and the combat skills to guard a harem, as well as the asexuality to be trusted to guard a harem. Eunuchs are highly reliable and loyal as well, because they have no families of their own to provide a basis for personal ambitions that might conflict with the goals of the man whose orders they execute. Uncle Tom stereotypes may be trusted to avoid even the appearance of sexuality in the presence of White people.

When Uncle Tom is configured to emphasize the eunuch facet of the stereotype, the character can be big, strong, and muscular to the extreme. Feats of strength, loyalty, and even technocratic skill have been exhibited by eunuch stereotypes. These visually virile males perform feats of strength and skill with unquestioning loyalty on orders from their White male leader. The television series *The A-Team* provided the most popular Black eunuch stereotype during the 1980s while the award-winning *Hill Street Blues* television series offered a more sophisticated approach to the eunuch stereotype. The Black male continuing characters on *Hill Street Blues* were among the most fully drawn Black characterizations created prior to September 1984 in a series that survived on network television for a season or more. Casual observation suggests mature, masculine images of Black men with the physical attributes and combat skills to be competent policemen. Their characterizations are as three-dimensional as others on the series. But some White police officers on the series reveal relationships with parents, children, and spouses or lovers. The White relationships are seldom ideal, but the Black police officers reveal no such relationships.

The Black men and women on *Hill Street Blues* were not shown in familial situations that provide models for ensuring cultural stability or perpetuating traditions that promote spiritual and physical survival. No Black policeman has a continuing mature relationship. Instead, they have exotic, picturesque affairs with Black women who were the tragic mulatto stereotypes of the 1980s: prostitutes and drug addicts who die within a few episodes. The only memorable Black mother on the series was a drug addict who was clearly unable to care for her child. Of course, the boy's father was absent and unmentioned, so the boy's only hope for survival was his foster parent, a single White policewoman.

The Cosby Show premiered in the fall of 1984. The A.C. Nielsen ratings ranked the series number three for the 1984-85 season. In the four seasons that followed, *The Cosby Show* was ranked number one in the Nielsen ratings with a larger percentage share of the television viewing audience than any other show in the history of television. In the 1989-90 season, the show held a strong number two spot and finished in fifth place for the 1990-91 season. A significant measure of a show's popularity is its ability to retain viewers for the time slot that follows. In the time slot following *The Cosby Show*, the show's spinoff, *A Different World*, ranked number two in 1987-88, its premiere season, and number four in 1989-90. *All in the Family* and *I Love Lucy* are the only comedies to achieve a similar degree of commercial success. The only noncomedy programs to achieve similar success before 1990 were *Gunsmoke*, *Bonanza*, and *Dallas*.[131] Prior to *The Cosby Show*'s emergence as arguably the most popular series in television history,[132] every successful television series with Black characters had at least one Black stereotype among the featured characters.

In addition to its other accolades, many have said *The Cosby Show* is the first successful television show with no stereotypical Black characters. *The Cosby Show* employed and listed in its credits a consultant whose job was to make sure the show's African American images were positive. Yet the show's efforts in this regard seem to be at odds with the perceptions of the White viewers who made *The Cosby Show* the most phenomenal financial success in television history. These White viewers, via the 1992 People's Choice Awards,[133] designated Bill Cosby the favorite male performer and the show the favorite comedy series of the 1984-85 season. Prior to *The Cosby Show*, White viewers only supported television shows with Black continuing characters when at least one Black character conformed to some Black stereotype; yet White viewers in historic numbers were comfortable with the Black characters they saw on *The Cosby Show*. Did these White viewers change, or did they get a message that Cosby did not intentionally send? Did they see some stereotype that the show's production staff failed to see? Ironically, the Black viewers who complained about stereotyping contended the characters were not really Black, or they were not Black enough, basing their objections on the presumption that "real" Black characters cannot possibly be physicians or attorneys or have children who do not do drugs or get pregnant before they get married.

Functions of the Fool

The Eurocentric tradition of the fool as a dramatic device may explain how millions of White viewers managed to receive a message that differs from the one *The Cosby Show* sought to send, and differs from the one most African Americans received. The court jester or fool in Medieval Europe was a person with a special relationship to a king or other lord of a medieval manor. By dressing and acting as the fool, a court jester could speak bluntly and frankly to high-ranking aristocrats. A person of lower rank, who developed a relationship with a king or other lord of a manor who tolerated blunt and frank remarks in a context of humor might be called that aristocrat's fool even if the person was not a jester by trade.

The character Falstaff in Shakespeare's *The Merry Wives of Windsor* and *King Henry IV, Part Two* exemplifies the fool as a dramatic device. Falstaff was Prince Hal's sidekick and functioned as his fool. As a character who meets the criteria Eurocentric dramatic heroes must exhibit, Prince Hal was never hungry or sleepy or afraid. As Hal's alter ego, Falstaff experiences the human frailties that Eurocentric heroes do not. This convention allows the dramatist to indicate the hero is in danger or tired or hungry without forcing the hero to exhibit such frailties himself. Twentieth century motion picture Westerns made extensive use of the fool as a character type and conveyed the concept to a far larger audience than Shakespeare's plays enjoyed. Gabby Hays was Roy Rogers' sidekick; Pat Buttram was Gene Autry's; Edgar Buchanan, as Red Connors, rode with Hopalong Cassidy; Tonto, played by Jay Silverheels, rode with his "kimosabe" known as the Lone Ranger; and Leo Carillo, as Poncho, rode with the Cisco Kid.

The fool's principal function in the dramatic action is to serve as a foil. Foils are relatively minor characters who accomplish the task of focusing attention on or telling the audience something about a major character. Theatre and literature borrowed the term "foil" from the jewelry maker's vocabulary where highly reflective metal foil is placed behind a gemstone to reflect light, making the gem appear brighter than it would seem otherwise. Referring to a character as a foil implies the character's main function is to make some other character shine brighter. All foils are not fools but all fools are foils.

Some fools are also coons. Early 1800s American theatre developed and marketed a Black stereotypical fool character type known as the coon. Theatre historians generally credit (or discredit) Thomas "Jim Crow" Rice with originating and popularizing the coon stereotype. Rice, a White vaudeville performer, claimed his Jim Crow character was an imitation of a Black youngster with a physical disability that he saw dancing and singing a song called "Jump, Jim Crow." Rice had not been very successful until he began doing his blatantly bigoted mockery of a disabled Black youth by wearing rags and blackening his face with burnt cork. The routine was such an enormous success in America and England in the 1830s and 1840s that the term "Jim Crow" became the nomenclature for the system of barriers preventing Black Americans from fully participating as citizens of the USA, entitled to equal protection of life and access to liberty and the pursuit of happiness. Donald Bogle describes coons as "those unreliable, crazy, lazy, subhuman creatures good for nothing more than eating watermelons, stealing chickens, shooting crap, or butchering the English language."[134] These traits make them objects of laughter and tools of bigotry in comedies or as comic relief in serious drama.

In the mid-1830s, numerous iterations of coon stereotypes appeared in vaudeville venues and theatres and later in motion pictures and television. Nearly all the early coon stereotypes were played by White actors in blackface. By the advent of network television, most coon roles were played by Black actors, but as late as the 1950s, White actors continued to perform coon routines in blackface in live venues, motion pictures, and even on network television. Some of these coon stereotypes functioned as foils in the tradition of the fool character type while more outrageous coon stereotypes were presented solely to make fun of Black people in the Thomas "Jim Crow" Rice tradition.

Mantan Moreland as Birmingham Brown in the *Charlie Chan* motion picture series and Eddie Anderson as Jack Benny's servant Rochester on radio, television, and motion pictures are two widely seen examples of the coon stereotype as a foil for the hero. Two characters on the *Amos 'n' Andy* show that aired on radio and television exemplify coon stereotypes that seem to serve no purpose other than to make fun of Black people. As his name implies, the character known as Lightning did everything extremely slowly—an exemplar of the lazy shiftless qualities so often alleged by bigots to be a character trait among Black men. A character named Calhoun was a practicing attorney, who in mythical *Amos 'n' Andy* America did not exhibit the requisite literacy to pass a high school English course, let alone the bar exam of some state in the USA. Civil rights organizations and the predominately Black National Bar Association objected to this mockery of the legal profession. After ignoring the protests for many years, Calhoun's identity unceremoniously shifted from attorney to businessman.

Following the 1950s, a new genre of Black sidekicks emerged in adventure dramas and murder mysteries. These new sidekicks are less dependent than their predecessors on foolish antics. They exist in programs with White heroes who reverse traditional preconceptions of nobility by finding nobility in White males who are not aristocrats and thereby make Eurocentric heroism seem more egalitarian. These new heroes have sidekicks who reflect egalitarian ideals and exhibit traits that reverse the superstitious, fearful, docile, lazy, shiftless traits of prior Black sidekicks who were more obviously coons.

The television series *McCloud* employed the popular "fish out of water" premise and placed a White Western marshal on assignment with the New York Police Department. A key visual image in the series showed Marshall McCloud pursuing a criminal on horseback on a busy Manhattan street. McCloud's Black sidekick served the purpose in the dramatic structure traditionally assigned to the fool. McCloud's sidekick worried about him when he was in danger, violated police procedures, or performed some outrageous feat in order to save someone (usually a "fair maiden") in distress or capture the bad guys. McCloud's sidekick was a highly professional, slightly conservative, competent, and experienced police detective who also happened to be Black. Joe Broadhurst did not exhibit any of the characteristics Black Americans complained about in pre-1960s characters. He moved with characteristically New York quickness. He spoke with good diction. Neither his behavior nor his clothing was exaggerated. He had the intelligence, competence, and work ethic to do his job well. Although his function was structurally that of the fool who is a foil, he was not a fool in the contemporary sense of the word. Broadhurst provoked laughter because he was the hero's total opposite. McCloud was relaxed, dressed in casual western wear, spoke with a regional dialect, and was unconventional in every possible way. Broadhurst never relaxed, always wore a coat and tie, did not speak with a regional or ethnic dialect, and was conventional in every way. The series derived its comic relief from Broadhurst's embarrassment and worry over McCloud's disregard for conventional police procedures and Broadhurst's efforts to keep NYPD's administration from finding out about McCloud's unorthodox tactics.

Hawk in *Spencer for Hire* functioned structurally as Spencer's fool, but in reverse. Spencer's uniqueness as a TV detective was his cultivated interior beneath the "blue collar" exterior. Since Spencer's character exhibited sensitivity and vulnerability, Hawk had to be the opposite. Recognizing the structural function of the fool clarifies a number of factors about Black images in television drama. The use of extraordinary costumes is in keeping with the court jester tradition. In contrast to Spencer's costumes, Hawk's were flamboyant: silk suits with silk turtleneck shirts, a white full-length leather coat, a hat, leather gloves, and ever present sunglasses. Hannibal's sidekick on *The A-Team*, B. A. Barracus, was even more visually bizarre. His haircut, clothes, and outlandish gold jewelry gave an even clearer contemporary costuming parallel to the traditional court jester.

In television situation comedies about a family, the role of the fool is traditionally portrayed by the father. This tradition goes back to the pretelevision era when the most popular comedies about a family were *Dagwood* of the newspaper comic strips, and *The Life of Riley* and *The Adventures of Ozzie and Harriet* on the radio. The prototype television family, *The Adventures of Ozzie and Harriet*, began as a radio program in 1944, moved to television in 1952, and continued on ABC television until 1966. Although the father character appears to be overtly stupid in many television situation comedies, such shows as *The Adventures of Ozzie and Harriet* and *Father Knows Best* portrayed fathers as intelligent and competent while still making the humor grow out of the manner in which the father contrasts with one or more other members of the family. A large part of the humor in these situation comedies grows out of the father's portrayal as rigid and pompous while other family members are flexible and pragmatic in their approach to various situations the family confronts.

Into the long tradition of the fool as a dramatic device and the father as the contrasting element from which a domestic situation comedy's humor grows, *The Cosby Show* emerged in 1984. Cosby was not the first Black father in a network television situation comedy. Redd Foxx first appeared in *Sanford and Son* on NBC in 1972, solidly in the tradition of the father functioning structurally as the fool. Whereas Heathcliff Huxtable, the father on *The Cosby Show*, is a medical doctor, Fred Sanford operated a junkyard for a living. Fred Sanford was more exaggerated than Heathcliff Huxtable in his rigidity and pomposity as well as other traits that generated humor. A number of Black people who found no significant fault with *Sanford and Son*'s father-son relationship strenuously objected to the Sapphire stereotype presented by Aunt Esther, sister of the senior Sanford's late wife. Both Sanford and Huxtable established high acceptability levels among Black and White viewers. Sanford's acceptability among White people centered around his nonthreatening age and socioeconomic status. In contrast, the size of Huxtable's family and his relationship with his wife establish him as a virile male and his occupation indicates intellectual and economic capacity to act in his own best interest and in the best interest of his family. Huxtable's success does not require help or advice from a

White person. His popularity among Black viewers is due, at least in part, to the fact that he exists in a Black environment. We see him with Black friends and family. His relationship with his wife provided the first such image to sustain in a television series. He does not seem inferior to Whites socioeconomically or as the butt of their jokes. Huxtable is only the butt of humor inflicted by his own family and friends in a manner that does not make him seem inferior or subservient.

Despite its positive signs of Blackness, *The Cosby Show* provides sustenance for whatever stereotypical and bigoted views White people may hold by offering an opportunity to laugh at a Black man, even though the Black man is portrayed as having both economic and social status. Further, the Eurocentric tradition of the fool as a dramatic device enables White people to associate Huxtable with traditional family situation comedies where the father functions structurally as the fool and thereby derive a level of comfort from the Huxtable character.

While one cannot exclude Cosby's immense talent as a factor in *The Cosby Show*'s success, the show's popularity among both Black and White viewers provided leverage for similar characters to appear in primetime television network comedies. After *The Cosby Show*'s success in 1984, networks scurried to introduce primetime programs with mostly Black casts. *Charlie & Co.*, starring Flip Wilson, premiered on CBS in the fall of 1985. Jaleel White, who later achieved stardom as Steve Urkel on *Family Matters*, played Flip Wilson's son. Although Flip Wilson had hosted a successful comedy-variety hour, *The Flip Wilson Show*, for four years (number two in the Nielsen ratings for the 1970-71 and 1971-72 seasons), *Charlie & Co.* had difficulty sustaining the 1985-86 season, and the series was not renewed for a second season. *The Cosby Show*'s success also leveraged opportunities for other Black male characters who presented virile male images. But other shows in the same era did not survive on network television despite the high quality of their actors and scripts. Such shows as *Bay City Blues*, with Bernie Casey; *Frank's Place*, with Tim Reid; and *Good Times*, with John

Amos come to mind. In the case of *Good Times*, the show survived but the father character did not.

Frank's Place, starring Tim Reid and Daphne Maxwell Reid and set in New Orleans premiered in the fall of 1987. Playwright Samm-Art Williams was the story editor for the series. The show's New Orleans restaurant setting introduced characters from a variety of walks of life that rank among the most fascinating assortments of characters ever congregated in a television series. While the plots were entertaining and humorous, the strength of the series was the engrossing conglomeration of characters who inhabited Frank's recently inherited restaurant. *Frank's Place* is among our favorite network television programs ever. Despite its critical acclamation as one of the best shows of the 1987-88 season, *Frank's Place* was canceled after its first and only season in which its time slot was changed four times.[135] The show's poor ratings could have been due to the difficulty the show's audience had in adjusting to its erratic schedule, or to the discomfort White viewers had in accepting the broad array of well-defined Black characters or both. Although *Charlie & Co.*, *Frank's Place*, and others with well-defined, nonstereotypical Black characters premiered in the years following *The Cosby Show*'s first year, none were able to sustain sufficient sponsorship for a second season.

Family Matters premiered in the fall of 1989. In its first season, the emphasis centered on the domestic activities of the Winslow family, father, mother, their three children, grandmother, and the recently widowed sister of the mother and her young son. At first, *Family Matters* seemed destined to travel the road of *Charlie & Co.* and *Frank's Place*. But the show's focus had changed by the beginning of the second season. The obnoxious next-door neighbor, Steve Urkel, a Black teenaged male, became the center of attention and the character emerged as an update of the coon stereotype.

A frequently used device for early coons had them pursuing and getting rebuffed by a woman who was obviously deserving of someone better than a coon. Urkel began as the intellectual nerd next door pursuing Laura, the Winslows' teenage daughter. Laura rebuffed Urkel at every opportunity. In the first season, a few Black intellectuals objected to making the intellectual Black teenager the butt of jokes and a failure at attracting the girl, but Urkel was not the center of attention. Response from White viewers in the first season revealed a potential gold mine, so the show's focus shifted from the Winslow family's domestic issues to Urkel's buffoonery echoing the *Good Times*' 1974 to 1975 shift in focus from the parents played by John Amos and Esther Rolle to their son, J.J., a coon stereotype played by Jimmy Walker.

The 1990s Urkel update of the coon stereotype has greater negative potential for Black people than the traditional coon stereotype. Young Black men are not inspired to emulate the traditional coon stereotype. The lesson young Black men learn from such stereotypes is to avoid any resemblance to them. On the other hand, making a smart, highly motivated teenager a coonlike source of derision and laughter reinforces the idea that young Black males should shun intellectual pursuits. Urkel is smart and he excels in school, but his glasses are thick, his trousers are several inches above the level that Black teenagers consider acceptable, his socks contrast with his trousers to emphasize they are what Black teenagers two generations ago laughingly called "high water," he carries his body in a manner that is contrary to the posture young Black men generally seek to achieve, and he speaks in a high-pitched nasal voice while most Black males his age try to cultivate a low, resonant tone. This thoroughly laughable visual and auditory image sends the message that young Black males who excel intellectually are seen as objects of ridicule by the society as a whole and especially by young Black females.

Urkel's usual visual image is ludicrous enough, but his appearance sometimes becomes far more preposterous. The episode that aired on Valentine's Day 1992 presents Urkel as a cupid in a skin-tight pink body suit over which he wears white boxer shorts with large red hearts. Atop his head is a curly blond wig. Despite the excellent character portrayals by other cast members, White viewers do not see a domestic situation comedy when they watch *Family Matters*. Instead, they see a coon show featuring Steve Urkel. As late as the 1990s, White viewers seemed comforted by Urkel's image of Black manhood.

The Supernegro

The "superNegro" is a modernization of the noble savage stereotype, notably exemplified by Sidney Poitier in such films as *Guess Who's Coming to Dinner?* and *Brother John*. Other than the obviously stereotypical characters and those on *The Cosby Show* and its spin-off *A Different World*, the most popular Black characters on primetime network television, appear in an environment where most of the principal characters are White. These characters never seem to have complex relationships with other Black people. By presenting the Black character and his or her goals in an environment in which White characters and their goals clearly prevail, each of these characters is diminished in the eyes of White viewers. The television series *In the Heat of the Night* exemplifies this phenomenon. The television series is based on a group of characters and a locale created in several feature films that starred Sidney Poitier as Virgil Tibbs, a successful big-city policeman, and Rod Steiger as the chief of police in the small Mississippi town of Sparta where Virgil Tibbs was born and reared.

In the television series, Virgil Tibbs and his wife Althea provide a view of a mature African American marriage in which both husband and wife have jobs that while less affluent than the Huxtables', require intelligence, initiative, and a college education. Each character is dedicated and caring both in the workplace and in their relationships with each other. However, the episodes do not focus on Virgil and Althea Tibbs; they are a small part of a larger picture. The series focuses on the entire town of Sparta, Mississippi, its police department, and the sundry murders and other crimes that are requisite to a primetime television detective series. Virgil and Althea Tibbs are seen in a context in which White characters prevail in numbers and in power.

When Black people receive a positive message in the portrayal of a Black character on television, they tend to presume White people who see the same program receive the same message. Black people may see a television program in which a Black husband and wife such as Virgil and Althea Tibbs are portrayed in a manner that is acceptable to them, while millions of White viewers see the same program without having their stereotypical views disturbed. When White people see *In the Heat of the Night* Virgil and Althea Tibbs may very well be invisible as they see White folks in Sparta, Mississippi getting along with Sparta's law-abiding Black citizens, proof that racism is a thing of the past, even in Sparta, Mississippi. Despite several Black characters who seem not to be stereotypes, *In the Heat of the Night* was one of the top three programs in the 1992 People's Choice Awards Favorite Television Dramatic Series category.[136]

L.A. Law, the 1992 People's Choice Awards winner in the Favorite Television Dramatic Series category, includes in the cast, a Black male attorney named Jonathan Rollins as a continuing character. Rollins does not seem to fit a stereotype, but on closer examination, he is a "superNegro" stereotype. No Black character other than Rollins gets enough attention to impact the show's popularity. Rollins occasionally appears in relationships with his parents and with Black women. What initially appeared to be a romantic relationship between the handsome Black attorney and an attractive Black woman who was enrolled in law school turned out to be two more contemporary Black stereotypes. She is in the process of divorcing her husband, making her a single-parent stereotype. More significantly, her soon-to-be ex-husband is a violent anti-intellectual who did not want his wife to go to law school because it heightens his awareness of his own failure as a breadwinner.

While Rollins' relationship with other Black people seems fleeting at best, *L.A. Law* exploited still another contemporary stereotypical image, that of the new urban Buck, by placing the successful, affluent Black man in a torrid romance with a White woman. America's favorite law firm has hired one Hispanic man and one Black man and each of these super-successful men of color has eventually found love and happiness with a White woman. The theme of these *L.A. Law* plot threads implies connection to a White lover allows persons of color to achieve personhood in the White world. But this thematic thread reminiscent of *No Place to Be Somebody* is not the main focus of the *L.A. Law* series. The characters of Jonathan Rollins and his Hispanic counterpart Victor Sifuentes are diminished by placement in a context where White characters prevail in numbers and in power.

In contrast, the early 1990s provided a look at an interracial love affair from the point of view of a Black male. In Spike Lee's film *Jungle Fever*, the Black male/White female relationship is one that is more of the hormones than of the heart. The thematic element of the film that focuses on the relationship takes a position that is essentially opposite to the theme of *No Place to be Somebody*. The audience is definitely not left with the impression that the successful young Black architect in *Jungle Fever* enhances his self-esteem as a result of his sexual encounter with a White secretary in the firm where he is employed as an architect. Instead, the audience sees a successful young architect who achieved personhood as a husband, father, son, brother, and friend in his African American "pre-jungle fever" environment. His interracial affair destroys rather than enhances his personhood.

In *L.A. Law, In the Heat of the Night*, and several other successful television dramatic series of the early 1990s, the Black characters are shown in environments where they are in the minority. While many of these characters seem less stereotypical than earlier Black characters on primetime television, their significance is reduced in the eyes of White viewers through variations of a dramatic device that places a Black character in a context that makes her or his goals subservient to some White person's goals. This contextual device creates an illusion of the Uncle Tom stereotype in the sense that many White Americans are comfortable enough with these Black characters to regard the series in which they appear as among their favorite.

Eurocentric values inspired the saying, "'dog bites man' is not news, but 'man bites dog' is news." Awareness of this concept may aid in understanding the creation and perpetuation of non-White stereotypes. Portrayals of non-Whites by White Americans generally follow the trend of ignoring the normative, ignoring those things that the non-White group itself regards as better than normative, and focusing instead on those things that White people find unusual, picturesque, and subnormative.

Deviant behavior is regarded as newsworthy by the Eurocentric Americans who control the dissemination of news, as well as by many decision makers in the Eurocentric American theatre. Although this fascination with deviant behavior affects decisions about White subject matter as well as Black, its impact on African American images is more negative. Visual images of Black Americans in stage, television, and motion picture dramas focus on such deviant stereotypes as pimps, prostitutes, and members of street gangs with overwhelming frequency. Ordinary, working-class Black people are not picturesque. Black businessmen and professionals are even less picturesque. They "look White," meaning they do not blatantly deviate from Eurocentric American norms to the extent that they may be readily ridiculed. Joseph Papp and the theatre he founded undoubtedly produced more plays by Black playwrights in New York than any other White producer. In contrast to this laudable accomplishment, Papp has been quoted as saying, "Whenever the black realizes that he's as fucked up as anybody else, then I say, 'Okay, I'll do the play.'"[137]

Such images as B. A. Barracus played by Mr. T are too obviously bizarre to pose a threat to mature African Americans' notions of what is real. Although such characters reinforce Black stereotypes, there is little likelihood that even relatively unsophisticated Black adults would regard these images as plausible in any context other than an action-adventure fantasy. On the other hand, many Black images in current circulation seem sufficiently plausible to cause notions of what is real to shift toward stereotypical images of Black life. These more plausible stereotypical images of Black people are especially insidious in their ability to distort Black people's views of what is normal or true. Concern about these stereotypes is necessary because American society increasingly regards the images presented in theatre, television, and film as real and true. Black Americans are not immune to this phenomenon. To decide which theatre and media images are disseminated to the American public and which images are not is to manipulate what people regard as real and not real.

An endless supply of these stereotypical images could, arguably, result in a massive shift in what is regarded as real toward a view of what is real according to the values of the WEPPEOs who control theatre, television, and film. Thus the need increases for Afrocentric theatre presenters to understand and respond to this phenomenon. The need to present theatre to African American audiences that is both plausible and true is more urgent than most people wish to believe.

Afrocentric theatre has functioned as a force that encourages critical thinking and recognizes that most of life's questions do not have simple or easy answers. Stereotyping of any variety encourages people to accept simple easy answers when real answers are complex and difficult. The overwhelming impact of American media may cause African American audiences to regard Afrocentric truth as implausible and Eurocentric theatre, television, and film stereotypes as truth. To the extent that African Americans allow their view of reality to be altered by this stereotyping, Black people's sense of truth may shift to a reality that is nearly as oppressive as physical bondage.

Chapter Eleven

Asking Critical Questions

"Any question that has an easily articulated answer isn't worth writing a play about." —Itamar Moses, October 2008, *American Theatre*

To ask critical questions, one must engage in critical thinking, which Michael Scriven and Richard Paul define as "the intellectually disciplined process of actively and skillfully conceptualizing, applying, analyzing, synthesizing, and/or evaluating information gathered from or generated by observation, experience, reflection, reasoning, or communication as a guide to belief and action."[138]

Encouragement of independent thought does not mean every opinion is as good as any other. Fundamental intellectual standards include:

Clarity: If a statement is unclear, we cannot determine whether it is accurate or relevant because we don't know what it is saying.

Accuracy: Is that really true? How can we find out if that is true?

Precision: More details or more specificity is needed.

Relevance: Is that connected or related to the question or issue?

Depth: How does that address or consider the complexities, the problems, or the most significant factors?

Breadth: Do we need to consider another point of view? Is there another way to look at this question? What would this look like from a markedly different point of view?

Logic: When one thinks, a variety of thoughts come together into some order. When the thoughts are mutually supporting and make sense in combination, the thinking is logical.

Fundamental Issues

Is "What is right?" a legitimate question to ask of a work of theatre art? When people seek to pose a more significant question than what happened next, they often ask "Is it real?" questions. While such questions are appropriate, especially when addressing issues of stereotyping, "Is it real?" discourse often makes presumptions about what is "human nature" or "universal" that ignore differences in cultural perspective. These different beliefs often affect people's views about a play's authenticity, legitimacy, or veracity: whether angels in general or deceased ancestors in particular influence natural phenomena to someone's benefit; whether polygamy is a good and worthwhile family structure; whether polytheism is a more primitive form of religious thought than monotheism; whether greed is human nature and is good because it is the driving force behind capitalism and capitalism is the lynchpin of America's greatness. None of these beliefs are universal and each can affect a culture's theatre. Many plays presume a point of view about witches, ghosts, or God that persons with a different cultural perspective might consider primitive.

In an unfortunately persistent scenario, television stations present news about "welfare mothers," teenage mothers, unwed mothers, or single parents on welfare, with accompanying visual images of young brown-skinned females who appear to be either Hispanic or African American. In fact, there are more White than either Black or Hispanic females who fall into the above categories. These images will provoke discerning observers to ask:

1. Are these stories factual? Are they truthful? Is there a difference between fact and truth?
2. Are people who get paid to disseminate their views about news and art obliged to present the whole truth, and nothing but the truth?
3. Are they obliged to persist until they have verified all the facts?
4. How does one verify facts and uncover the truth?

Every culture's art disseminates truths from the perspective of its value system. Americans are inundated with commodities passing for art that are manufactured and marketed more for profit than for disseminating truth. Making a profit is not inherently wrong or evil, but it sometimes overwhelms a manufacturer's or distributer's original purpose. The desire to preserve fame and fortune may diminish an artist's zeal to proclaim truth. Different cultures tell of a messenger who proclaims the truth, and the response is, "Kill the messenger!" A character in the play and motion picture *A Few Good Men* makes the point that some people "can't handle the truth." Discerning questions that describe or evaluate theatre differentiates entertainment whose primary purpose is to make a profit from art that disseminates truth.

While critical questions about race are requisite to understanding "diversity" and "multiculturalism" in the arts, such questions are often banned from polite discourse. Considerate Americans must learn to discuss these simple, but fundamental questions without offending members of another group.

5. What is and how do we determine who is Black, Negro, Colored, African American?
6. What is an Afrocentric Perspective?
7. How do we determine whether or not an African American artist is Afrocentric?

8. What do Black American artists experience that is different from what White American artists experience?
9. Do African American artists face barriers that White American artists do not?
10. How might differing experiences make a Black American's art different from a White American's art?
11. If Afrocentric artists have different ways of working or different goals, how do we describe and evaluate their work?
12. Do or should people of different races, ethnic groups, cultures, or ages all use the same criteria to determine whether or not a work of art is "good?"

The relationship between performing art's intrinsic value and its dollar value can be seen by comparing the costs in any specific geographic area of live theatre and symphonic music to popular music concerts and professional sports. Various levels of government spends billions of dollars to sustain and support selected artists and the arts they create. The fact that most taxpayer-subsidized art is Eurocentric and not highly valued in an Afrocentric context does not mean most White people value it either. These publicly supported arts cannot sustain themselves in America's market-driven economy because most Americans do not want to pay to experience them.

13. Do the people who will not pay to experience this kind of art know it is supported by their tax dollars?
14. Do most taxpayers think public funding for the arts is appropriate and worthwhile, or do they believe it is inescapable?
15. What kind of art do America's various cultural segments value?
16. Can you describe the characteristics that cause you to value the arts you value?
17. Do standards for evaluating art differ based on what this society calls race?

Plays are best examined from a point of view that allows observation in a larger context that considers: (1) the world of the play and why things happen as they do in that world; (2) the playwright's point of view; and (3) the production values that represent the collaborative efforts of many theatre artists.

Foundation Questions

Some foundation questions delve into the process of creating theatre, others address the playwright's process and goals, and others address how audience members experience the play. One of the simplest and most direct approaches to foundation questions is:

18. What was the playwright trying to do?
19. Did she or he succeed?
20. Was it worth doing?

But these questions raise additional ones:

21. How does one determine what the playwright was trying to do?
22. Can one say a playwright succeeded without first learning what the playwright's goals were?
23. Are certain choices the playwright made in constructing the play apparent? Why did the playwright make those choices?
24. How does a script become a collaborative work of theatre art? Who gets to collaborate and how?
25. As an audience member, did you feel like a participant or an observer? Were you drawn in to the production?
26. Did the play seem to flow or did it seem static? Did the play's tempo and rhythm contribute to your sense of involvement?
27. What did you think about and feel at the end of the production? In retrospect, what did you think and feel about the production in its entirety a full day or more afterward?

ASKING CRITICAL QUESTIONS

Some foundation questions lead to questions that delve more specifically and deeply into a play's use of the six components of theatre Aristotle described: plot, character, theme, dialogue, music (mood and rhythm), and spectacle. Although some Eurocentric theatre analysts have sought to clarify or modernize Aristotle's approach, they generally formulate their analysis around the six components.

28. Do all the production's components form a coherent whole? If not, which components seem not to fit? Why?

    Example: We wrote a play with multiple changes in time and place. We indicated in the script's notes that scenery, props, and costumes must be sufficiently sparse to not slow down the tempo or interrupt the action. We have seen several productions of the play with beautiful scenery, props, and costumes that evoked an appropriate time and place. However, some of the productions were weakened when the action literally came to a halt to move scenery and props.

29. Which components do the playwright or the production staff emphasize or diminish?
30. Which components seem to enhance the playwright's vision?
31. Do some components seem to detract or distract from the playwright's vision?

Style Questions

Asante says an "ism" is a position from which the world is viewed. An "ism" is based on an assumption of power and authority as a way of looking at the world. The style called *realism* views the world from a place of Marx's perspective on economic history, Darwin's perspective on biology, and Freud's perspective on psychology. Proponents of realism named their "ism" in a way that makes their view appear to be the only "real" place from which to view the world. Proponents of realism describe other "isms" in a way that suggests no other position or viewpoint is "real." Other points of view (e.g. classicism, symbolism, impressionism) are rhetorically distanced from reality. Realism further suggests the aim of theatrical performance is to create a faithful representation of reality. Some cultures do not want their art to create faithful representations of reality.

32. What constitutes good and truth with regard to the specific manner in which the play ought to be presented?
33. How do the actors act? Do they seem like real people in a real situation or do they seem to be performing?
34. How do production elements such as scenery, costumes, lighting, and sound contribute to the play's success?
35. What is the play's ideological context? How does the playwright seem to feel about the world of the play? Are there differences between the audience's and the play's reality (time and place of the action; how people relate to some superior force, other types of people; what constitutes "other")?
36. What are the world of the play's significant stated or unstated characteristics? How do characters relate to the environment? Do the characters shape the environment or does the environment shape them? Are the characters comfortable [or alien] in the world of the play? Does the world of the play have significant characteristics that are different from your world?

Example: The men play checkers in *Ceremonies in Dark Old Men* and chess in *Goin' a Buffalo*. The men in both plays exhibit intelligence, focus, discipline, and ample work ethic to complete complex and arduous tasks, yet they do not earn a living at a legal job. Each of these playwrights presumes its intended audience has sufficient prior information to know these men cannot "just get a job" and that racism is a pervasive force that severely limits not only their characters' choices, but also their hopes and aspirations.

Example: Knowledge about racial discrimination in 1950s America enables an audience to know Troy Maxon in August Wilson's *Fences* might very well have been a better baseball player than many in the major leagues. Likewise, Walter Lee Younger in Lorraine Hansberry's *A Raisin in the Sun* has legitimate cause to be angry and legitimate reason to believe he has the requisite work ethic to succeed at running a small business. As with all plausible protagonists, Troy Maxon and Walter Lee Younger have flaws. But their flaws do not obviate the truth that the overwhelming unseen antagonist in each of these plays is racism.

37. At the time and place the play was written, who held political and economic power? Does the playwright endorse or challenge the idea that those who have power and privilege deserve it?
38. At the time and place the play was written, who made up the audience? Why did they attend? What did they expect? How did they behave? What impact does the nature of the play's intended audience have on the play?
39. What impact does the playwright's and the production's source of support seem to have on the play? At the time and place the play was written, how were theatrical productions financed? Were other approvals such as government or church required?
40. Does the play fit a traditional form such as tragedy, comedy, melodrama, satire, farce? If so, which? If not, why not?
41. What in the play reminded you of something you have read or experienced? How did that reminder affect your understanding of the play? Did the play make you think of something in your life in a different way?
42. After finding critical analyses or journalistic reviews of the play, what are the main points expressed in these published opinions? Do you agree or differ with these opinions?
43. How can you use this secondary source material to enhance your thesis/argument?

Texture Questions

The texture encompasses dialogue through hearing, spectacle through seeing, and the mood through feeling.

44. What meaning is conveyed by what the audience's eyes see?
45. Does the information conveyed by settings, costumes, makeup, lighting, etc. enhance the play's structure?

    Examples: In *Fences*, what does it mean to see Troy make progress in building a fence as the play progresses? What does it mean to see him with a baseball bat in his hand? In *A Raisin in the Sun*, what does it mean to see Lena Younger carry a potted plant out of her apartment at the end? What does it mean to see Benetha change to more Afrocentric clothing and hairstyle?

46. When the eye sees a specific environment on stage, one may ask: Why are these characters in this place? Does the environment have some impact on the characters who inhabit it? Does the nature of the place tell the audience something about the characters who inhabit it?
47. Does the eye see different categories of things, places, people (rich/poor, male/female)? Does the environment (setting) contribute to the audience's understanding of these categories?
48. How does the eye see differences between categories of things, places, people? Do different categories of people look or behave differently? How does a production use preconceived notions about different categories of things, places, people to help convey the play's thematic messages?

    Examples: the Jew in *The Merchant of Venice*, the Moor in *Othello*, the Black man in *Six Degrees of Separation*, ideas about being "highborn" in Elizabethan and Restoration plays; twentieth-century ideas about being Black in plays by Eugene O'Neill, Lillian Hellman, Kaufman, and Hart; ideas about being White in plays by Ed Bullins, Amiri Baraka, James Baldwin.

49. For what kind of theatrical space was the play written? What is the impact of any assumed or presumed theatrical convention?
50. How does what the audience's ears hear establish mood, tempo, rhythm, and plausibility; convey information, ideas, and themes; reveal character?
51. What relationship does the play's language have to everyday colloquial usage?
52. How does "what the audience's ears hears" differ from what a reader sees written on a page?
53. Does the script offer potential for nommo (word power) when spoken by the actors? Afrocentric viewpoints eschew Eurocentric literary evaluators who laud "heightened" language for such linguistic imagery as metaphors, similes, analogies, allegories, tropes, and symbols for essentially decorative purposes. Instead, Afrocentric points of view tend to value linguistic imagery that is functional.
54. Does the play have symbols? Hearing words or seeing an object may evoke meaning beyond the identity of the word or object itself. Even character's names can contain symbolic meaning.
55. What is the play's main symbol? Are there additional symbols? What do you think the symbol(s) means to the playwright? Does the symbol enhance or enrich the meaning of the play for you?

Example: In August Wilson's *The Piano Lesson*, the central conflict revolves around an actual piano that must be seen by the audience. The piano is not just a piano, it is a symbol of a family's legacy that the family's ancestors value and endeavor to protect.

56. Does the play contain dramatic irony? Dramatic irony occurs when the audience is privy to some significant information that one or more characters do not know.

Structure Questions

The structure encompasses the plot, character, and theme.

Plot: Only what the audience actually observes is considered plot. When a character tells other characters that something happened, what the character says happened is not plot because the action was not observed by the audience. Only the act of the character saying the thing (not the thing) is plot. While this distinction may seem trivial, it becomes significant if what the character said was not true. Plots often have complications, reversals, and twists. Answering questions about the plot enables a description of the events that move the play from the beginning through the middle to the end and facilitates describing the through-line of the play or creating a plot outline.

57. Who or what is the protagonist?
58. What is the protagonist's goal or desire?
59. What does the protagonist do or discover in each scene that is relevant to the goal?
60. Why did the playwright include the scene?
61. Who is working against the protagonist?
62. What is the play's principal conflict or question? Does it involve an internal conflict in one character? One character against another? One group against another?
63. What is the source that gives rise to the play's conflict?
64. What could the characters have done to prevent or resolve the conflict?
65. How does the beginning generate needed information about the time, place, mood, and style of the play and about the past that enables the audience to make sense of the play's present action?

ASKING CRITICAL QUESTIONS

66. What is the moment at which the play's action begins?
67. What sets the action in motion? How is the conflict introduced?
68. What are the given circumstances, locale, time, environmental conditions, initial attitudes, and relationships of characters, etc.?
69. What are the complications, the series of events (discoveries) that carry the action forward? How does the play move from one complication to another? Are there reversals when the fortunes of a serious character take a decisively downward turn or when the fortunes of a comic character begin to rise? Are there discoveries or recognitions by a main character regarding the relevance of a person, thing, or situation previously unknown or inadequately understood?
70. What is the moment of decision or no return for the main character?
71. How are the complications/conflicts resolved?
72. Do the play's pieces fit together to form a whole? In Afrocentric theatre, the pieces often fit together as a whole without creating a linear or logical or chronological series of events. Sometimes, the parts do not seem to fit except in retrospect. Sometimes, the story begins at the end and circles back to the end at the end.

Character: Asking questions about a character may reveal a larger or deeper issue than a character who just made a series of bad choices. Sometimes characters reveal issues by changing over the course of the play. In other instances, a character does not change but more of the character is revealed over the course of the play. The analogy of peeling away the layers of an onion is often used to illustrate how such characters are revealed.

73. What is the underlying issue the playwright seeks to reveal by showing a character? From the playwright's point of view, what caused the choices that incite the character's conflict or dilemma?
74. How does the character respond to the consequences of those choices?

75. Does the character change? How? What causes the change? Is it just an outward change in appearance or behavior, or a deeper change in values or ideals? How does the audience know the change has taken place? Is it consistent with the character's previously exposed values? Is the change adequately motivated?
76. Instead of a change, does the character reveal deeply rooted traits not previously exposed? Does the revelation come as a complete surprise or was there reason to suspect the character might be capable of the behavior?
77. Do relatively minor characters seem to be present mostly to focus attention on or tell us something about a major character? Such characters are often called "foils." The implication of calling a character a foil is that the character's main function is to make some other character shine brighter.

Example: In *A Raisin in the Sun*, Travis functions as a foil for his father. When Lena insists that Travis hear his father's conversation with Lender, Walter is forced to reveal his true character and refuse to accept money if he agrees to stay out of Clybourne Park. In some instances, heroes require a foil because the audience must learn things about them that they are too modest or fearless or embarrassed to say or do themselves.

78. Does the play have contrasting characters? What do the contrasts tell us about the play?

Example: *Strivers Row* contains two contrasting groups. The strivers pretend to be wealthier and more Eurocentric than they actually are in contrast to the ordinary working-class Black folks who are, for the most part, unassuming and unpretentious.

79. What character moves you in what way?

ASKING CRITICAL QUESTIONS

80. Describe a choice a character makes. Does the choice seem good or bad? Is your point of view about the choice different from the playwright's?
81. What are the physical, social, psychological, and moral traits of the principal characters?
82. How is character revealed in the play? Is this a traditional Eurocentric or Afrocentric way to reveal character?
83. How does the playwright cause characters to be sympathetic or unsympathetic? Does the playwright's effort in this regard succeed with you?
84. Do you find the characters interesting?
85. Do you find the characters plausible?

Theme: *A Handbook to Literature*, fifth edition, provides a definitive statement of theme:

> A central or dominating idea in a work . . . . the abstract concept that is made concrete through its representation in person, *action*, and *image* in the work. No proper *theme* is simply a subject or an activity. Both *theme* and *thesis* imply a subject and a predicate—not just vice in general, say, but some such proposition as "vice seems more interesting than virtue but turns out to be destructive."[139]

86. Does the play contain an identifiable expression of the theme?
87. What does the playwright want the audience to know? What is the overall impact or idea the play conveys? What is the play about (not to be confused with what happens in the play)? What major ideas or topics or implications does the play address?
88. Since there is generally more than one possible view of the theme, which do you find most plausible?
89. How does the playwright convey meaning or theme?

Examples: by making the audience laugh at inappropriate behavior; by creating contrasts or similarities; by putting the words in the mouth of a plausible character. Sometimes the playwright states the theme directly in a character's dialogue. A playwright might also state the theme by having a character that the audience has reason to distrust say the opposite of the theme.

90. A key question about any comedy: What is the playwright getting people to laugh at?
91. What larger (*e.g.* social, ethical) issues does the play address?
92. What is revealed by looking deeper beneath the surface? Does the work expose some deeper truth? If so, what? If not, does the playwright's failure in this regard make it a mediocre play?
93. What is the root cause of any pathology (greed, violence, deceit, hypocrisy) portrayed in the work? Is the pathology endemic to the character's genetic (*e.g.* aristocratic, racial) background, or to the character's social or economic condition, or to the environment?
94. Is the character a surrogate or allegorical representative of a much larger group or issue?
95. What are the philosophical (or cultural) assumptions upon which the play is built?
96. Does the title illuminate the play's theme?

Examples: What do the characters say about fences in the play entitled *Fences*? Lorraine Hansberry's title, *A Raisin in the Sun*, is taken from a poem by Langston Hughes entitled "Harlem." Hughes asks in the poem, "What happens to a dream deferred?" One of several answers Hughes posits is, "Does it dry up like a raisin in the sun?"

Constructing Themes

A theme is a one-sentence statement about a play that articulates the main idea the play expresses from the playwright's view of "the world of the play." One way to approach writing a theme sentence is to complete the sentence: "The playwright wants the audience to believe that . . . ." When composing a theme statement, do not evaluate the playwright's point of view or include character's names.

The theme statement includes three components:
    A. A subject or topic that describes what the play is about.
    B. An evaluative modifier from the playwright's point of view.
    C. An action verb.

If one word can fill both functions, the evaluative modifier and the action verb may be the same word.

Developing a theme statement requires considering ideas about each of the three components. *A Raisin in the Sun* is built on the conflict that arises from how the Younger family will spend the money from Walter Younger, Sr.'s life insurance. Many have concluded the subject or topic that describes what the play is about is money. If one pursues this course, one needs to ask: How deep is the issue of money? Does it cause conflict, or simply expose issues already present in individual characters and relationships? Is it representative of some larger issue? If money is not the root cause of the conflict, what is? Others have asked: What is the root cause of Walter's desire to own a liquor store? Does Walter want to help or hinder his sister's "dream"? Some have concluded the money's significance is that it ignites hope to achieve a deferred dream. They have reasoned Walter's refusal to take Lender's offer of money and move to Clybourne Park indicates the play is not about money. Following the idea that the money is a foil:
    A. Subject or topic: human worth and dignity
    B. Evaluative modifier: intrinsic worth is more important than money
    C. Action verb: substitute, replace, supplant, purchase

Possible theme statements:

Human worth and dignity:
- — cannot be purchased with or replaced by money
- — has intrinsic worth, more important than money

A different approach to constructing a theme for *A Raisin in the Sun* might involve consulting secondary source material. The play's title is taken from a Langston Hughes poem that asks, "what happens to a dream deferred" and answers, "Does it dry up like a raisin in the sun?" What is the "dream"? What causes it to be deferred? How does the family's current living situation compare to Clybourne Park? Is Lena's goal to move into a White neighborhood? Could Lena take the money and buy a "nice" house somewhere else? How long has Walter Sr. been dead? Who is head of the household? What does Walter Lee think about his job, his mother's job, his wife's job? How do each of the other family members feel about Beneatha's desire to become a doctor? If the subject or topic is dreams, evaluative modifiers and action verbs could lead to several possibilities such as:

Dreams:
- — are the linchpin of life, and when pursued, they may lead to fulfillment
- — generate hope, and hope can be fulfilled through hard work and dedication
- — too long deferred induce hopelessness, which in turn leads to self-destructive behavior

News media offers another source of theme ideas. Lorraine Hansberry stated in a television interview: "The most ordinary human being has within him or her an enormous profundity."[140] Following the possibility of ordinary people as subject or topic and profound ideas as the evaluative modifier, an approach to the theme might lead to such a possibility as:

Ordinary people:
- — express profound ideas
- — can pursue profound ideas to actualization

Examples of other questions one might raise when constructing a theme statement for some other plays:

Dutchman: Why the speech about Bessie Smith?

Contribution: When watching "war movies," how do audiences respond when enemy soldiers are killed? When Americans watched a WWII film fifty years ago, how did they respond when American soldiers killed Nazi soldiers or Japanese soldiers? When viewing a typical western (or an action adventure film), how do you feel when the hero kills the villain? Who is the villain in this play and why does he deserve to be killed? The audience realizes what Mrs. Grace Love has done and Eugene Love does not. What is the significance of this dramatic irony? Why does the playwright name the protagonist Grace Love? Why does the playwright have Grace Love sing the songs she sings at the beginning of the play?

Fences: Why does Troy oppose his son's desire to pursue sports? Troy cannot afford to pay for his son to go to college and he does not want his son to get an athletic scholarship. Is Troy opposed to his son's desire to pursue sports or to attend college, or both?

Ceremonies in Dark Old Men: Why don't these men have jobs? Is it because they are lazy or greedy or without sufficient moral fiber to avoid a life of crime? What motivates them to pursue an illegal business? Are the "normal" opportunities to start a legal business open to them?

Goin' a Buffalo: Do most people who live in Los Angeles think Buffalo is a better place to live? What is the underlying cause of this desire to move to Buffalo? Why would a "street walker" want to go to the U.S. city with the largest annual snowfall?

Questions that seem simple on the surface turn out to be not as simple when pondered in depth. The "real world" is replete with complexity, ambiguity, and uncertainty. A belief system based in the ideology of White supremacy and its obligatory racial stereotypes encourages the interpretation of Black theatre in shallow, simple, uncomplicated, obvious ways. Learning to appreciate dramatic art from more than one cultural perspective can enhance one's ability to recognize and cope with the world's complexities, ambiguities, and uncertainties.

END NOTES

1. Mavor Moore, address to the International Council of Fine Arts Deans, Washington, D.C., October 24, 1982. The Canada Council is similar to but broader in scope than the National Endowments for the Arts and Humanities in the USA.
2. Molefi Kete Asante, *Afrocentricity: The Theory of Social Change* (Buffalo: Amulefi Publishing Co., 1980) was our original source, but we have chosen to use a more succinct but less accessible quote from a paper Dr. Asante presented at the International Conference on Black Communication in Bellagio, Italy in 1979, entitled "Intercultural Communication: An Afrocentric Inquiry into Encounter," which was published in *International Conference on Black Communication* (New York: The Rockefeller Foundation, 1980), 5-6.
3. For examples of this documentation, see Robert Farris Thompson, "African Influence on the Art of the United States," in *Black Studies in the University*. ed. Armstead L. Robinson, Craig C. Foster, and Donald H. Ogilvie (New Haven: Yale University Press, 1969), 122-170; Ivan Van Sertima, *They Came Before Columbus* (New York: Random House, 1976); and for an overview of African cultural values as retained in Africa to use as a basis for comparison with African cultural retentions in the Americas, see John S. Mbiti, *African Religion and Philosophy* (New York: Praeger, 1969).
4. Carter G. Woodson, *The Mis-Education of the Negro* (Washington, D. C.: The Associated Publishers, Inc., 1933), xiii.
5. [W.E.B. DuBois], "Krigwa Players Little Negro Theatre: The Story of a Little Theatre Movement," *The Crisis*, 32, No.3 (July, 1926), 134.
6. A. Peter Bailey, "The Contemporary Black Theatre Movement," *The Crisis*, 90, No.2 (February, 1983), 22.

7. W. E. B. DuBois, *The Souls of Black Folk* (1903; rpt. New York: New American Library, 1969), 45.
8. Carlton Molette, "Aristotle's Union of Rhetoric and Dramatic Theory," *The Southern Speech Journal*, 34, No.1 (Fall 1968), 47-51, suggests that the art versus rhetoric dichotomy is a false one, even in as Eurocentric a conceptual framework as Aristotle's.
9. Maulana Karenga, *Kawaida Theory: An Introductory Outline* (Inglewood, California: Kawaida Publications) Karenga devotes a chapter to each of the seven elements that comprise a culture.
10. The process used to determine the meaning of words is described by the editors: "*The World Book Dictionary* is based on an extensive quotation file containing more than three million quotations collected by experienced readers over a period of twenty-five years. These are culled from a wide sampling of contemporary magazines, newspapers, scholarly and technical journals, and books. Through an extensive reading program, the dictionary staff of editors and researchers constantly accumulates information on words, meanings, and usages," 4.
11. Cheryl M. Fields, "Controversial Book Spurs Scholars' Defense of the Legacy of Margaret Mead," *Chronicle of Higher Education* (May 11, 1983), 28. The quote is by George E. Marcus, chairman of the anthropology department, Rice University, Houston, Texas.
12. Jacob H. Carruthers, "The Wisdom of Governance in Kemet," *Kemet and the African Worldview*, eds. Maulana Karenga and Jacob Carruthers (Los Angeles: University of Sankore Press, 1986), 3.
13. Cheikh Anta Diop, *Civilization or Barbarism: An Authentic Anthropology*, trans. Yaa-Lengi Meema Ngemi, ed. Harold J. Salemson and Marjolijn de Jager (Brooklyn: Lawrence Hill Books, 1991), 362.
14. Maulana Karenga, selected and retranslated, *Selections from The Husia*, (Los Angeles: The University of Sankore Press, 1984), 95.
15. Karenga, 41-42.
16. Diop, *Civilization or Barbarism*, 129.
17. Cheikh Anta Diop, *The Cultural Unity of Black Africa* (London: Karnak House, 1989), 148.

END NOTES

18. Morris Massey, *What You Are Is Where You Were When*, video cassette (Farmington, Michigan: Magnetic Video Corporation, 1976).
19. Feagin and Vera, *White Racism* 1995, ix.
20. Race: Are We so Different? A Project of the American Anthropological Association. www.understandingrace.org.
21. Derald Wing Su, "Dismantling the Myth of a Color-Blind Society." *Black Issues in Higher Education*, November 6, 2003, back cover.
22. Molefi K. Asante, *Erasing Racism*. (Promethius Books, 2003), 16.
23. *August Wilson: The American Dream in Black and White*. Produced and Directed by Tony Knox. Princeton, NJ: Films for the Humanities and Sciences, 1990. Videocasette.
24. Kariamu Welsh-Asante, ed. *African Aesthetics: Keeper of the Traditions* (Philadelphia: Temple University Press, 1987), 53. For a larger discussion see Molefi Kete Asante, *The Afrocentric Idea*.
25. Farai Chideya, *Don't Believe the Hype: Fighting Cultural Misinformation about African-Americans* (New York: Penguin Books USA, 1995), xvii and xx.
26. Oscar G. Brockett, *History of the Theatre* (Boston: Allyn and Bacon, 1968) and Sixth Edition (Boston: Allyn and Bacon, 1991), 10-11.
27. Cheikh Anta Diop, *The African Origin of Civilization: Myth or Reality*, trans. Mercer Cook (Westport: Lawrence Hill and Company, 1974), 230.
28. Brockett, 9.
29. Brockett, 9.
30. E. A. Wallis Budge, *From Fetish to God in Ancient Egypt* (New York: Dover, 1988), 263.
31. Herodotus, *History*, Book II, trans. George Rawlinson (New York: Tudor, 1928), 99, quoted in Diop, *The African Origin of Civilization*, 234.
32. Brockett, 10.
33. Brockett, 7.
34. Budge, *From Fetish to God in Ancient Egypt*, 23.
35. Budge, 23-24.
36. Diop, *Civilization or Barbarism*, 337.

37. Diop, 337.
38. Sir Banister Fletcher, *A History of Architecture on the Comparative Method* (New York: Charles Scribner's Sons, 1963), 27.
39. Fletcher, 30.
40. Diop, 320.
41. Brockett, 8.
42. Cheikh Anta Diop, "Origin of the Ancient Egyptian," *General History of Africa*, Chapter 1 in Vol 2 (The UNESCO Press, 1981), in *Egypt Revisited*, Vol. 10, *Journal of African Civilizations*, ed. by Ivan Van Sertima (New Brunswick: Transaction Publishers, 1989), 9.
43. Cheikh Anta Diop, *Precolonial Black Africa* (Westport: Lawrence Hill and Company, 1987), 212-234. Diop documents this migration with linguistic evidence and describes it from the perspective of physical artifacts and social patterns.
44. Several writers attribute different first names to Mr. Brown. James Hatch and Omanii Abdullah, *Black Playwrights, 1823-1977: An Annotated Bibliography of Plays* (New York: R. R. Bowker, 1977), 29; call him Henry Brown. Jonathan Dewberry, "The African Grove Theatre and Company," *Black American Literature Forum*, 16, No.4 (Winter, 1982), 128; says William Henry Brown. Oscar G. Brockett, *History of the Theatre*, 6th ed. (Needham Heights, MA: Allyn and Bacon, 1991), 422; says James Brown. Fannin S. Belcher, Jr., *The Place of the Negro in the Evolution of the American Theatre, 1767-1940*, Diss. Yale 1945 (Ann Arbor: University Microfilms International, 1969), 292; states "There is no infallible evidence that 'James' was his first name, but it seemed the most probable one . . . in the . . . New York City Directory for 1820 and 1821." George A. Thompson, Jr., *A Documentary History of the African Theatre (*Evanston: Northwestern University Press, 1998), 3. The most thorough study to date, based on New York city tax records and censuses, Thompson says his name was William Alexander Brown.
45. Benjamin Brawley, *The Negro Genius* (New York: Dodd, Mead and Company, 1937), 59. Brawley puts William Wells Brown's birth year in 1815, give or take a year. Brawley states William Wells Brown escaped

from slavery in 1834 when he was about nineteen years old. Even if we allow for a reasonable margin of error in William Wells Brown's birth date, it is clear he would not have been old enough to start a second career in 1817 as owner-manager of a theatre. Certainly, William Wells Brown was not a free adult living in New York in 1817.

46. George C. D. Odell, *Annals of the New York Stage* (New York: Columbia University Press, 1928), III, p.35 lists the "first reference with which I am familiar" as *The National Advocate*, August 3, 1821.

47. See Herbert Marshall and Mildred Stock, *Ira Aldridge: The Negro Tragedian* (New York: Macmillan Company, 1958), 31. They quote the *Anglo-African Magazine* of January 1860, having asserted on p.11 that it is "the only known piece of printed matter dealing with Aldridge's early life, and the correctness of which is confirmed by his own statement in a letter to the author some months after its publication. It was written by Dr. James McCune Smith, a schoolmate of Aldridge at the African Free School in New York."

48. "Professionalism" in the theatre is generally addressed by two standards: (1) artistic quality and (2) financial remuneration that allows pursuit of their art on a full-time basis. Participation by such actors as Ira Aldridge and James Hewlett provides reason to assume the African Company met minimum standards of artistic quality of their time and place. Ticket prices address the issue of financial remuneration. Admission prices at New York theatres in 1822 and 1823 as cited by Odell are: "The price of admission for the African Company" box, 75 cents; pit, 50 cents; gallery, 37-1/2 cents (p.70). "Tickets at Vauxhall Gardens . . . were high 50 cents" (p.79). "With Hilson's arrival, the prices at the City Theatre were raised to 75 cents in the boxes, and 50 cents in the pit; the gallery remained at 25 cents" (p.66). "Bad luck in Warren Street is indicated by the fact that admission to the pit was not reduced to 25 cents" (p.68).

49. Odell, 70, and Laurence Hutton, "The Negro on the Stage," *Harpers*, 79 (June, 1889), 133.

50. Brockett, *History*, 335 and 377.

51. George A. Thompson, Jr., *A Documentary History of the African Theatre* (Evanston: North western University Press, 1998), 87 and 138.

52. Brockett mentions this is an event of some significance beginning with the 2nd edition (1974) of his *History of the Theatre* (pp.376-377); however, there is no mention of the African Company in the 1st edition.
53. We spent some weeks in St Vincent and the Grenadines gathering information about Chatoyer. Much of that information was garnered through interviews and from materials not readily available in the USA.
54. "Psyches different between races, psychologists say." *Houston Chronicle*, 22 May 1983, Sec.3. p.4. col.1.
55. As quoted in Marshall and Stock, pp.33-34 from *The National Advocate*, Sept. 21, 1821; on pp.34-36 from *The American* of January 10, 1822.
56. As quoted in Marshall and Stock, pp.33-34 from *The National Advocate*; p.38 from the *Star* of December 22, 1825; also, see Plate 2, between p.40 and 41.
57. As quoted in Marshall and Stock, 34-36.
58. Marshall and Stock pp.37-39.
59. As quoted in Marshall and Stock, p.39 from a letter by Ira Aldridge to Dr. James McCune Smith, who was according to Marshall and Stock (p.11), "a schoolmate of Aldridge at the African Free School in New York. Dr. Smith studied at the University of Glasgow, BA, 1832; MA, 1833; MD, 1834. He became an important figure in the medical profession in New York as well as a scientific writer of note."
60. Doris E. Abramson, *Negro Playwrights in the American Theatre, 1925-1959* (New York: Columbia University Press, 1969), inside front dust cover, x, 14.
61. William Wells Brown, *The Escape; or a Leap for Freedom* (Boston: 1858; rpt. Philadelphia: Rhistoric Publications, n.d.).
62. John Hope Franklin, *From Slavery to Freedom* (New York: Vintage Books, 1969), 232.
63. William Wells Brown, Act I, Scene 1, pp.17-20 and Act I, Scene 2, p.23.
64. William Wells Brown, Act I, Scene 1, pp.18-21 and Act III, Scene 5, p.33.

END NOTES

65. Loften Mitchell, *Black Drama* (New York: Hawthorn Books, Inc., 1967), 30-31.
66. Donald Bogle, *Toms, Coons, Mulattoes, Mammies, and Bucks: An Interpretive History of Blacks in American Films* (New York: Viking Press, 1973), 10.
67. Ibid, 16.
68. Barbara and Carlton Molette, "The Ripoff King," *The Informer and Texas Freeman* (Houston), 15 October, 1977, 6.
69. William Cockerham, "One of the Biggest Frauds in History?" *Houston Chronicle*, August 23, 1981, Zest, 8 and 39.
70. Ibid.
71. Ibid.
72. Arthur M. Schlesinger, Jr., *The Age of Jackson* (Boston: Little, Brown and Company, 1945), 427.
73. Schlesinger, 450.
74. Ed Siegel, "Edward Albee, still playing rough: 'Slugging,' not comforting, is this master's aim," March 7, 2004. Copyright 2006, Globe Newspaper Company.
75. Thorstein Veblen, *The Theory of the Leisure Class* (1899; rpt. New York: New American Library, 1953).
76. Henry Louis Gates, Jr., "The Chitlin Circuit," The New Yorker, February 3, 1997, 44-55. From the 1920s to the present, 'chitlin circuit' performances have been immensely popular in and useful for Black American communities.
77. Martha Hyer, *Ethnic Dance: Roundtrip to Trinidad*, featuring Geoffrey Holder and Carmen deLavallade. Produced for the National Educational Television and Radio Center by the Lowell Institute Cooperative Broadcasting Council, WGBH, Boston, 1960. Black and white film, twenty-nine minutes.
78. *August Wilson: The American Dream in Black and White*, produced and directed by Tony Knox, Films for the Humanities and Sciences, Princeton, N.J., 1990.

79. August Wilson, "The Ground on Which I Stand." *American Theatre*, September, 1996, 14-16, 71-74. Also published in several anthologies and under separate cover.
80. Ben Brantley, "In the Rush to Progress, the Past is Never Too Far Behind." *New York Times*, May 9, 2007. nytimes.com/learning/teachers/featured_articles20070511friday.html
81. August Wilson, "A World of Ideas." Interview by Bill Moyers. WNET/New York and WTTW/Chicago, 1988.
82. Lewis Nkosi, *Home and Exile* (London: Longmans, Green and Company, Ltd., 1965), 108.
83. Efua Sutherland, "The Drama-Theatre Argument: A Clash of Concepts," *Encore* (National Association of Dramatic and Speech Arts, 1970), 3-8.
84. Malidoma Patrice Somé, *Ritual* (New York: Penguin Group, 1993), 67.
85. Earl L. Stewart. *African American Music: An Introduction* (Shirmer Books, imprint of Simon & Schuster Macmillan, 1998), 166.
86. Kwanzaa is celebrated by many African-Americans and some consider it an alternative to Christmas. Kwanza is a week long, from December 26 to January 1. Ceremonial aspects honor family, children, community, and nation. Presents are given to children as a token of the fruits of the labor of the parents and as a reward for being contributing members of the family.
87. Henri Frankfort, *Ancient Egyptian Religion* (New York: Harper & Row, 1948), p.viii.
88. Mbiti, 2.
89. Diop, *African Origin of Civilization*, 230.
90. George and Portia Kernodle, *Invitation to the Theatre* (New York: Harcourt Brace Jovanovich, Inc., 1971), 209.
91. Temple University Press, 1987, 58-70.
92. Stewart, 5-8.
93. Nkosi, 111.
94. Although there is no substitute for experiencing actual Afrocentric church services, several excellent examples of Afrocentric sermons are available

END NOTES

as audio recordings. Rev. C. L. Franklin, *The Twenty-Third Psalm*, Chess, 9309, n.d., provides such an example.

95. Opinions that were expressed in widely read and respected periodicals in the early 1970s illustrate the manner by which African-American theatre is demeaned by calling it propaganda. The sampling of such articles includes a spectrum of Eurocentric writers, including a Pulitzer-Prize-winning playwright who happens to be African-American.

   Eric Bentley, "Must I Side With Blacks or Whites?" *New York Times*, Arts and Leisure, 23 January 1972, 1 and 12.

   Charles Gordone, "Yes, I am a Black Playwright, But . . .," *New York Times*, Arts and Leisure. 25 January 1970, 1 and 11.

   Walter Kerr, "We are Left with Only the Nightmares," *New York Times*, Arts and Leisure. 6 December 1970, 5 and 7.

   Hilton Kramer, "Black Art and Expedient Politics," *New York Times*, Arts and Leisure. 7 June 1970, 19.

96. Ned A. Bowman, "A Roundup of Recent Theatre Buildings." *Theatre Design and Technology*, No.5 (December 1968), 20.

97. Woodie King, *Black Theatre: The Making of a Movement* (San Francisco, California, newsreel, 1978).

98. Hillyard Robinson earned a BA and MA in architecture from Columbia University, joined Howard University's School of Architecture faculty in 1924. He designed the Howard University building constructed in 1961 that contains the Ira Aldridge Theatre and Crampton Auditorium, as well as a museum space and facilities for the academic departments of art, drama, and music.

99. Mbiti, 17-19.

100. Earl L. Stewart. *African American Music: An Introduction* (New York: Shirmer Books imprint of Simon & Schuster Macmillan, 1998), 8-9.

101. Stewart, 23.

102. Stewart, 10-11.

103. Stewart, 11.

104. Molefi Asante, *The Egyptian Philosophers: Ancient African Voices From Imhotep to Akhenaten* (Chicago: African American Images) 50. It is not clear if Kagemni wrote the text or the text was written to him by his mentor.
105. Asante, 52.
106. Although *The Signifying Monkey* is described in such works as Roger D. Abrahams' *Deep Down in the Jungle*, 1st revised ed. (Chicago: Aldine, 1970), 113-119, 142-146, 153-156; and Langston Hughes and Arna Bontemps, ed., *Book of Negro Folklore* (New York: Dodd, Mead and Company, 1958), 363-366, audio recordings offer better insight into oral presentations. Abrahams mentions several recordings on 145-146.
107. Abrahams, 100-103, 120-129; and Hughes and Bontemps, 366-367.
108. J. C. deGraft-Johnson, *African Glory* (Baltimore: Black Classic Press, 1986), 129.
109. Richard Coe, "Soul Plays," *Washington Post*, 30 Oct. 1970, Sec. D, 8.
110. Abram Hill, *Strivers Row*, TS, p.I-2-67. The play script of this African-American classic, first performed in 1940, was first published in 1991.
111. Langston Hughes, *Simply Heavenly* (New York: Dramatists Play Service, Inc., 1959), 62.
112. Hughes, 30-31.
113. Hughes, pp. 20-21 for dialogue leading to the song. Langston Hughes, book and lyrics, *Simply Heavenly*, music and orchestration by David Martin, with Claudia McNeil, Melvin Stewart, and Anna English, Columbia, OL 5240, n.d.
114. Hughes, 62.
115. Hughes, 72.
116. Joseph A. Walker, *The River Niger* (New York: Hill and Wang, 1973), dedication page.
117. William Branch, "A Medal for Willie," in *Black Drama*, ed. Woodie King and Ron Milner (New York: New American Library, 1971), 470-471.
118. Douglas Turner Ward, in *Classic Plays from the Negro Ensemble Company*, ed. Paul Carter Harrison and Gus Edwards (Pittsburgh: University of Pittsburgh Press, 1995), xxiv.

END NOTES

119. Philip Hopkins, "A review of *Russell Simmons Def Poetry Jam on Broadway*," http://www.theatermania.com/broadway/russell-simmons-def-poetry-jam-on-broadway_17987/.
120. Personal interview with the newspaper critic whose identity will not be revealed since confidentiality was requested at the time, November 8, 1971.
121. Ralph Ellison, *Invisible Man* (New York: The New American Library, 1952), 7.
122. Carlton and Barbara Molette, *Rosalee Pritchett* (New York: Dramatists Play Service, 1972), 4.
123. Barbara and Carlton Molette, *Presidential Timber* (Atlanta: unpublished script, 2010), 17.
124. Assertions about audience response are based on observations of audience responses to a 1976 production of *The Escape*, produced by Texas Southern University's School of Communications.
125. Ossie Davis, *Purlie Victorious* (New York: Samuel French, Inc., 1961), 37 and 63.
126. Compare Ernest J. Gaines, *The Autobiography of Miss Jane Pittman* (1971; rpt. New York: Bantam, 1979); to the made-for-TV motion picture based on the Gaines novel with the same title, starring Cicely Tyson, screenplay by Tracy Keenan Wynn, produced by Robert W. Christiansen and Rick Rosenberg, directed by John Korty, CBS-TV Special, 1974, video disc rpt.
127. Douglas Turner Ward, *Day of Absence* (New York: Dramatists Play Service, 1966), 41.
128. James Baldwin, *Blues for Mister Charlie* (New York: Dell Publishing Co., Inc., 1964), 5.
129. Baldwin, 6.
130. Ann Hodges, "People make their choices," *Houston Chronicle*, 15 March 1984, Sec.5, p.6, cols. 1-3; and the display advertisement "People's Choice Awards" on the same page cols. 4-5. This material can probably be verified in the March 15, 1984, issue of any major metropolitan newspaper in the USA.

131. Alex McNeil, *Total Television* (New York: Penguin Books, 1991), 1060-1062. Data after 1989-1990 season was obtained by telephone from the research director of the NBC affiliate station in Baltimore, Maryland.

132. At least two factors leave room for doubt when comparing the popularity of television programs that first aired decades apart: (1) Cable television's rapid growth and (2) America's growth in both population and number of viewing devices per family.

133. "Country Singers are People's Choice," *Baltimore Sun,* 19 March 1992, D1. We focus on the People's Choice Awards to the exclusion of other such awards because People's Choice Awards are determined by a poll conducted by the Gallup organization. Most other award winners are selected by critics, industry colleagues, or some other effort to generate what will be regarded by the general public as "expert opinion." We are interested in discovering and commenting on the general public's views rather than those of industry colleagues, newspaper critics, or any other form of expert opinion.

134. Donald Bogle, *Toms, Coons, Mulattoes, Mammies, & Bucks* (New York: The Viking Press, Inc., 1973), 8.

135. Alex McNeil, 276.

136. "Country Singers are People's Choice," *Baltimore Sun,* 19 March 1992, D1.

137. Faye Levine, *The Culture Barons* (New York: Thomas Y. Crowell, 1976), 102.

138. Summarized from Michael Scriven and Richard Paul, www.sonoma.edu/cthink/University/univlibrary/cthistory.nclk

139. Holman, C. Hugh and William Harmon. *A Handbook to Literature*, fifth edition. (New York: Macmillan, 1986), 502.

140. Lorraine Hansberry. Produced and written by Ralph J. Tangney. Films for the Humanities, 1975.

BIBLIOGRAPHY

Works Cited

Books and Articles

Abrahams, Roger D. *Deep Down in the Jungle*. 1st rev. ed. Chicago: Aldine Publishing Company, 1970.

Abramson, Doris E. *Negro Playwrights in the American Theatre, 1925-1959*. New York: Columbia University Press, 1969.

Asante, Molefi Kete. *The Afrocentric Idea*. Philadelphia: Temple University Press, 1987.

—*Afrocentricity: The Theory of Social Change*. Buffalo: Amulefi Publishing Co., 1980.

—*Erasing Racism*. Amherst: Promethius Books, 2003.

—"Intercultural Communication: An Afrocentric Inquiry into Encounter." In *International Conference on Black Communication*, Bellagio, Italy, 1979. Ed. Bruce E. Williams and Orlando L. Taylor. New York: The Rockefeller Foundation, 1980.

—"Location Theory and African Aesthetics." *The African Aesthetic*. Ed. Kariamu Welsh-Asante. Connecticut: Praeger, 1994: 53.

Bailey, Peter A. "The Contemporary Black Theatre Movement." *Crisis* 90, No.2 (1983): 22-25.

Barashango, Ishakamusa. *Afrikan Genesis*. Silver Spring: Fourth Dynasty Publishing Company, 1991.

Belcher, Fannin S., Jr. *The Place of the Negro in the Evolution of the American Theatre, 1767-1940*, Diss. Yale, 1945. Ann Arbor: University Microfilms International, 1969.

Bentley, Eric. "Must I Side With Blacks or Whites." *New York Times*, Arts and Leisure, 23 January 1972: 1+.

Bogle, Donald. *Toms, Coons, Mulattoes, Mammies, and Bucks: An Interpretive History of Blacks in American Films*. New York: Viking Press, 1973.

Bowman, Ned A. "A Roundup of Recent Theatre Buildings." *Theatre Design and Technology*. No. 5 (1968): 10-23.

Brantley, Ben. "In the Rush to Progress, the Past is Never Too Far Behind." *New York Times* 9 May 2007. *New York Times Online*. 11 June 2007.

Brawley, Benjamin. *The Negro Genius*. New York: Dodd, Mead and Company, l937.

Brockett, Oscar G. *The Essential Theatre*. New York: Holt, Rinehart and Winston, 1980.

—*History of the Theatre*. Second ed. Boston: Allyn and Bacon, 1974.

—*History of the Theatre*. Sixth ed. Boston: Allyn and Bacon, 1991.

Chideya, Farai. *Don't Believe the Hype: Fighting Cultural Misinformation About African Americans* (New York: Penguin Books USA, 1995).

Cockerham, William. "One of the Biggest Frauds in History?" *Houston Chronicle*. 23 August 1981, *Zest*, 8+.

Coe, Richard. "Soul Plays." Rev. of *Dr. B. S. Black* by Carlton Molette. *Washington Post*, 30 October 1970, Sec. D, 8.

DeGraft-Johnson, J. C. *African Glory*. Baltimore: Black Classic Press, 1986.

DewBerry, Johnathan. "The African Grove Theatre and Company." *Black American Literature Forum*. 16, No. 4 (1982): 128-131.

Diop, Cheikh Anta. *The African Origin of Civilization: Myth or Reality*. Translated by Mercer Cook. Westport: Lawrence Hill and Company, 1974.

—*Civilization or Barbarism: An Authentic Anthropology*. Translated by Yaa-Lengi Meema Ngemi. Edited by Harold J. Salemson and Marjolijn de Jager. Brooklyn: Lawrence Hill Books, 1991.

—*The Cultural Unity of Black Africa*. London: Karnak House, 1989.

—*Precolonial Black Africa: A Comparative Study of the Political and Social Systems of Europe and Black Africa, from Antiquity to the Formation of Modern States*. Translated by Harold Salemson. Westport: Lawrence Hill and Company, 1987.

DuBois, [W.E.B.] "Krigwa Players Little Negro Theatre: The Story of a Little Theatre Movement." *The Crisis*. July 1926: 134-136.

—*The Souls of Black Folk*. 1903; rpt. New York: New American Library, 1969.

Ellison, Ralph. *Invisible Man*. New York: New American Library, 1952.

BIBLIOGRAPHY

Fields, Cheryl M. "Controversial Book Spurs Scholars' Defense of the Legacy of Margaret Mead." *Chronicle of Higher Education.* 11 May 1983, pp.28-29.

Fletcher, Sir Banister. *A History of Architecture on the Comparative Method.* Seventeenth Edition. New York: Charles Scribner's Sons, 1963.

Franklin, John Hope. *From Slavery to Freedom.* New York: Vintage Books, 1969.

Gaines, Ernest J. *The Autobiography of Miss Jane Pittman.* 1971; rpt. New York: Bantam, 1979.

Gordone, Charles. "Yes, I am a Black Playwright, But . . ." *New York Times*, Arts and Leisure, 25 January 1970: 1+.

Harrison, Paul Carter and Gus Edwards ed. *Classic Plays from the Negro Ensemble Company*, Pittsburgh: University of Pittsburgh Press, 1995.

Hatch, James V., and Omanii Abdullah, ed. *Black Playwrights, 1823-1977: An Annotated Bibliography of Plays.* New York: R. R. Bowker Company, 1977.

Hodges, Ann. "People make their choices." *Houston Chronicle,* 15 March 1984, Sec. 5, p. 6, cols. 1-3.

Holman, C. Hugh and William Harmon. *A Handbook to Literature*, Fifth Edition. New York: Macmillan, 1986

Hughes, Langston, and Arna Bontemps, ed. *Book of Negro Folklore.* New York: Dodd, Mead and Company, 1958.

Hutton, Laurence. "The Negro on the Stage." *Harper's.* June 1889: 133.

Karenga, Maulana. *Kawaida Theory: An Introductory Outline.* Inglewood: Kawaida Publications, 1980.

—Selected and Retranslated. *Selections from the Husia: Sacred Wisdom of Ancient Egypt.* Los Angeles: The University of Sankore Press, 1984.

Karenga, Maulana and Jacob H. Carruthers, eds. *Kemet and the African Worldview.* Los Angeles: University of Sankore Press, 1986.

Kerr, Walter. "We are Left with Only the Nightmares." *New York Times*, Arts and Leisure, 6 December 1970: 5+.

Kernodle, George and Portia Kernodle. *Invitation to the Theatre.* New York: Harcourt Brace Jovanovich, Inc., 1971.

Kramer, Hilton. "Black Art and Expedient Politics." *New York Times*, Arts and Leisure, 7 June 1970: 19.

Levine, Faye. *The Culture Barons.* New York: Thomas Y. Crowell, 1976.

Marshall, Herbert and Mildred Stock. *Ira Aldridge: The Negro Tragedian*. New York: Macmillan Company, 1958.

Mbiti, John S. *African Religion and Philosophy*. New York: Praeger, 1969.

McNeil, Alex. *Total Television*. New York: Penguin, 1991.

Mitchell, Loften. *Black Drama*. New York: Hawthorn Books, Inc., 1967.

Molette, Barbara and Carlton Molette. "The Ripoff King." *The Informer and Texas Freeman* (Houston). 15 October, 1977: 6.

Molette, Carlton. "Artistotle's Union of Rhetoric and Dramatic Theory." *The Southern Speech Journal*. 34, No. 1 (1968): 47-51.

Moore, Mavor. Address to the International Council of Fine Arts Deans, Washington, D.C. 24 October 1982.

Nkosi, Lewis. *Home and Exile*. London: Longmans, Green and Company, Ltd., 1965.

Odell, George C. D. *Annals of the New York Stage*. New York: Columbia University Press, 1928. Vol. III.

"Psyches different between races, psychologists say." *Houston Chronicle*, 22 May 1983, Sec. 3, 4, col. 1.

Schlesinger, Arthur M., Jr. *The Age of Jackson*. Boston: Little, Brown and Company, 1945.

Stewart, Earl L. *African American Music: An Introduction*, Shirmer Books, an imprint of Simon & Schuster Macmillan, 1998.

Sutherland, Efua. "The Drama-Theatre Argument: a Clash of Concepts." *Encore*, 1970: 3-8.

Thompson, Robert Farris. "African Influence on the Art of the United States." In *Black Studies in the University*. Ed. Armstead L. Robinson, Craig C. Foster, and Donald H. Ogilvie. New Haven: Yale University Press, 1969: 22-170.

Van Sertima, Ivan. ed. *Egypt Revisited*. Vol. 10, *Journal of African Civilizations*. New Brunswick: Transaction Publishers, 1989.

—*They Came Before Columbus*. New York: Random House, 1976.

Veblen, Thorsten. *The Theory of the Leisure Class*. 1899; rpt. New York: New American Library, 1953.

Wilson, August. "The Ground on which I Stand." *American Theatre*, September, 1996: 14-16, 71-74. Also published in several anthologies and under separate cover.

Woodson, Carter G. *The Mis-Education of the Negro*. Washington, D. C.: The Associated Publishers, Inc., 1933.

The World Book Dictionary. 1979 ed.

Film, Video, and Audio Recordings

August Wilson: The American Dream in Black and White. Produced and Directed by Tony Knox. Princeton, NJ: Films for the Humanities and Sciences, 1990 (VHS).

Autobiography of Miss Jane Pittman. Writ. Ernest J. Gaines. Screenplay by Tracy Keenan Wynn. Prod. Robert W. Christiansen and Rick Rosenberg. Dir. John Korty. CBS-TV Special, 1974. Video disc rpt.

Ethnic Dance: Roundtrip to Trinidad. Writ. Martha Hyer. With Geoffrey Holder and Carmen deLavallade. Prod. National Educational Television and Radio Center by the Lowell Institute Cooperative Broadcasting Council, WGBH, Boston, 1960. Black and white film. 29 minutes.

Franklin, C. L., Rev. *The Twenty-Third Psalm*. Chess, 9309, n.d.

Griffith, D. W., dir. *The Birth of a Nation*. Mutual, 1915.

King. Writ. and dir. Abby Mann. Prod. Paul Maslansky. NBC. February 1978.

King, Woodie, Jr. *Black Theatre: The Making of a Movement*. San Francisco: California Newsreel, 1978.

Massey, Morris. *What You are is where You were when*. Farmington, Michigan: Magnetic Video Corporation, 1976.

Wilson, August. Interview by Bill Moyers. "A World of Ideas." WNET/New York and WTTW/Chicago, 1988.

Plays by Black Playwrights

Baldwin, James. *The Amen Corner*. New York: Dial Press, 1968. First prod. 1954.

—*Blues for Mister Charlie*. New York: Dell Publishing Co., Inc., 1964. First prod. 1964.

Branch, William. "A Medal for Willie." In *Black Drama*. Ed. Woodie King and Ron Milner. New York: New American Library, 1971. First prod. 1951.

Brown, [James]. *King Shotaway*. Script not extant. First documented prod. 1823.

—*Tom and Jerry, or Life in London*. Adapted from play by Pierce Egan. Script not extant. First prod. c. 1822.

Brown, William Wells. *The Escape: or a Leap for Freedom*. 1858; rpt. Philadelphia: Rhistoric Publication, n.d. Date of first production unknown.

Childress, Alice. *Wedding Band*. New York: Samuel French, 1973. First prod. 1967.

—*Wine in the Wilderness*. New York: Dramatists Play Service, 1969. First prod. 1969.

Cotter, Joseph S. *Caleb, the Degenerate: A Study of the Types, Customs, and Needs of the American Negro*. 1901; rpt. in *Black Theatre USA*. Ed. James V. Hatch. New York: Free Press, 1974. First production unknown.

Davis, Ossie. *Purlie Victorious*. New York: Samuel French, 1961. First prod. 1961.

Elder, Lonnie. *Ceremonies in Dark Old Men*. New York: Samuel French, 1965. 1969.

Fuller, Charles. *A Soldiers' Play*. New York: Samuel French, l982. First prod. 1981.

Gordone, Charles. *No Place to be Somebody*. New York: Bobbs-Merrill Company, 1969. First prod. 1969.

Hansberry, Lorraine. *A Raisin in the Sun*. New York: Random House, 1959. First prod. 1959.

Hill Abram, *Strivers Row*. TS. First production 1939.

Hughes, Langston. *Mulatto*. 1931; rpt. in *Five Plays by Langston Hughes*. Ed. Webster Smalley. Bloomington: Indiana University Press, 1963. First prod. 1935.

—*Simply Heavenly*. New York: Dramatists Play Service, Inc., 1959. First prod. 1957.

Lee, Leslie. *First Breeze of Summer*. New York: Samuel French, 1975. First prod. 1975.

Mason, Judi Ann. *Livin' Fat*. New York: Samuel French, 1974. First prod. 1976.

Matheus, John. *Ti Yette*. In *Plays and Pageants from the Life of the Negro*. Ed. Willis Richardson. Washington, D. C. The Associated Publishers, 1930. First production unknown.

Mitchell, Loften. *Star of the Morning*. In *Black Theatre USA*. Ed. James V. Hatch. New York: Free Press, 1974. First prod. 1955.

—*Tell Pharoah*. In *The Black Teacher and the Dramatic Arts*. Ed. William R. Reardon and Thomas D. Pawley. Westport: Negro Universities Press, 1970. First prod. 1968.

Molette, Carlton. *Dr. B. S. Black*. In *Encore*, 14 (1970), Tallahassee. First prod. 1969.

Molette, Carlton and Barbara. *Rosalee Pritchett*. New York: Dramatists Play Service, 1972. First prod. 1970.

Shine, Ted. *Contribution*. New York: Dramatists Play Service, 1970. First prod. 1969.

—*Idabel's Fortune*. TS. First prod. 1969.

Walker, Joseph. *The River Niger*. New York: Hill and Wang, 1973. First prod. 1972.

Ward, Douglas Turner. *Day of Absence and Happy Ending*. New York: Dramatists Play Service, 1966. First prod. 1965.

Williams, Samm-Art. *Home*. New York: Dramatists Play Service, 1979. First prod. 1979.

Young, Clarence. *Perry's Mission*. TS. First prod. 1971.

Additional Works Recommended

Anthologies of Plays by Black Playwrights

Asante, Molefi and Abu S. Abarry. *Africa Intellectual Heritage*. Philadelphia: Temple University Press, 1996.

Barksdale, Richard, and Keneth Kinnamon, ed. *Black Writers of America*. New York: The Macmillan Company, 1972.

Branch, William, ed. *Black Thunder: An Anthology of Contemporary African American Drama*. New York: Mentor, 1992.

Couch, William, Jr. *New Black Playwrights*. Baton Rouge: Louisiana State University Press, 1968.

Elam, Harry, Jr., and Robert Alexander, ed. *Colored Contradictions: An Anthology of Contemporary African American Plays*. New York: Penguin Books, 1996.

Hamalian, Leo and James V. Hatch, ed. *The Roots of African American Drama: An Anthology of Early Plays, 1858-1938*. Detroit: Wayne State University Press, 1991.

Harrison, Paul Carter. *Totem Voices: Plays from the Black World Repertory*. New York: Grove Press, 1989.

—and Gus Edwards, ed. *Classic Plays from the Negro Ensemble Company*. Pittsburgh: U. of Pittsburgh Press, 1995.

Hatch, James V., ed. *Black Theatre USA: Forty-Five Plays by Black Americans, 1847-1974*. New York: The Free Press, 1974.

—and Leo Hamalian. *Lost Plays of the Harlem Renaissance, 1920-1940*. Detroit: Wayne State University Press, 1996.

Jackson, Pamela Faith and Karimah. *Black Comedy: Nine Plays*. New York: Applause Books, 1997.

King, Woodie and Ron Milner, ed. *Black Drama*. New York: New American Library, 1971.

Ostrow, Eileen Joyce, ed. *Center Stage: An Anthology of 21 Contemporary Black American Plays*. Oakland: Sea Urchin Press, 1981; reprint, Urbana-Champaign: University of Illinois Press, 1991.

Patterson, Lindsay, ed. *Black Theatre*. New York: Dodd, Mead and Company, 1971.

Perkins, Kathy A., ed. *Black Female Playwrights: An Anthology of Plays before 1950*. Bloomington: Indiana University Press, 1990.

—and Roberta Uno, eds. *Contemporary Plays by Women of Color*. New York: Routledge, 1996.

Reardon, William R. and Thomas D. Pawley, ed. *The Black Teacher and the Dramatic Arts: A Dialogoe, Bibliography, and Anthology*. Westport, CT: Negro Universities Press, 1970.

Richardson, Willis, ed. *Plays and Pageants from the Life of the Negro*. Wash., D.C. The Associated Publishers, 1930.

Turner, Darwin, ed. *Black Drama in America: An Anthology*, Second ed. Washington, D.C. Howard University Press, 1994.

Wilkerson, Margaret B., ed. *Nine Plays by Black Women*. New York: Mentor, 1986.

BIBLIOGRAPHY

Books

Ani, Marimba, *Yurugu: An African-centered Critique of European Cultural Thought and Behavior,* Africa Work Press, Inc., 1994.

Allen, Theodore W. *The Invention of White Race.* New York: Verso. 1994.

Asante, Molefi Kete and Abu S. Abarry, ed. *African Intellectual Heritage.* Philadelphia: Temple U. Press, 1996.

ben-Jochannan, Yosef A.A. *Africa: Mother of Western Civilization.* Baltimore: Black Classic Press, 1988.

Bernal, Martin. *Black Athena: The Afroasiatic Roots of Classical Civilization.* Vol 1, *The Fabrication of Ancient Greece 1785-1985.* New Brunswick: Rutgers University Press, 1987.

—*Black Athena: The Afroasiatic Roots of Classical Civilization.* Vol 2, *The Archaeological and Documentary Evidence.* Brunswick: Rutgers University Press, 1991.

Berger, John, et al. *Ways of Seeing.* London: British Broadcasting Corporation and Pelican Books, 1972.

Bogle, Donald. *Toms, Coons, Mulattoes, Mammies, and Bucks: An Interpretive History of Blacks in American Films.* Viking Press, 1973.

Boyer, Horace Clarence. *The Golden Age of Gospel.* Chicago: University of Illinois Press, 2000.

Brisbane, Robert H. *Black Activism: Racial Revolution in the United States 1954-1970.* Valley Forge: Judson Press, 1974.

Craig, E. Quita. *Black Drama of the Federal Theatre Era: Beyond the Formal Horizons.* Amherst: The University of Massachusetts Press, 1980.

Diop, Cheikh Anta. *The African Origin of Civilization: Myth or Reality.* Translated by Mercer Cook. Lawrence Hill and Company, 1974.

Edwards, Gus. *Advice to a Young Black Actor: Conversations with Douglas Turner Ward.* Portsmouth: Heinemann, 2004.

Elam, Harry, Jr. and David Krasner, ed. *African American Performance and Theater History.* Oxford: Oxford University Press, 2001.

Feagin, Joe R. *Racist America.* New York: Routledge, 2000.

Floyd, Samuel A., Jr. *The Power of Black Music*. New York: Oxford University Press, 1995.

Gayle, Addison, Jr., ed. *The Black Aesthetic*. Garden City, NY: Anchor Books, 1971.

Harrison, Paul Carter, Victor Leo Walker II, and Gus Edwards, ed. *Black Theatre: Ritual Performance in the African Diaspora*. Philadelphia: Temple University Press, 2002.

Hatch, James V., and Omanii Abdullah. *Black Playwrights, 1823-1977: An Annotated Bibliography of Plays*. R.R. Bowker Co., 1977.

Hay, Samuel A., *African American Theatre: An Historical and Critical Analysis*, Cambridge U. Press, 1994.

Hill, Anthony with Douglas Q. Barnett. *Historical Dictionary of African American Theater*. Scarecrow Press, Inc., 2009.

Hill, Errol, ed. *The Theatre of Black Americans*. 2 vols. Englewood Cliffs: Prentice Hall, 1980.

Hill, Errol G. and James V. Hatch. *A History of African American Theatre*. Cambridge: Cambridge University Press, 2003.

James, George G. M. *Stolen Legacy*. New York: Philosophical Library, 1954; reprint, Newport News: United Brothers Communications Systems, 1989.

Jones, LeRoi. *Blues People*. New York: William Morrow and Company, 1963.

Kamalu, Chukwunyere. *Foundations of African Thought*. London: Karnak House, 1990.

Karenga, Maulana. *Kawaida Theory: An Introductory Outline*. Inglewood: Kawaida Publications, 1980.

Kent, George E. *Blackness and the Adventure of Western Culture*. Chicago: Third World Press, 1972.

King, Woodie Jr. *The Impact of Race: Theatre and Culture*. New York: Applause, 2003.

MacDonald, J. Fred. *Blacks and White TV: Afro-Americans in Television Since 1948*. Chicago: Nelson-Hall,1983.

McAllister, Marvin. *White People Do Not Know How to Behave at Entertainments Designed for Ladies and Gentlemen of Color*. Chapel Hill: The University of North Carolina Press, 2003.

BIBLIOGRAPHY

Mahone, Sydne. *Moon Marked & Touched by Sun: Plays by African American Women*. New York: Theatre Communications Group. 1994.

Marshall, Herbert and Mildred Stock. *Ira Aldridge: The Negro Tragedian*. Macmillan Company, 1958.

Mitchell, Loften. *Black Drama*. New York: Hawthorn Books, Inc., 1967.

—*Voices of the Black Theatre*. Clifton, NJ: James T. White and Company, 1975.

Oguibe, Olu. *The Culture Game*. Minneapolis: University of Minnesota Press, 2004.

Richards, Dona Marimba, *Let the Circle be Unbroken: The Implications of African Spirituality in the Diaspora*. The Red Sea Press, 1993.

Sampson, Henry T. *Blacks in Black and White: A Source Book on Black Films*. Metuchen, NJ: Scarecrow Press, 1977.

Smith, Arthur L. aka Molefi Asante. *Rhetoric of Black Revolution*. Boston: Allyn and Bacon, 1969.

Southern, Eileen. *The Music of Black Americans, Third Edition*. New York: W.W. Norton and Company, 1971.

Spellman, A.B. *Black Music*. New York: Schocken, 1973.

Tate, Greg, ed. *Everything But the Burden*. New York: Harlem Moon Broadway Books. 2003.

Thompson, George A. *A Documentary History of the African Theatre*. Evanston: Northwestern University Press, 1998.

Tildon, J. Tyson. *The Anglo-Saxon Agony*. Philadelphia: Whitmore Publishing Co. 1972.

Van Sertima, Ivan and Larry Williams, ed. *Great African Thinkers: Vol 1, Cheikh Anta Diop*. Incorporating *Journal of African Civilizations*, Vol. 8, No. 1. New Brunswick: Transaction Books, 1989.

Williams, Chancellor. *The Destruction of Black Civilization: Great Issues of a Race from 4500 B.C. to 2000 A.D.* Chicago: Third World Press, 1976.

Wilson, William Julius. *The Declining Significance of Race: Blacks and Changing American Institutions*, third ed. Chicago: University of Chicago Press, 2012.

Woll, Allen. *Dictionary of the Black Theatre: Broadway, Off-Broadway, and Selected Harlem Theatre*. Westport, CT: Greenwood Press, 1983.

INDEX

A

A-Team, The, 231, 233, 238
Abramson, Doris, 70
Abydos Passion Play, 54–55
Achilles, 95
Ackamoor, Idris, 207
Adventures of Ozzie and Harriet, The, 239
African American Music: An Introduction (Stewart), 146, 171
African Company, The, 61–62, 64–67
African Grove, 45, 64
Afrocentric Idea, The (Asante, M.), 44, 144
Afrocentricity: The Theory of Social Change (Asante, M.), 3
Afrophobia, 28–29
Ain't Misbehavin', 81
Aldridge, Ira, 61, 66
Ali, Mohammed, 183
American, The (newspaper), 65
American Anthropological Association, The, 32
Amos, John, 240, 242
Amos 'n' Andy, 194, 199, 237
Anderson, Eddie, 187, 237
Ansa, Kwame (African chief), 184
Antigone, 177
Aristotle, 143, 253
Art Ensemble of Chicago, 136–37
Asante, Molefi Kete, 3–4, 42–44, 47, 144, 174, 206, 253
Association of Black Psychologists, 63
Atlanta University, 91
Autry, Gene, 235
avant-garde nationalism, 136

B

Bailey, A. Peter, 8
Baldwin, James, 153, 224, 257
Baldwin, Joseph, 63
Baraka, Amiri, 8, 69, 257
Bay City Blues, 240
Beaty, Daniel, 207
Benny, Jack, 187, 237
Bernstein, Leonard, 172
Berry, Chuck, 85
Beulah, 194, 199
Billy the Kid, 95
Birth of a Nation, The, 81
Black Caribs (Garifuna), 63
Black Drama (Mitchell), 75
Black Theatre: The Making of a Movement (King, W.), 161
Black Theatre Network, 69
Blackwell, Otis, 89
Blues Brothers, 84
Blues for Mr. Charlie (Baldwin, James), 224
Boatner, Joe, 90–91
Bogle, Donald, 81, 236
Bohannan, Laura, 100–102
Bonanza, 234
Bonner, Marita, 69
Boone, Pat, 84
Branch, William, 70, 202
Brantley, Ben, 125
British School of Egyptology, 57
Brockett, Oscar G., 52–55, 58–59
Brother John, 243
Brown, Birmingham, 237
Brown, James, 146, 173

Brown, William Alexander, 61, 70
Brown, William Wells, 61, 69–72, 218
Browne, Theodore, 69
Brownsville Raid, The (Fuller), 69
Buchanan, Edgar, 235
Buckwheat, 189–90
Budge, E. A. Wallis, 55
Bullins, Ed, 69, 257
Butcher, James, 70
Buttram, Pat, 235

C

Caleb, the Degenerate (Cotter), 70
Calloway, Cab, 206
Canada Council, 2
Capone, Al, 95
Carillo, Leo, 235
Carter, Steve, 70
Cartwright, Samuel, 63
Casey, Bernie, 240
Cassidy, Hopalong, 235
Celebration of Blackness, 161, 165
Ceremonies in Dark Old Men (Elder), 69, 223, 254, 265
Charles, Ray, 45, 85
Charlie & Co., 240–41
Charlie Chan (film series), 237
Chatoyer, Joseph (Black Carib chief), 63
Chicago Defender, The, 192
Childress, Alice, 69, 187, 194
Chinese classical opera, 118
Chip Woman's Fortune, The (Richardson), 69
chitlin circuit, 110
Chubby Checker, 84–85, 90
Cisco Kid, The, 235
Civilization or Barbarism (Diop), 57
Clara's Ol' Man (Bullins), 69
Cleage, Pearl, 70
Cleveland School of Music, 91
Cockerham, William, 90
color-blind casting, 40
Colored Museum, The (Wolfe), 70

Confession Stone, The (Dodson), 69
Connors, Red, 235
Contendings of Horus and Set, The (Gardinier), 56–57
Contribution (Shine, T.), 69, 187, 194, 265
Contributions (collection of three plays by Shine, T.), 69
Cosby, Bill, 234, 239–40
Cosby Show, The, 230, 232–35, 239–41, 243
Cotter, Joseph S., 70
cradle of civilization, 30
Crandall, Prudence, 67–68

D

Dallas, 234
Darwin, Charles, 35, 95, 253
Darwinism, 204
Darwin's theory of evolution, 35
Davis, Ossie, 70, 187, 192, 218
Day of Absence (Ward, D.), 69, 210–12, 222–23
Dean, Phillip Hayes, 70
Death of a Salesman, 176
Debussy, Claude, 172
Declining Significance of Race, The (Wilson), 41
Democratic Review, 96
Dhambala, 119–20
Different World, A, 234, 243
Diff'rent Strokes, 232
Diop, Cheikh Anta, 22, 57, 59
Dodson, Owen, 69
"Don't Be Cruel," 89
double consciousness, 9, 16, 164–65, 167
dozens, the, 179, 182–83
Dr. B. S. Black, 185
Dreamgirls, 81
DuBois, W. E. B., 7, 9, 69, 165
Duke Ellington, 173
Dutchman (Baraka), 8, 69, 265

INDEX

E

Eastwood, Clint, 94
Edmonds, S. Randolph, 69
Edwards, Gus, 70
Egan, Pierce, 61–62
Elder, Lonne, 69, 223
Ellington, Duke, 173
Ellison, Ralph, 211, 213, 228
Eminem, 84
Emperor Jones, The, 81
English, Dianna, 94
Erasing Racism (Asante, M.), 42
Escape: or A Leap for Freedom, The (Brown, W. W.), 61, 69–71, 74, 218
Ethnic Dance: Roundtrip to Trinidad, 119
Evans, Don, 70

F

Family Matters, 240–41, 243
"Fare Thee Well, Titanic," 214
Father Knows Best, 239
Fences (Wilson, A.), 255–56, 262, 265
Fetchit, Stepin, 185–86
"Fever," 89, 245
Few Good Men, A, 250
Fletcher, Sir Banister, 58
Flip Wilson Show, The, 240
Foxx, Redd, 239
Franklin, Aretha, 146
Franklin, John Hope, 71
Franklin, Rev. C. L., 146
Frank's Place, 240–41
free jazz, 136
Freud, Sigmund, 95, 253
Freudian psychoanalysis, 209–10
From Slavery to Freedom (Franklin, J.), 71
Fuller, Charles, 69
Funnyhouse of a Negro (Kennedy), 69

G

Gaines, Ernest J., 220
Gallup poll, 230, 232
Gardiner, Alan, 56
Gardiner, Howard, 79
Garifuna (Black Caribs), 63
Gershwin, George, 172
Gibson, P. J., 70
Glass Menagerie, The, 151
Glengarry Glenn Ross, 151
Goin' a Buffalo, 254, 265
Gone with the Wind, 194
Good Times, 240–42
Gordone, Charles, 215–16
Graven Images (Miller), 69
Griffith, D. W., 81
Grimke, Angelina, 69
"Ground on Which I Stand, The" (Wilson, A.), 125–26
Guess Who's Coming to Dinner?, 243
Gunsmoke, 234

H

Haley, Bill, and the Comets, 84
Hall, Katori, 23
Hall, Stuart, 15
Hamlet (Shakespeare), 101–3, 150
Handbook to Literature, A, 261
Hansberry, Lorraine, 69
Happy Ending (Ward, D.), 209–10, 213
Hardy Holtzman Pfeiffer Associates, 160
Harriet Beecher Stowe, 216
Harrison, Paul Carter, 70
Hartford Courant, 90
Hays, Gabby, 235
Hellman, Lillian, 257
Herodotus, 55
Hewlett, James, 61, 65–66
Hildy, Franklin J., 52
Hill, Abram, 69, 187, 208
Hill Street Blues, 231, 233
Hitler, Adolf, 34, 92, 226
Holder, Geoffrey, 119
Holder, Laurence, 70
Hopkins, Philip, 205
Hotel, 231
"Hound Dog," 84, 88–89
Howard University, 162, 186

Hughes, Langston, 69, 187, 192, 222, 262, 264
Humperdink, Englebert, 84
Hurston, Zora Neale, 70

I

I Am My Own Wife, 151
Ibsen, Henrik, 143
Idabel's Fortune (Shine, T.), 187, 194
I Love Lucy, 234
Imhotep, 58–59
Ink Spots, 90–91
Institute of the Black World, 161
In the Heat of the Night, 243–45
Invisible Man (Ellison), 211, 228
Ionesco, Eugène, 143
Ira Aldridge: The Negro Tragedian (Marshall, Stock), 64–65
Ira Aldridge theatre, 162
"It Don't Mean a Thing If It Ain't Got That Swing," 173

J

Jackson, Michael, 230–31
Jackson, Samuel L., 208
James, Jesse, 95
Jim Crow, 76, 236
Joan of Arc, 177
Joe Turner's Come and Gone (Wilson, A.), 70
Johnson, Georgia Douglas, 69
Jones, Rhodessa, 207
Jones, Tom, 84
Joplin, Janis, 84
Jordan, Louis, 206
Jordan, Michael, 122
Jungle Fever, 245
Just Our Luck, 232

K

Kagemni, 174
Karenga, Maulana, 18, 138
Katherine Dunham Dance Company, 162
Kaufman and Hart, 257

Kemet, 22, 52, 54–55, 57, 59–60, 117
Kemites, 22–23, 53–55, 57, 60–61, 104, 117, 140
Kennedy, Adrienne, 69
Kenny, Bill, 90
Kernodle, George and Portia, 143
King (TV miniseries), 220
King, Martin Luther, Jr., 23, 117, 195, 220
King, Woodie, 161
Kingfish, 199
King Henry IV, Part Two (Shakespeare), 235
King Shotaway, 62–64, 66
Kwanza, 138

L

L.A. Law, 244–45
Lathan, Stan, 205
Leadbelly, 181, 214
Lee, Leslie, 70
Legree, Simon, 217–18
Lewis, Jerry, 80, 188
Liber, Jerry, 88
Life of Riley, The, 239
Little Rascals, The, 189
Little Richard, 85
Livin' Fat, 213
Lone Ranger, The, 235

M

Maat, 22, 53
Macbeth, Robert, 161
"Make It Funky," 173
manifest destiny, 5, 96–97, 105
Marie, Teena, 84
Marshall, Herbert, 64
Martin, David, 192
Marx, Karl, 253
Marxism, 152
Mason, Judi Ann, 70, 213
Massey, Morris, 24
Matheus, John, 222
Mbiti, John S., 140, 166

INDEX

McCloud, 237–38
McIver, Ray, 70
Medal for Willie, A (Branch), 202
melting pot myth, 30
Memphite Drama, 54, 104
Memphite stele, 104
Menes, 54
Merchant of Venice (Shakespeare), 256
Merry Wives of Windsor, The (Shakespeare), 235
Midnighters, The, 84–85
Miller, May, 69
Mingus, Charlie, 136
Mis-education of the Negro, The (Woodson), 5
Mitchell, Loften, 70, 75
Modern Jazz Quartet, 137
Molette, Barbara, 74, 208, 213
Molette, Carlton, 208, 213
Moliere, 188
Mona Lisa, 103–4
Moore, Mavor, 2
Morehouse College, 142
Moreland, Mantan, 237
Morris Brown College, 161
Mountaintop (Hall, K.), 23
Mount Rushmore, 93
Moynihan Report, 41, 199
Mr. T., 230–31
Muddy Waters, 85
Mulatto (Hughes), 69, 222
Murphy, Eddie, 189–90

N

National Advocate, 64
National Bar Association, 237
National Black Theatre Festival, The, 47, 206–7
National Conference on African-American Theatre, 69
Nat Turner (Edmonds), 69
Natural History (magazine), 100
Natural Man (Browne), 69
N'dao, Chiek, 93
New Lafayette theatre, 160
New York Times, 125
Nielsen ratings, 240
Nkosi, Lewis, 146
nommo, 144–45, 257
No Place to be Somebody (Gordone), 215–16, 245
Noyes Academy, 67
Nubian, 60

O

Oedipus Rex, 103, 150
Old Man Pete (Edmonds), 69
O'Neill, Eugene, 257
"On the Slave Market," 61, 63
Osiris, 55–57
Osiris and Horus, myth of, 55
O'Sullivan, John L., 96
Othello (character), 47–49, 175, 177, 221
Othello (play by Shakespeare), 48, 100, 221, 256
Otis, Johnny, 88
Our Gang, 189–90
Our Lan' (Ward, T.), 69
Owens, Daniel, 70
Oyamo, 70

P

Pan-African Congress, 57
Parker, Thomas Andrew "Colonel," 88
Parks, Rosa, 195
Park Theatre, 65
Passing Strange (Stew), 205–6
Paul, Richard, 248
Pawley, Thomas, 70
Penney, Rob, 70
People's Choice Awards, 230, 232, 234, 244
Perry, Tyler, 46, 80, 188–89
Peterson, Louis, 70
Piano Lesson, The (Wilson, A.), 257
Pitts-Wiley, Ricardo, 207
Plantation (Shine, T.), 69
Plato, 118
Platonic philosophy, 151

Poetics (Aristotle), 143
Poitier, Sidney, 243
Poncho, 235
Porgy, 81
Power, Will, 207
Presley, Elvis, 84–85, 87–90
Ptah-Hotep, 22
Pulitzer Prize, 125, 215
Purlie Victorious (Davis), 187, 192, 218
Purple Flower, The (Bonner), 69

R

Rachel (Grimke), 69
Radio Golf (Wilson, A.), 125–26, 203
Raisin in the Sun, A (Hansberry), 1, 69, 81, 197, 199–201, 215, 255–56, 260, 262–64
Ravel, Maurice, 172
Reid, Daphne Maxwell, 241
Reid, Tim, 240
Rene, Otis, 88
Rice, Thomas "Jim Crow," 76, 236
Richard III (Shakespeare), 64–66
Richardson, Willis, 69
River Niger, The (Walker), 201
Roberts, Vera Mowry, 52
Robey, Don, 89
Robin Hood, 95, 213
Robinson, Hillyard, 162
Rochester, 185–87, 237
Rogers, Roy, 235
Rolle, Esther, 242
Rosalee Pritchett (Molette, C.; Molette, B.), 213
Ross, John, 70
Royal Coburg Theatre, 66
Russell Simmons Def Poetry Jam, 205

S

St. Vincent, 62–63
Sakkara (Saqqara), 57–60
Salaam, Kalamu ya, 70
Sanchez, Sonia, 70
Sanford and Son, 239

sankofa, 16
Sapphire, 194, 199, 239
Saturday Night Live, 189
Schlesinger, Arthur, Jr., 96
Scotsboro Boys, The, 81
Scriven, Michael, 248
Shabako, 54
Shakespeare, William, 6, 48, 64–65, 100, 175–76, 188, 221, 235
Shange, Ntozake, 69
Shine (character), 181–82, 214
Shine, Ted, 69, 187, 194
Shoes (Shine, T.), 69
Signifying Monkey, The, 178–79, 183, 204
Silverheels, Jay, 235
Simmons, Russell, 205
Simon, Neill, 188
Simple Takes a Wife (Hughes), 192
Simply Heavenly (Hughes), 82, 187, 192–93
Sinatra, Nancy, 84
Six Degrees of Separation, 256
Slaveship, 8
"Sleepy Time Down South," 88
Snefru, 174
Soldier's Play, A, 215
Somé, Malidoma Patrice, 133
Sousa, John Philip, 170
Spelman College, 130
Spence, Eulalie, 70
Spencer for Hire, 238
Stalin, Joseph, 92
Star of Ethiopia, The (DuBois), 69
Star of the Morning (Mitchell), 75
Steiger, Rod, 243
Step Pyramid of Zoser, 58
Stew, 205–6
Stewart, Earl L., 173
Stock, Mildred, 64
Stoller, Mich, 88
Stone Mountain, 93
Stowe, Harriet Beecher, 216, 218
Stravinsky, Igor, 172
Strivers Row (Hill), 69, 187, 190–91, 208, 260

INDEX

Sunday Morning in the South, A (Johnson), 69
Sun Ra, 136
Sutherland, Efua, 130, 162
Sweet Sweetback's Badass Song, 185
syncopation, 171–72

T

Talented Tenth, The (Wesley), 69
Taylor, Cecil, 136
Theory of the Leisure Class (Verblen), 109
Thicke, Robin, 84
Thornton, Willie Mae "Big Mama," 84, 88–89
Titanic, The, 181, 183, 204, 214
Ti Yette (Matheus), 222
Tolson, Melvin, 70
Tom and Jerry, or Life in London (Egan), 61–62
Tonto, 235
Trouble in Mind (Childress), 69
Tsegaye, G. M., 57
"Twist, The," 84
Tyson, Cicely, 220

U

Uncle Tom, 216–19, 231–33, 245
Uncle Tom's Cabin (Stowe), 216, 218–19
urban folk hero, 62
Urkel, Steve, 240–43

V

Vanilla Ice, 84
Van Peebles, Melvin, 185
Veblen, Thorstein, 109

W

Walker, Jimmy, 242
Walker, Joseph, 70
Ward, Douglas Turner, 69, 209–10, 222
Ward, Theodore, 69
Ward, Val Gray, 162
Warner, Malcolm Jamal, 207
Wayne, John, 94
Webster, 231–32
Welsh-Asante, Kariamu, 44
WEPPEO, 10–11, 109, 111, 123, 130, 210
Wesley, Richard, 69
Whalum, Wendell P., 142
White, Jaleel, 240
Whitman, Walt, 97
Who's Afraid of Virginia Woolf, 151
Williams, Bert, 185
Williams, Samm-Art, 70, 241
Wilson, August, 43, 70, 79, 124–26, 202–3, 240, 255, 257
Wilson, Flip, 240
Wilson, William Julius, 41
Wilson, Woodrow, 81
Wine in the Wilderness (Childress), 187, 194
Winfield, Paul, 220
Wolfe, George C., 70
Woodson, Carter G., 5, 128, 165
Wynn, Tracy Keenan, 220

Z

Zoser, 58–59

ABOUT THE AUTHORS

Barbara and Carlton Molette have collaborated as scholars, playwrights, and theatrical designers. They have presented papers for international and U.S. professional organizations, published articles and two editions of *Black Theatre: Premise and Presentation*. Members of the Dramatists Guild since 1971, their playwriting collaborations began with *Rosalee Pritchett*, premiered by the Morehouse-Spelman Players and presented by the Negro Ensemble Company, Free Southern Theatre, several university theatres, and published by Dramatists Play Service and in *Black Writers of America*.

Ten-minute plays include *Out of Time*, produced by Turtle Shell Theatre on West Forty-third Street, New York in 2011, *Move the Car* opened May 31, 2012, at Warehouse Performing Arts Center in North Carolina. Atlanta's Essential Theatre premiered *Tee Shirt History* on July 11, 2012.

Their musical, *Dr. B. S. Black*, in collaboration with Charles Mann, was coproduced at Atlanta's Peachtree Playhouse by Theatre of the Stars and Just Us Theatre with Samuel L. Jackson in the title role, and produced by other theatres in Washington, D.C., Houston, and Memphis. *Fortunes of the Moor* premiered at the Frank Silvera Writers' Workshop in New York and has been presented at other venues, including the National Theatre of Ghana, ETA Creative Arts in Chicago, and several universities, including Western Michigan, Brown, Ohio State, the universities of Louisville, Pittsburgh, and Connecticut. Miami's M Ensemble Theatre produced the premiere of *Our Short Stay*. *Prudence* premiered at the Connecticut Repertory Theatre. Readings of *Presidential Timber* were presented at the National Black Theatre Festival, Woodie King's New Federal Theatre in New York, New Life Productions in Columbia, South Carolina, and by

AFROCENTRIC THEATRE

Bowie State University at the Kennedy Center in Washington, D.C. Other full-length plays that premiered in Atlanta include *Noah's Ark* (published in *Center Stage*, University of Illinois Press), and *Booji*, also presented by Texas Southern University on KPRC-TV, Houston. Other ten-minute plays include *Widgets, A Fond Farewell, Silver Tongue, Kin Ship, Last Supper,* and *The Great Xmas Race*.

Barbara Molette was born in Los Angeles and attended public schools there. She earned a BA from Florida A & M University, an MFA from Florida State University, and a PhD from the University of Missouri. Professor emerita and former chair of the English Department at Eastern Connecticut State University, she has taught at Spelman College, Texas Southern University, and Baltimore City Community College, where she was director of Writing across the curriculum. She was president of the National Conference on African American Theatre, administrative fellow for the Mid-Missouri Associated Colleges and Universities, and director of arts in education programs for the Mayor's Advisory Committee on Art and Culture in Baltimore. She has conducted workshops on writing, scriptwriting, staff development, humanities, costuming, and makeup design for teachers and theatre artists, and served as consultant to government agencies and businesses. Her play, *Perfect Fifth*, won third place in the WMAR-TV television competition and was produced by Arena Players of Baltimore.

Carlton Molette was born in Pine Bluff, Arkansas, attended public schools in Kansas City, Missouri, earned a BA degree from Morehouse College, an MA from the University of Iowa, and a PhD from Florida State University. Theatrical credits include over 100 productions as playwright, producer, director, designer, publicist, stage manager, actor, and technician. He is professor emeritus of dramatic arts and African American studies at the University of Connecticut. He served on the faculties of Spelman College, and Atlanta, Howard, and Florida A & M universities, as director of the Atlanta University summer theatre, chair of the division of fine arts at Spelman College, founding dean of the School of Communications at Texas

ABOUT THE AUTHORS

Southern University, dean of arts and sciences at Lincoln (MO) University, and vice president for academic affairs at Coppin State University. He has also served as guest director at the University of Michigan; seminar leader at the University of Iowa's Afro-American Summer Drama Institute; consultant for universities, colleges, theatre companies, government agencies, and businesses; and on the boards of arts organizations in Atlanta, Baltimore, and Houston.